Praise for *Startup Leadership*

"Derek Lidow is right: entrepreneurs, not mere ideas, lead companies to their full potential. Lidow puts this powerful idea to work, alongside the full breadth and depth of his own experiences running growth companies, in *Startup Leadership*. I recommend this book for every founder—regardless of your stage—because Lidow's invaluable insights, personal leadership strategies, and framework will help you improve the trajectory of your success."

—**Rich Karlgaard**, publisher, *Forbes* magazine; board director; investor; entrepreneur; and author, *The Soft Edge*

"Trust me because I've seen and done virtually everything that's possible in business today. Whether you're an investor, board member, CEO, accelerator, small business owner, or aspiring entrepreneur, *Startup Leadership* is mandatory reading. Thanks to the smart and detailed advice of serial success story Derek Lidow, the book will help de-risk virtually any enterprise. It will also expand your levels of innovation, profits, culture, and success. I recommend you get a copy—and give a copy to someone who needs it."

—**Bruce Hack**, advisor, angel investor, board director, and former CEO, Vivendi Games

"The entrepreneur's journey is often misunderstood as an idea coming to life. In fact, it is entrepreneurs themselves who must learn to create and lead an organization. *Startup Leadership* provides aspiring and experienced entrepreneurs powerful tools to grow as leaders."

—**Brian O'Kelley**, founder and CEO, AppNexus

"This is not another book on how to build a successful startup. Lidow demystifies relationship building, negotiation, and vision creation with clarity and balance. He shows what it takes to become a more confident leader who builds startups with less risk and better outcomes. Your transformation into a better-equipped entrepreneurial leader begins now."

—**Natasha Gajewski**, founder and CEO, Simple Health Inc.

"If any book contains the secrets of entrepreneurial success, this is it! I recommend *Startup Leadership* to both budding and proven entrepreneurs."

—**Greg Olsen**, founder, Epitax and Sensors Unlimited

"*Startup Leadership* is the handbook for leadership all entrepreneurs should read while scaling their business."

—**Chris Kuenne**, founder-entrepreneur, Rosetta

"A must-read for aspiring and experienced entrepreneurs!"

—**Jeremey Donovan**, author, *How to Deliver a TED Talk*

"This book fills an important gap among books about entrepreneurship, and Derek Lidow shows what it really takes to make a successful startup. *Startup Leadership* focuses on the essential, yet elusive, leadership elements required to navigate a venture from idea to self-sustainability. Future entrepreneurs will be thankful to have this companion along for the entire journey."

—**John Danner**, professor, Haas School of Business, UC Berkeley

"Finally, an easy-to-read and digestible blueprint for entrepreneurs that will empower them to build and lead sustainable enterprises. Lidow encapsulates years of trial and error and teaches what's required for successful entrepreneurship with a clear methodology."

—**Jeanne Gray**, founder and CEO, AmericanEntrepreneurship.com

"Finally, from the true-life experiences of a highly successful entrepreneur, comes a how-to book that is more than an academic compendium. Derek Lidow captures the essence of the leadership qualities needed for success, not just in the formation and early stages of a venture, but along the path to a significant stand-alone business. This hands-on book is an instant classic."

—**Ricardo B. Levy**, professor, Stanford University, and author, *Letters to a Young Entrepreneur*

STARTUP
LEADERSHIP

HOW SAVVY ENTREPRENEURS TURN THEIR
IDEAS INTO SUCCESSFUL ENTERPRISES

Derek Lidow

JB JOSSEY-BASS™

A Wiley Brand

Published by Jossey-Bass
A Wiley Brand
One Montgomery Street, Suite 1200, San Francisco, CA 94104-4594
www.josseybass.com

Jossey-Bass books and products are available through most bookstores. To contact Jossey-Bass directly call our Customer Care Department within the U.S. at 800-956-7739, outside the U.S. at 317-572-3986, or fax 317-572-4002.

Wiley publishes in a variety of print and electronic formats and by print-on-demand. Some material included with standard print versions of this book may not be included in e-books or in print-on-demand. If this book refers to media such as a CD or DVD that is not included in the version you purchased, you may download this material at http://booksupport.wiley.com. For more information about Wiley products, visit www.wiley.com.

Library of Congress Cataloging-in-Publication Data
Lidow, Derek, 1953-
   Startup leadership : how savvy entrepreneurs turn their ideas into successful enterprises / Derek Lidow. – First edition.
      pages cm
   Includes bibliographical references and index.
   ISBN 978-1-118-69705-4 (cloth); ISBN 978-1-118-84567-7 (pdf);
ISBN 978-1-118-84565-3 (epub)
   1. New business enterprises. 2. Leadership. I. Title.
   HD62.5.L525 2014
   658.1'1 – dc23

                                                                 2013042360

Printed in the United States of America
FIRST EDITION
HB Printing   10 9 8 7 6 5 4 3 2 1

To my muse, partner, and true love, Diana

CONTENTS

PREFACE

The objective of this book is to help entrepreneurs succeed—all types of entrepreneurs, in all stages of developing their idea into a tangible enterprise. The premise of this book is that entrepreneurs, not ideas, lead their enterprises to success. These pages describe fundamental capabilities that enormously enhance an entrepreneur's chances of success; capabilities that can be enhanced through understanding and practice. This book takes a very different tack from what you find in most books on entrepreneurship, or even what you find in most business books. We do not talk about money, or products, or customers. We do talk about how you and the people you find and motivate need to work together in order to produce more value than you could have done alone.

This book is about leadership, and the particular type of leadership required to take an initial idea to the point where it has become an enterprise that produces value and is self-sustaining. Startup leadership is perhaps the most challenging form of leadership because the founder starts alone, or with very few people who are willing to dedicate themselves to his success. Most entrepreneurs fail not because they were incapable, but rather because they had nobody coaching them on how to prepare and respond to the myriad of challenges they will face. My book provides that advice and coaching. Using an analogy, my book is not about childbirth; rather, it is about early child rearing—bringing a child up from birth to the point where he leaves home because he has found a great job and a nice place to live. Most business books treat enterprises as if they were grown adults, not addressing the stages at which they are fragile infants, developing adolescents, or teenagers.

The widely accepted belief that half of the new jobs and economic growth come from new enterprises is actually misleading; brand-new firms account for only a few percent of the jobs in any given year. The more accurate statement is that virtually all the new job creation and economic growth comes from firms that have taken the entrepreneur's original idea and transformed it into scalable activities that teams of people are motivated to work on together. These firms account for over 60 percent of all job creation.[1] (A footnote number indicates that a citation or further discussion can be found in the chapter notes in the back of the book; you can also find these at www.dereklidow.com.)

Most entrepreneurial enterprises hire at most one or two other people and stop growing.[2] These firms go out of business quickly, replaced by another one- or two-person enterprise, usually in the same business, but run by a different entrepreneur. Less than 10 percent of all the enterprises that launch create any measurable value beyond what the entrepreneur could earn working for someone else. Surprisingly, many large firms encourage entrepreneurial actions by their management that result in the same creation of low value. These traps are easy to fall into without the skills discussed in this book.

Many of the firms that succeed at creating value still go out of business or shrink precipitously because they do not make themselves self-sustaining.[3] Customers and economic conditions always change, and any enterprise—or any internal department, for that matter—must be able to innovate and change in order to prevent itself from atrophying and decaying. Firms have to create value and be self-sustaining in order to create economic value. These firms are led by entrepreneurial leaders—a very small subset of all entrepreneurs, estimated by some to be fewer than one in fifty.[4]

It has constantly fascinated me to watch who has become successful and who has not. This fascination dates back to when I finished graduate school and started working for a company in Silicon Valley. The mid-seventies were the start of the golden age of the semiconductor industry, and the world hasn't been the same since. Thousands of impressive people played essential roles in the success of the global semiconductor, computer, and electronics industries and in the success of the individual companies they founded and led. A few of these people are very famous; many more are not as famous, but their contributions are justifiably well respected in their markets and by their peers. My fascination, however, is with the thousands of impressive people who tried but failed to make a lasting mark. I want to understand why some people can successfully take their ideas and turn them into something that has a positive effect on the world, while other people, many with even greater experience and talents, fail to leave a mark.

My interest in success and failure started as a purely selfish desire to figure out how to get ahead in an exciting industry. I did well in school and received my PhD in applied physics from Stanford at the age of twenty-two, so I of course felt that I could tackle any problem the real world would send my way. I was surprised to find that my credentials and technical experience did not entitle me to being immediately chosen to lead. Why did some people care what I had to say and wanted to help me succeed while others clearly did not? I wanted to understand what was happening, so I could be successful. I also wanted to understand so that I could help other people be successful. Over the past thirty-five years I have remained fascinated with success and failure. I have constantly observed, I have read avidly, and I have sought out others to hear their stories or get their advice. I even founded a company, iSuppli, part of whose mission was to track who was successful in the tech world and who was not. I have put to use what I have learned, frequently with eye-opening results.

I now teach entrepreneurial leadership at Princeton University, and my interest in success and failure has become an academic pursuit. What enables some people to turn their ideas into value-producing self-sustaining enterprises while others are unable to? I have found that the fundamental challenges in the founding and growing of a successful semiconductor company are no different from those for founding and growing any other type of enterprise. What creates a successful enterprise is fundamentally the same for all entrepreneurs.

Doing my research, I have found gems of universal truth relative to taking ideas and then getting people to help you turn the idea into a real value-producing and self-sustaining enterprise. Each gem is universal, meaning it can be applied broadly across cultures and business scenarios. Each gem is well supported and consistent with all available evidence, but to make this book as readable as possible I have put all supporting footnotes, references, and analysis into chapter notes that you will find at the back of the book.

To make this book more memorable and valuable, it is organized around a series of stories about entrepreneurs and the actions that led to their success—or failure. Each story illustrates a gem of truth directly applicable to growing an idea into a value-producing, self-sustaining enterprise. All of the stories are about real people, but for many I have changed the facts and circumstances to hide real identities. I use real names where the name of the entrepreneur may add an extra dimension to the story; in those cases I have not changed facts or situations.

January 2014
Princeton, New Jersey

Derek Lidow

Success Requires More Than Entrepreneurship

Success, defined in whatever monetary and emotional terms you choose, requires more than being able to form a company around your idea. Ideas, and the companies formed around them, come and go. Very few create any tangible lasting value or emotional fulfillment. Even more heartbreaking is the all-too-common situation in which an entrepreneur succeeds in starting a new enterprise only for the enterprise to stagnate and slowly die. Entrepreneurs are commonly removed when outside investors are part of a startup. The following true story of Adam is an excellent example of an entrepreneur that started a great company only to be forced out because he could not deal with the competitive and organizational pressures that entrepreneurial leaders must face. As we shall see over the next twelve chapters, entrepreneurs like Adam[1] can succeed in seeing their ideas become value producing and self-sustaining enterprises once they are armed with a basic set of startup leadership skills.

Adam passionately wanted to be an entrepreneur from the time he was in high school. He taught himself to program computers, and by age fourteen he was already earning money making websites for local small businesses. He went to an excellent university and majored in economics while taking all the classes on entrepreneurship that were offered. Upon graduation, Adam sought more hands-on experience, accepting a job at a major computer company. He did well at the company but did not feel satisfied being "a cog in a big machine," and after two years he accepted a job at a software startup. Although he wasn't part of the startup's founding team, he was given responsibility for a small group of programmers developing a new feature for the startup's existing product, which improved the management of market research companies. Adam's team delivered its product enhancement on time—a significant accomplishment in software development, a field in which almost all projects run behind schedule. When Adam felt his accomplishments were not properly acknowledged by the startup's founders, he decided that he needed to start his own firm.

The opportunity was practically at hand—the startup, which had struggled to find new customers and to keep its existing customers satisfied, shut its doors within six months. Adam was elated to be out of a job; he felt he knew how to better address the software needs of the market research community, and now he had a chance to prove it. Just four years out of college, Adam launched his company, Gale Solutions (named after his mother). He raised money from two wealthy former classmates and a few family friends. He hired three people from the defunct startup: two former classmates and another person from the large software company that had first employed him.

Capturing the first few customers proved to be much harder than Adam had expected. Market research firms were interested, but he could not get them to actually commit to buying his software. He got a break when Josh, a top executive of a customer Adam had been courting, was hired to be the CEO of another market research firm. Josh, already familiar with Gale's software, called and said he wanted to use it. The enterprise finally had its first customer. Adam and his team delivered the software, and after six months of working closely with Josh on some critical modifications, the software finally produced meaningful efficiencies. After two years Adam finally had a real example of how well his software worked. Armed with an excellent customer reference, Adam made six more sales in the next thirteen weeks.

Gale Solutions survived those first two years on family loans and Adam's maxed-out credit cards. Fortune smiled on Adam again when Josh offered to introduce him to a well-known venture capitalist, Gerry. Josh gave Adam and his enterprise glowing recommendations, and Gerry soon offered to invest. Needing money and impressed with the reputation of such a successful venture capitalist, Adam gladly accepted a $3 million investment in return for 50.1 percent ownership of Gale. The investment enabled Adam to expand his enterprise and hire a sales force and a CFO.

Running his fast-growing company was a struggle for Adam, but he still relished it. He worked twelve-hour days dealing with customer issues, authorizing pricing for contracts with new customers, reviewing progress on new software updates, signing checks, working with his top engineers on new versions of the software, as well as dealing with employee issues. The more successful the company became, the more employee issues he had to deal with. One of these was of particular concern.

Adam respected his new VP of sales, who had run sales for a successful software supplier. Adam also respected his VP of product management, who was smart and fearless in negotiating final deal terms. But the two VPs hated one another, and Adam often had to stop their shouting matches. Adam felt they both made good points, but he was unable to get either of them to listen to what the other had to say.

Adam had another problem: his engineering team kept missing their deadlines for software updates. He sensed that the complexity of the software was getting beyond his engineers' ability to control it. He was sure he could help them if only he could spend more time with the team.

Adam was disappointed that Gerry was not available to give more advice. He saw Gerry every six weeks for exactly two hours at board meetings, where Gerry asked excellent questions and gave very pointed advice, such as "You need a more experienced head of accounting" or "You have got to step up to fix the problem between product management and sales; hire a counselor if you must." Adam hired an experienced CFO to improve accounting and other financial tasks, but the CFO's son fell ill and she soon went on leave. When Adam spoke about hiring a counselor to the VP of sales, the VP responded, "We are doing just fine as we are!" and that he would quit if Adam inserted another person into the brew.

Although growing a company was exhausting, most nights Adam still fell asleep feeling very accomplished. So it was all the more devastating when Gerry took him to a rare lunch and, after congratulating him on some favorable customer reviews, told him that it was time for him to step aside as CEO. He needed to let a more experienced executive take over and build the company to the point where it could be sold for a hefty valuation.

"Where did I go wrong?" Adam asked, holding back his tears.

Gerry laid it out: "You have done a good job, but to make this company really valuable, we need to make changes. The sales force is good but not great. They argue way too much with the person you brought in for marketing. Invoices are sent out late, and you no longer deliver your latest software enhancements on time. Your success has finally brought competitors into the market, and they have more money to spend on sales and marketing than we can make in five years. They will blow us out of the water if we don't change quickly. We need a strong, experienced CEO to make sure the company keeps growing and becomes valuable."

Adam was speechless, so that was that.

Stories like Adam's are repeated every day. Entrepreneurs that accept money from professional investors are more likely to be removed as CEO—as the leader—the more successful their enterprises become.[2] It's true that if Adam had not accepted money from Gerry, he wouldn't have been pushed aside—but Gerry was right in his contention that the major competitors Gale Solutions' success had attracted would have likely blown him out of the water. Adam was doomed to suffer major setbacks either way.

The real world is brutal, and most entrepreneurs do not understand what it takes to succeed with their dreams. Specifically, there is a big gap between getting a company to the starting blocks and getting the company to the point where it can stand on its own. This gap is where the entrepreneur and his enterprise are extremely vulnerable and where inadvertent mistakes can be economically fatal. When the enterprise is very immature and fragile, every new hire, every customer, project, strategy, crisis, or pivot has disproportionately large impacts on the future well-being of the enterprise—and on whether the founder can continue as its leader.

Books on entrepreneurship, many of them excellent, focus on how you start a company, and these books finish with their advice once a hypothetical stream of customers show up. This book is about building an enterprise from the initial idea to the point where the company has become profitable and is self-sustaining.

My standard for entrepreneurial success is a basic one: you have to get your enterprise to the point where it is self-sustainable. If you can do that, you have proven yourself to be a real *entrepreneurial leader* (EL). This goal is attainable, and not just for the lucky or the specially gifted entrepreneur; given the proper skills and insights, most entrepreneurs can ultimately become successful—they can become ELs.

ENTREPRENEUR, OR ENTREPRENEURIAL LEADER?

Entrepreneurship is a calling that many aspire to. Almost half of the working population in the United States will try to become an entrepreneur during their working career. I am using the word *entrepreneur* in the classic sense of the word: someone who works to start a business as well as someone who leads a business they have started.[3] Fewer than half the people who try to start a business get it to the point where they actually get a paying customer. Even after the entrepreneur has found a real customer, about half give up and shut down within five years. Fewer than one in four entrepreneurs who start out remain in business for more than five years.[4]

Almost all entrepreneurs with businesses that have lasted five years have succeeded in making enough profit to stay in business, but few of these entrepreneurs ever grow their firm to the point where it is self-sustaining. By *self-sustaining*, I mean that the enterprise meets two criteria:

- It can operate whether or not the founder is active in the firm.
- It is able to gain new customers with new innovations in its products or services; that is, customers lost through aging and

shifts in the market can be replaced by other customers buying new products or services.

A self-sustaining firm is a valuable tangible asset. A firm that is not self-sustaining will go out of business. This is the unfortunate fate of the vast majority of all the profitable enterprises ever founded. It is estimated that less than 2 percent of all entrepreneurs get to the point where their enterprise has created tangible value and is self-sustaining.

Leading an enterprise all the way from conception to the point where it is producing value and is self-sustaining—which means you are succeeding as an EL—is much more challenging than starting a company. If you want to see your idea reach its full potential, if you want to enjoy the fulfillment that comes from having made a tangible difference in the world, if you want to achieve financial success, then you must aspire to be an entrepreneurial leader.

Adam was an excellent entrepreneur, but he was not an entrepreneurial leader. He didn't have to lose both his job and the control over his idea and his company. But he just didn't understand what he needed to know—that what he had done (and done very well) to establish his company as a viable enterprise in a potentially competitive field was not all that he needed to do to lead his enterprise successfully to self-sustainability. What had worked so well even weeks before now no longer worked. Adam's business had moved into a different stage of maturity, with a different set of challenges and needs, requiring a different deployment of leadership skills.

STAGES, SKILLS, AND SELFISH SELFLESSNESS

Like infants becoming children, then adolescents, and then teenagers, enterprises go through stages of maturity. I will describe four stages that entrepreneurial leaders must understand and manage; these stages define times when changes in leadership skills are required. Without understanding these four stages, an entrepreneur cannot completely understand what *changes* are required in their leadership to move the enterprise closer to being self-sustaining. Sometimes entrepreneurs figure out that they need to change before it is too late, but often only after bad things have happened to the enterprise and to the trust the team would otherwise have had in its leader. I will describe these four stages and the leadership expectations of each in Chapter Three.

Becoming an entrepreneurial leader requires that you develop specific skills; fortunately, these skills do not require extreme abilities of any sort. You do not have to be born with any special traits. Indeed, you can even have major weaknesses, but you must understand what they are and be willing to mitigate them to the point where they do not interfere. Self-awareness and self-knowledge are the foundation of the EL skill set.

Adam was not very self-aware. He knew he was smart and a nice person, and he thought that was all he needed to be able to figure out how to solve any problem. He did not realize that his strengths that derived from his personal set of motivations, traits, and skills had corresponding weaknesses. He had no clue that his affability was related to his aversion to conflict, which actually fostered the relationship problems he had spent so much time solving. Being a nice guy had its dark side. Similarly, he couldn't see that his perfectionism resulted in his inability to delegate, which in turn meant he was prioritizing his time ineffectively. As we'll see, he wasn't skilled at understanding relationships, motivating others, or the nuances of leading through change. He just kept on applying his logic and his natural charm to implement only temporary solutions to each new problem he inadvertently caused for himself.

The first half of this book explores the required EL skill set in depth, including:

- *Self-awareness:* How to work with your own motivations, traits, and skills—your capability mix.
- *Relationship building:* How relationships form and how you make them stronger.
- *Motivation:* How you motivate others to want to help you be successful.

- *Leading change:* How to make people willingly change what they have been doing successfully.
- *Enterprise basics:* Understanding the leadership needs of all enterprises as they mature.

These skills are not difficult to master if you are motivated to do so. What makes becoming an entrepreneurial leader most challenging is learning how to be selfish and selfless at the same time. Properly using these straightforward skills requires the EL to find a personal balance between these otherwise conflicting characteristics. Entrepreneurs have to be selfish: the very fact of their starting an enterprise means they want others to change their habits or even their lives to accommodate how the entrepreneur thinks the world should work. As we'll see in Chapter Two, genuine selfishness is at the root of entrepreneurial success. On the other hand, leadership requires that you make those who follow you feel that they will be successful in achieving their own personal desires. Balancing selfishness with selflessness—understanding how, when, and why each of these serves enterprise success—is tricky when you are unaware what you need to do it. Finding that balance through the practice of these fundamental skills of startup leadership will be a recurring theme of this book.

The startup leadership skills we explore here apply broadly to any enterprise and any entrepreneur. That is, they give almost any motivated entrepreneur the ability to transform ideas into a tangible and self-sustaining reality. This tangible reality could be a for-profit company, a non-profit philanthropy, an all-volunteer organization, a new division within a larger existing enterprise, a new political group, or even a rock band. Startup leadership applies equally to leading a tribe or an extended family. Because these skills apply so broadly, I tend to refer to the EL as leading an *enterprise*, the most generic term for a group of people formed for the purpose of accomplishing a specific task. From time to time I may use the term "company" or "business" if that is more suitable in a specific context, but my overall intent is always for these concepts to apply more broadly.

This book has two parts after this chapter. The first, Chapters Two through Seven, discusses the skills you need to master to become an entrepreneurial leader. The second, Chapters Eight through Twelve, shows how to apply these skills to five major challenges faced by every EL.

PREREQUISITES: MASTERING THE SKILLS OF STARTUP LEADERSHIP

To lead others, you must first lead yourself, and leading yourself requires that you must realistically understand your capabilities—both strengths and weaknesses. What you are capable of achieving is a combination of your motivations, your traits, and your skills, all of which are interdependent. Chapter Two distinguishes among motivations, traits, and skills and gives you tools to inventory and map your capabilities. These insights will allow you to leverage your strengths and mitigate your weaknesses so that you can build and lead an enterprise.

Chapter Three talks about the enterprise itself and what it needs from its leaders to succeed, using a simple model of enterprise development. There are only three components that impact an enterprise's ability to create value, which every entrepreneurial leader needs to understand: projects, processes, and culture. Chapter Three discusses what these are and how each must be nurtured for any enterprise to develop to maturity. Enterprise maturity, in turn, can be understood in terms of four distinct stages, during which the EL must provide different types of leadership to see that projects are successfully launched and completed, that processes are efficiently controlled, and that a culture evolves that enables the people who staff the enterprise to operate passionately and productively.

Entrepreneurial leaders never act alone in getting the world to adopt their ideas, so the EL must build strong relationships with other people who will help her achieve her vision. In Chapter Four we discuss the essence of all relationships: the existence of a shared objective. There are three categories of shared objectives—cooperative, competitive, or retreating—and our relationships are a dynamic mix of all three types. Understanding cooperation, competition, and retreat puts the EL in an excellent position to structure her relationships to further the needs of the enterprise.

Motivation is to groups as relationship building is to individuals, and motivational skills are the subject of Chapter Five— understanding how to motivate scores of people to align their actions to your desires. Motivating others requires creating job tasks that make people feel autonomous, masterful, and purposeful, and not controlled, insecure, and lost.

The final skill we discuss in Part One is leading change. The EL's challenge is that once the enterprise has been created, he must constantly change the lives of the people around him for the sake of satisfying the changing needs of customers. New projects must be launched, new processes inaugurated, legacy processes improved, and cultures adjusted. Many entrepreneurs are scared of change and resist it, thereby imperiling the future of their enterprises and the well-being of all their employees and stakeholders. To successfully change what people are currently satisfied doing, an EL must ensure that five prerequisites of change are in place and stay in place; these are discussed in Chapter Six.

That's it. No other general skills are required of an entrepreneurial leader. To lead the creation of a specific type of enterprise, the EL may need to have mastered some industry or marketplace specific skills: for example, it would be virtually impossible to start a law firm without having attended law school. Some enterprises are started by teams of founders rather than by one person, and the requisite industry skills may need to be mastered by only one of the founders in order for the startup to be credible. Many other important skills can be hired into the enterprise when and as needed—for example sales, accounting, and process management—and are not skills that every EL needs to master.

By Chapter Seven you'll have a sense of your motivations, your traits, and your skills, including how comfortable you feel building relationships, motivating others, and leading change. You will also understand how each of these skills must be utilized as an enterprise matures through its four stages. You will need to decide what you are going to do about it. Creating a *personal leadership strategy* (PLS) generates an understanding of the specific steps you will need to take to successfully launch and grow your idea into a tangible reality. You will need to mitigate some of your traits. You may even have to explore the reasons for some of your motivations in order for you to *really* want to mitigate the traits that could prevent you from being successful. There will likely be some skills you need to acquire or get better at performing. You will need to identify people who can help you and who want to help you. Each EL must develop her own strategy for how to be successful.

Armed with a PLS, we can move on to Part Two, which is about how you apply this knowledge and insight to five challenges all ELs encounter as they develop their enterprise: creating entrepreneurial strategy, structuring the enterprise, hiring and firing, forming and leading teams, and leading through crisis.

APPLICATION: WHAT AN ENTREPRENEURIAL LEADER DOES

It is common for enterprises to fail because their leaders tried to implement fantasy strategies. There is widespread misunderstanding about how strategy applies to fledgling or fragile enterprises; business strategy as it is practiced today applies to fully mature enterprises and is irrelevant to entrepreneurial leaders. Chapter Eight describes how ELs must create and implement entrepreneurial strategies that are consistent with the enterprise's stage of maturity. Entrepreneurial strategy emphasizes that *any activity that is not focused on maturing the enterprise to the next stage is a waste*. For example, the strategy in stage one is all about how best to find the customers you are looking for with the least investment of time and without spending all the available money. If you do not find your customer, or enough customers, then you are out of business, and all other expenditures of time and money are wasted and distracting relative to achieving the only milestone that matters to your survival at that moment. ELs find "entrepreneurial strategy" to be a major competitive advantage and straightforward to implement, and by the end of Chapter Eight an EL will know how to put together very compelling strategies.

Another common mistake of entrepreneurs that ELs avoid is creating a dysfunctional organization that cannot implement the enterprise's strategy no matter how well it may be conceived. Organizational structures facilitate certain actions and impede others. It does great damage to an enterprise and its culture when an entrepreneur selfishly implements an organizational structure that impedes her team's ability to implement the strategy or operate productively. Understanding how to structure the company to utilize the talents of the team and to grow efficiently is a major strength of ELs. Chapter Nine is not about how to draw organization charts, but about aligning formal structures with informal ones so that the organization can execute entrepreneurial strategy. This alignment requires the EL to practice all of her skills.

Many enterprises fail because they cannot, or do not know how to, find and keep great employees. Small and growing enterprises need each and every employee to perform their assigned tasks productively and passionately; every person counts. Chapter Ten explains that hiring and firing is not a skill, but rather the result of successfully constructed projects and processes. With good hiring and firing, the EL builds a powerful team.

The ability to form and lead effective teams is something ELs need to do themselves as well as help others do successfully. Most enterprises deliver disappointing products and suffer from poor productivity because their teams are poorly led—eventually going out of business after wasting plenty of money. Chapter Eleven discusses the skill mix needed to lead successful teams, and also gives special attention to two specific kinds of team: the board of directors and the sales team, on which the fate of the EL and the enterprise depends.

Leaders are expected to successfully lead their teams through crises regardless of whether the crisis was preventable or not. Many entrepreneurs just give up when the first crisis hits. Unfortunately, crises get more challenging to survive as enterprises mature, and the fear of crises makes many entrepreneurs prevent their enterprises from growing and maturing at all. This deliberate reluctance to make any change leads to the eventual death of the enterprise and the entrepreneurial dreams that go with it. Leading through a crisis— the subject of Chapter Twelve—is a special case of leading change, and is a capability of all successful ELs.

Most people can be successful as entrepreneurial leaders once they dedicate themselves to getting the skills and help necessary. Everyone will need a great deal of help to succeed. Everyone will need to change. Everyone will need to be selfless. A good dose of selfishness is also required, but we have that naturally. If you are not willing to change, or ask for help, or be selfless toward those who help you, then you will not be successful growing any idea into a sustainably valuable entity.

Although being an entrepreneurial leader will enable you to create significant value with just an idea, it will not enable you to do the impossible. The final chapter is designed to help you understand what you can reasonably expect to accomplish, given your motivations, traits, and EL skills. The answer will be different for every person, but almost all of us have something to contribute to the welfare of others—and it is improving the welfare of others that creates value. You can create value. The big question is, do you want to do it?

The payoff is very large for getting this right: fulfillment, financial success, status, and well-being. The risk is large too, and it's not just financial: when a young enterprise is not successful, the entrepreneurs experience frustration, stagnation, economic hardship, and unhappiness.

If you want to be a successful entrepreneurial leader, if that is your real motivation, then read this book and use it. It will enormously increase your chances of success.

PART ONE

PREREQUISITES: MASTERING THE SKILLS OF ENTREPRENEURIAL LEADERSHIP

This part of the book describes the motivations and skills required to be an entrepreneurial leader. ELs, either instinctively or through coaching, understand that their strong selfish motivations are a prerequisite to entrepreneurial success because they enable them to act selflessly, as required of all successful leaders.

The skills of an entrepreneurial leader require no special traits to master, but they cannot be overlooked or ignored. The five required skills are self-awareness, relationship building, motivation, effectively leading change, and mastering the basics of how enterprises operate and mature.

The first part ends with a discussion of how entrepreneurial leaders hold themselves accountable, through the formulation of a personal leadership strategy (PLS), for finding their motivations and investing the energy and time to master these five skills.

Are You Selfish Enough to Be Selfless?

We start with two questions: "How much do you want to be an entrepreneurial leader?" and "Are you capable of being an entrepreneurial leader?" The answers to both lie in how well you know yourself. It is virtually impossible to turn your idea into something valuable and tangible if you are not motivated to do so. You must know what it is that you absolutely want to accomplish. Once you know what you want, you can answer the question of whether you are capable of getting it. What you are capable of achieving will depend not only on your motivations but also on your traits and your skills. We'll spend this chapter getting a clear picture of all three: motivations, traits, and skills.

Brian O'Kelley was twenty-nine-years old when he was fired as the CTO of Right Media, a company that Yahoo would spend $680 million to buy only a month after Brian's departure.[1] Brian had spent virtually every waking moment since graduating college trying to build successful new enterprises—four up to that point. After repeated failures, firings, and immense personal cost, Brian had succeeded in inventing a critical new advertising technology—only to find himself pushed out of the enterprise he had been instrumental making successful.

Brian's suffering amid repeated entrepreneurial failures finally led to an understanding of what it would take to lead a world-class team at a rapidly growing and maturing enterprise. His fifth startup, AppNexus, has successfully grabbed a significant share of the global advertising technology market from Google and Yahoo, a truly remarkable entrepreneurial accomplishment. Brian is thoughtful about his many failures and willing to share his startup leadership insights and epiphanies with others.

Brian started his first enterprise in high school when he bought a warehouse of obsolete computers from his local school district, enlisted friends, refurbished the computers, and sold them for twenty times what he paid for them. While he was studying computer science at Princeton, he and a friend got a contract to create software to automate TV studios, and he was almost expelled for breaking the rules against using university property for commercial purposes. Fortunately, Brian was able to convince the university to put him on probation, and he was able to finish his senior year.

In the fall of their senior year, Brian's roommate asked for his help on several projects involving building websites for some LA nightclubs and famous personalities. He convinced Brian to spend winter break in Hollywood to scope out the business potential. Talking to entertainment people in Hollywood confirmed for Brian that he had no interest in designing websites for nightclubs. He nevertheless became very intrigued with an opportunity he saw to sell tickets to nightclubs and concerts over the Internet (this was at the height of the dot-com bubble). Brian, his roommate, and another classmate with entertainment industry contacts decided to found a company that would get people to buy tickets online for local events. Within the next four months Brian raised half a million dollars and convinced nine graduating Princetonians to move to LA and work for the company. They were in business the day after they graduated from Princeton, calling their ticket-selling website LA2nite.

Within four months the business was out of money and had no real customers. There was a strong disagreement over the direction the company should take. Harsh words and recriminations led Brian's two cofounders to arrange for a psychoanalyst to try to get Brian to change the way he acted as CEO. Brian felt distraught and angry. Those four months had shown him that it would be much harder than he'd expected to make the company a success. On his own initiative Brian lined up someone willing to buy LA2nite for more money than their investors had put in. Rather than being happy with this news,

Brian's cofounders could not believe that he would want to sell their company—it had such great potential! Brian's best friend informed him that he had been voted out of the company, and Brian had no job, no company, and no choice but to go live in the basement of his parents' home in Georgia.

When you ask Brian about his motivation for founding LA2nite, he says, "It looked like an opportunity; Ticketmaster had a monopoly and was charging huge fees, and nobody was doing online ticket sales. We thought we could." Actions are driven by motivation. Consequently, for Brian or any entrepreneur who is motivated by an exciting opportunity, the motivation to continue the company goes away as soon as they no longer think their opportunity is exciting. Many entrepreneurs fail when they decide the effort "isn't worth it."

Five years later, after having been fired from two other enterprises he played a role in starting, Brian was broke and was working as a journeyman computer programmer for a company trying to create software to help advertisers make their internet advertising more effective. The founders of the company quickly realized Brian was extremely capable at understanding the complexities of the programs they needed to build, so they put him in charge of their nascent engineering team and gave him some stock options.

Brian's programs proved groundbreaking in the new business of advertising technology (referred to as "adtech"). The company, Right Media, grew quickly. But Brian was not happy. He had stopped communicating with the CEO, as he felt the CEO had made some very bad decisions, some of which Brian did not want to cooperate with him in implementing. Brian also insisted on controlling all decisions being made within the various departments and groups that worked for him. Brian had nineteen people reporting to him, and only he knew what all of them were doing and how they all needed to work together. After a year of fighting, the CEO was angry enough to fire Brian and strip him of a large number of the stock options that he had been awarded for his work and contributions. These lost stock options would have been enormously valuable just one month later when Right Media was sold to Yahoo.

Brian was furious. He felt ripped off. He also felt he had not gotten any of the credit he deserved for having conceived the programs and business models that revolutionized how companies place ads on the Internet. He wanted, more than anything he had ever wanted, to show the world that he was the person everyone should look to in order to understand the future of internet advertising. This burning need for credit and acknowledgment—for revenge, really—was Brian's motivation for founding AppNexus. But founding AppNexus wasn't easy. There were now large entrenched companies in the space. There were also rumors among the venture capital community about Brian being impossible to work with, and questions as to why anyone would want to invest in someone to start a new adtech company who had been fired from his last five jobs. Some savvy investors, however, knew that revenge is a powerful motivator and, when coupled with unique technical talents, can lead to a successful startup. Within a year Brian found financial backing to try again, and several years later, after a lot of hard work and having overcome enormous business and technical challenges, his new business was a huge financial success.

MOTIVATION IS POWER

Successfully taking an idea and turning it into something valuable and self-sustaining is extremely difficult, stressful, and demanding. The most challenging requirement for entrepreneurial success, however, is the requirement that you must change yourself—which every EL must do as his enterprise grows. Without a powerful motivation you will not make the required changes in yourself. Instead you will give up, often after having lost money, wasted precious years of your life, and having emotionally hurt people whom you cared for—just as Brian O'Kelley did with his first startup and just as a majority of failed entrepreneurs have done with theirs. Brian was motivated to start LA2nite when he felt the excitement of an overlooked opportunity, but he wanted to sell out as soon as he felt he was wrong about the business opportunity. At that point he did not have a strong enough motivation to make the leadership sacrifices required of an EL. Spotting a business opportunity was not enough. He needed something more completely selfish to drive him.

Your motivations drive your actions. They are your basic desires and fears. They are your *essential needs*. Your strongest motivations arise from the things that are the source of your happiness or that protect you from your primal fears. It wasn't until his fifth startup, AppNexus, that Brian's selfish motivation for starting his company was strong enough that he was willing to make all the selfless changes required of an entrepreneurial leader. His motivation was to prove to the world that he was the best person in the world to lead an advertising technology business. He felt he deserved that title and anything short of claiming it would be a failure too devastating to endure.

Some would call Brian's motivation "identity fulfillment"; others would call it revenge. An intense drive to fulfill your identity—in Brian's case, to be the best adtech entrepreneur alive—can be a powerful enough motivation to give you the energy, determination, and focus you need to make all the changes required of an EL. Here are some of the other motivations that often drive entrepreneurial leaders:[2]

- The desire to not have to work for anyone else—to be your own boss
- The desire to be rich
- Fear of starvation
- Fear of being humiliated in the eyes of a parent, a loved one, or a rival

These motivations are all completely selfish. They must be, in order to propel an entrepreneur to make the selfless sacrifices he needs to make growing his enterprise.

There are other motivations entrepreneurs mention that are usually not strong enough to drive both selfish and selfless actions, including:

- The desire to learn how to be an entrepreneur or successful business person

- The desire to do something fun or cool
- A feeling that the world needs your idea
- Not wanting to let that opportunity to make money pass you by

The major difference between these two lists is that the first is a list of essential needs and the second is a list of wants. The consequences of failure to fulfill the need to be an entrepreneur must be significant enough to drive the entrepreneur to overcome, *without any hesitation,* the hardships and traumas that must be endured to selflessly transform herself into the person her enterprise requires. There must be nothing else that is more important. If you hesitate to think about whether your idea is worth the trouble, then it is just a matter of time before you will want to bail out.

I meet many entrepreneurs. I always ask them, "Why did you start your company [or charity]?" They often tell me some variation of "I had a great idea that I thought the world needed." I then ask, "What if you could find somebody more experienced than you who could do a better job of successfully getting the world to adopt your idea? Would you be willing to hand over your idea to him?" Everyone always answers, "No," and then I ask them what they *really* want from their company. It usually takes another couple of rounds of question and answer before we get to what I recognize as the real motivations. They're often one of those in that first list. Even the most altruistic entrepreneurs who do not care about money or profit and who want to make the world a better place must accept that they have selfish desires. If they cared only about making the world a better place, then they would ultimately be more successful by working for an established philanthropy with more experience, resources, and contacts. Altruistic entrepreneurs selfishly want the world to become better *in the ways they want.*

Understanding your truest motivations is challenging and scary: these may not be consistent with the image you try to project. People are generally afraid to admit to their selfish motives, yet understanding and accepting these is a key to your future success. The process doesn't have to be complicated. Many people can find their core motivation by just honestly answering some tough questions. A classic method is to ask yourself the question, "If I were going to die today, what would make me feel my life had been a success?" It's a bit morbid, but it really gets to the point.[3] A less morbid variation could be, "What do I have to do to be completely satisfied with my life?"[4] Another method for finding your core motivation is to go to a trained therapist. The process will be more in-depth and involved—it will cost money—but it can be worth getting professional help if you cannot find out on your own what it is that you really want.

If you really want the possibility of succeeding in turning your idea into a self-sustaining enterprise, then the *truthful* answer to the question, "How much do you want to be an entrepreneurial leader, and why?" should be, "I want more than anything to be an entrepreneurial leader in order to . . . be rich, or be my own boss, or be successful in the eyes of my parents, or never ever feel hungry again . . ." or something else enormously selfish that means more to you than anything. Some entrepreneurs have succeeded in getting their enterprises part of the way to self-sustainability without deeply passionate motivations, and a tiny fraction of them have even been lucky enough to have made some money for their efforts. But I am not aware of any examples of entrepreneurial leaders who have built a self-sustaining enterprise without a passionate core motivation.

If you don't want to be an EL badly enough that you are willing to make enormous sacrifices and change yourself, don't despair: you can team up with somebody else who *does* feel that way. You can provide the EL with traits and skills they may not have and become a critical complement and essential founding teammate. As we will see, ELs are always on the lookout for major talent.

MOTIVATIONS, TRAITS, AND SKILLS: YOUR CAPABILITY MIX

To discover whether you are capable of being an entrepreneurial leader, we need to find out more of your motivations and also understand your traits and your skills. Your capabilities are the combination of your motivations, traits, and skills. Understanding your capability mix allows you to devise specific strategies for leveraging your strengths and mitigating your weaknesses to turn your idea into a tangible reality (how to put such a strategy together is the subject of Chapter Seven). The answer to the question, "Am I capable of being an entrepreneurial leader?" will hinge on the idea that you want the world to accept *and* your capability mix. So we are really answering the question, "What are the minimum capabilities I need to be credible in the eyes of the team I assemble to make my idea into a tangible reality?" We'll first deal with how you determine your capabilities, then figure out the minimum capabilities you'll need to be credible.

Motivations, traits, and skills define you; they are distinct but inter-related. You are born with your *traits* or they develop early in your life. They are tied to your physiology and to your psychology. Your traits influence what you feel and what you want, so they affect your moti-vations. I have traits that make me get bored with routine—it is just the way I am. I am therefore highly motivated to create new interest-ing situations for myself and to avoid repetitive tasks. It is important to understand what your traits enable you to do and what they inhibit you from doing—then you can figure out how to deal with them.

Skills are abilities to perform prescribed tasks. You learn skills; you are not born with them. Your mastery of a skill is influenced by your traits and your motivations. Skills likewise influence your motivations; achieving proficiency in some skill can make you feel you have satis-fied a motivation.

We have already talked about your motivations for becoming an EL, but you have other motivations in addition to the one that generates your greatest passion. These other motivations drive most of your everyday actions, like what you say and how you react. The motivations that drive your daily actions are important to understand because they drive your relationships—those you make and those you break. I was clueless about most of my motivations until the company I worked for assigned me an executive coach, someone who was a trained industrial psychologist. My executive coach pointed out that I had a strong "need to be needed," and this need drove some counterproductive competitive behavior that impeded my ability to lead larger groups of people and certain personality types. If I felt I had been excluded from a meeting or decision-making process in which I felt I had important points to make, then I would publically ask questions that would discredit the solutions they had proposed. I didn't realize what I was doing. Once this motivation was explained to me, then it was straightforward for me to change my behavior. I made it a goal to volunteer my ideas in a constructive and noncompetitive manner with subordinates, teammates, peers, and supervisors. With a simple change in behavior, I was soon being assigned to lead the most challenging projects. The change really just involved learning how to diplomatically offer suggestions. I also used my understanding of this motivation to overcome my trait of becoming bored with routine tasks. I now make routine tasks into fulfilling exercises by focusing on helping other people involved in the task. (When I discuss the skill of relationship building later, you will see how you can improve almost any relationship if you are motivated to do so.)

As you achieve some of your desires and overcome some of your fears, your motivations change (your most important motivations will change only with major events in your life), and you can learn to manipulate many of your subsidiary motivations that drive your daily actions and reactions. For example, you can often influence some of your motivations by deliberately sating some of your desires or getting help to successfully confront some of your fears (fear can motivate as much as desire). We all have many fears. Do you fear introducing yourself to strangers, or speaking in front of audiences, or delivering bad news, or making mistakes, or confronting someone who is belligerent, or . . . ? These fears limit you and what you can do. Adam, whom we met in Chapter One, had a fear of confrontation. He hated telling people he disagreed with them; this caused him to let people act in ways that were not in the best interest of his company. If Adam had realized that this fear would prevent him from being a successful EL, then he almost certainly would have been motivated to seek out help in overcoming it.

TRACKING DOWN YOUR TRAITS

Your traits are inborn or develop soon after birth. You cannot change them; you must learn to harness the strengths and mitigate the weaknesses they give you. You have hundreds of traits, some of which can help make it easier for you to become an EL and some of which can make it harder. No trait makes it completely impossible if you are willing to do the hard work to mitigate it—not shyness, or impulsiveness, or insensitivity to other people's emotions. Granted, some combinations of traits make it extremely difficult to achieve certain entrepreneurial ambitions: if you have the physical traits of being short, with poor hand-eye coordination, it becomes extra challenging to develop the skills to play basketball competitively enough to attract varsity high school athletes to your basketball camp. It is not impossible, but you will need to find basketball playing partners to help you achieve your dream.

Most of your traits, including personality traits, can be determined through straightforward testing, most of it free.[5] I list below the common traits that impact your ability to perform the essential skills of an EL. You need to do additional research beyond what we can discuss here to determine all the traits that could impact your ability to lead more specific entrepreneurial enterprises—such as a basketball camp.

Start your list by using the Myers-Briggs Personality Type Indicator (MBTI).[6] The MBTI is well established in the business world because it helps you better understand these traits: how you process information, how you relate to other people, and how you make decisions. The four Myers-Briggs personality dimensions or traits (introversion/extroversion, sensing/intuiting, thinking/feeling, and perceiving/judging) tell us a great deal about how we prefer to structure our relationships and how other people naturally want to structure theirs. MBTI is useful to understand because it can point to natural differences between how you and others act and react, and it can point to specific actions that can be taken to deal productively with those differences. In later chapters I'll refer to some of the situations in which an understanding of MBTI is useful, but for now, put it on your list of tools for determining your traits.

Next, figure out how you prefer to learn new things: verbally, visually, or kinesthetically (based on feel). You want to know how to put yourself in a position to learn new skills as easily as possible, as well as to understand how best to teach a skill to someone else.

Your intelligence, typically measured as intelligence quotient (IQ), plays a role in making it easier or harder to understand abstract concepts. If you understand your intelligence and your own level of skill at quickly understanding abstract or complex situations, then if necessary you can organize your enterprise to buffer you from having to make decisions in complex situations by yourself. You likely already have some understanding of your intelligence based on how easy it was for you to get good grades in school or high scores on standardized tests.

Your emotional intelligence (EQ) measures your ability to detect and understand other people's emotions. Your ability to quickly determine how to react to a person to convince them to do what you want is related to your EQ, and you need to understand whether this will be a challenge for you. You may already have a good sense of your EQ, based on people telling you that you are very empathetic or that you are a real people person. As with any trait, if your EQ is low then you will want to pay extra attention to finding partners and constructing your enterprise so you are not put in a position to have to respond appropriately to other people's emotions. As we will discuss in a moment, Brian O'Kelley has organized AppNexus in this way.

Three other traits can make a difference to your success as an EL: your physical stamina, your ability to stay mentally focused, and your control of your emotions. Natural physical stamina can give you a competitive advantage, allowing you to use your skills at a high level of mastery over long periods of time. Your ability to stay mentally focused for long periods can give you a competitive advantage in performing long-term intellectually demanding tasks, such as you might be called upon to do in a protracted negotiation. Each of us has a different level of intensity in how we emotionally react to stress and crises.[7] Does pressure make you calm, or do you become frantic and illogical? This trait can make a critical difference in what you are capable of doing by yourself, or with others, while under the many stresses that come from being an entrepreneur.

If you know the strengths and weaknesses related to your traits, you can construct strategies that leverage your strengths and mitigate your weaknesses. Brian O'Kelley has many traits that make it very difficult for people to work with him. He gets very emotional when things do not go right: he can scream and throw things. He tends to change his mind, frustrating his team by causing them to stop work on things he has decided are no longer important. When under stress he has a hard time understanding other people's emotions. He can be a control freak and a perfectionist to the point that no one can meet his expectations. There were reasons his best friend and partner engaged a psychoanalyst to intervene at LA2night to try and get Brian to understand how to be a better leader.

By the time Brian founded AppNexus, he was determined not to let his "quirks" get in the way of leading his team to adtech success. He spent time in therapy, he listened to his advisers, and he sought out and brought to AppNexus people who mitigated his weaknesses and complemented his strengths. With his complementary team in place, Brian now rarely finds himself in a position where he feels like throwing things or making people feel he doesn't care about them. People's appreciation of Brian's business and technical talents is no longer overshadowed by a fear of working with him. Brian is an excellent example of how troublesome traits can be mitigated.

DEVELOPING YOUR SKILLS

You need to be aware of your key skills and your level of proficiency in each of them. You do not need to list all of them, just those that could relate to forming and growing your idea into the enterprise you want. The following is a common depiction of the levels of proficiency:

- *Basic:* Can perform the task under nonstressful conditions
- *Competent:* Can perform the task under varying conditions with acceptable outcomes
- *Master:* Can consistently perform the task under very stressful conditions

- *Best-in-Class:* Can consistently perform the task under the most extreme possible conditions

Proficiency can improve with hours of practice and with experienced coaching, but what level of mastery you can achieve also depends on your traits and your motivations.

There are five skills that all ELs needs to master (best-in-class skills are not requisite for ELs):

- *Self-Awareness:* Understanding your motivations, traits, and skills
- *Enterprise Basics:* Understanding how an enterprise works and what an enterprise needs from its leader at each of its stages of maturity
- *Relationship Building:* Forming new relationships and making existing relationships stronger
- *Motivation:* Making others passionate about helping you become successful
- *Leading Change:* Leading people to willingly change what they already do successfully

I describe how you can acquire these skills in the following four chapters. These skills do not require any special traits, and they are all within the abilities of anyone with the driving motivation to be an entrepreneurial leader. Granted, some traits make developing some skills more challenging: if you struggle with numbers, you will have an enormous challenge becoming a great accountant, which is virtually required to start your own accounting firm. But if you do not have an innate ability to manipulate numbers, of course there are still countless other enterprises you can start.

Beyond these five essential skills, there are specific skills you may need to have in order to be perceived as credible at leading a team to turn your particular idea into a tangible reality. The specific skills you will need may not be obvious. Brian O'Kelley had a rare skill that he learned in college: how to create systems that can automatically scale over a network of different computers. This skill made him particularly effective at leading the technical design of the products that Right Media and AppNexus offered. Brian's technical knowledge also gave him the opportunity to learn how adtech functioned as a business—note that one valuable skill often develops the ability to learn other relevant and complementary skills. Brian knew the adtech business intimately, and he knew he would be a credible leader of AppNexus—provided he could lead himself to act in ways that would make people happy to work with him. Many people itching to be ELs already work in or around the type of business they want to lead. They can directly assess whether their industry-specific skills match or exceed those of the people running the business they work for or work with.

If you do not know what skills are required to lead the type of business you want to start, then you need to spend time to find out. The most direct way is just to ask some successful entrepreneurs in the relevant market. If you feel driven to start a chain of restaurants and you have never worked in the restaurant business, then read about founders of restaurant chains, big and small. Call the entrepreneurs up and ask them questions. If you are an admirer, tell them. Ask them what skills it takes to be a successful entrepreneur in their market. Are they all PhD computer scientists, trained chefs, or creative storytellers? You need to feel confident that you understand the bare minimum of skills you will need to master as well as the traits you need to mitigate to create a successful new enterprise in your industry of interest.

Profiles of relevant entrepreneurs are easy to find because many entrepreneurs love media attention.[8] Think of yourself competing with one of the entrepreneurs you have profiled. What skills would you need to do it better than he did? You don't have to have better skills than every one of the entrepreneurs you profiled, but if you can develop specific skills better than even one of them, you can feel yourself capable of being an EL in that business.

It is essential that you have a good grasp of the skills you have and the skills you lack. As you work to develop your idea, you will create a team, and missing skills can often be hired or developed in someone you have partnered with. What you need is enough skill to be credible in attracting a strong team to help you succeed. If you do not have previous experience working in the marketplace, then you need to assemble some people you respect and trust to tell you the truth about the skills you need. Tell them what skills you think you'll need and how you created your list. Use the people you have assembled to help you improve your list and also to give you confidence. In general, it is good to get advice from people who do not think exactly like you do and who have had different experiences.

It is virtually certain you will need to develop your skills to be successful in creating any new enterprise. You will need to develop or improve the five skills required to be an EL. It is certain that you will need help. Do not think of yourself as incapable just because you need help; think of yourself as the person who brings together a talented team of people who are excited about accomplishing a vision close to yours.

But there does need to be a good match between your capability mix and the industry you're interested in. As an extreme example of a minimum set of specific skills required to be a successful EL in a certain market, today's successful entrepreneurs in the semiconductor industry all have had extensive experience working in responsible positions in other semiconductor companies or in semiconductor divisions of big industrial enterprises. To be capable of being a semiconductor industry EL, you must either have the skill set of a top industry executive or be able to inspire a leading industry executive to want to partner with you. If your driving motivation is to be an EL in the semiconductor industry, you almost certainly will need to work many years in the industry, acquiring the skill set you need while meeting people with skill sets that complement yours—and who may be interested in working with you. If you are not motivated to do all of this, then you are not motivated to be a semiconductor EL. Less-developed and less-technical markets may require many fewer specific skills in order to be a successful EL. Franchisers provide the specific skills training required to be successful in the markets they serve.

The motivations of most aspiring ELs are not specific to an industry. If your motivation is to be rich or to be your own boss, then you do not really care what industry or market you break into. Consistent with your core motivation, you may need to flip your mindset from "I want to be an xyz [say, adtech] entrepreneur" to "I really just want to be rich, or my own boss, or . . ." The vast majority of all the wealth created by entrepreneurs is not in technology or highly specialized markets; rather, it comes from startups in mainstream businesses like retail, food, distribution, fashion, transportation, or construction. If you understand your true motivation, it is highly likely that you can find a market where the skills you already have, or can straightforwardly acquire, will make you capable of being an EL.

Knowing what you *can* accomplish will free you from some of the fears that are holding you back from trying to realize your dreams. Armed with an understanding of your motivations, traits, and skills, you can determine what you can accomplish by correlating them with people who have already been successful. If you meet the threshold set by anyone else who has been a successful entrepreneur, then you are capable of doing the same. The critical point of this chapter is that if you have an intense passion driving you to be an entrepreneur, you have the most important prerequisite to being a successful entrepreneur—an EL. Your driving passion will be your source of energy to make changes, to develop critical skills, and to endure the hardships and discomforts required of every entrepreneurial leader. The following chapters discuss the skills you will need to master. Chapter Seven summarizes how you can put together these skills to become the entrepreneurial leader your heart and soul are telling you is your destiny.

3

Enterprises Are Needy

Children are needy, and so are enterprises. Needs shift as the child or enterprise grows. If parents treat their teenager like an infant, trouble ensues. If an entrepreneur attempts to lead his growing enterprise the same way he did when the first prototype was built, trouble also ensues. A fledgling enterprise needs different things from its leader as it matures from an interesting idea into a value-producing, self-sustaining enterprise. Entrepreneurs are often insensitive to the trouble that comes from giving the wrong sort of attention and leadership to their enterprises. Once entrepreneurs are armed with some understanding about the basics of how their enterprises work and mature, they can avoid these troubles. Most ELs come by this knowledge the hard way, as they naïvely lead their enterprises into crises that could have been anticipated and avoided if they had only known about what their enterprises needed to mature properly. Some entrepreneurs are lucky enough to survive these crises and to learn from them; most are not.

Wendy Kopp is the founder of Teach For America (TFA) and one of the great entrepreneurial leaders of her generation.[1] Her accomplishments have changed the course of education in the United States. Yet Wendy started with no money or real-world experience, just an idea, which she turned into an enterprise that trains thousands of the brightest college graduates to successfully teach the country's most underprivileged students. TFA's revenues exceeded $270 million in 2011.[2]

Wendy's story is an outstanding example of how an entrepreneur with a good idea can become an EL just in time to save her enterprise from collapse. Entrepreneurial near-death experiences are frequently a catalyst for this transformation, but they do not have to be. Had Wendy known what her nascent enterprise really needed from her, she could have saved millions of dollars and spared herself years of wasted effort. Wendy started TFA upon her graduation from Princeton; she had had no opportunity to learn or even read about what new and fragile enterprises need (my Princeton class did not exist back then). In this chapter, we take a look at what it would have been important for Wendy to know.

PROJECTS, PROCESSES, AND CULTURE: THE THREE BASICS

Immature enterprises have only three parts that matter: projects, processes, and culture (these are essential to mature enterprises as well, but at different levels of scale and complexity). Everything an enterprise creates is the result of its projects, processes, and culture. This applies to all types of enterprises, regardless of whether their mission is to make money or create social good.

It is surprising, but even experienced business people can confuse projects and processes. *Projects* are a set of tasks performed by a team of people to create something new or to make something better. Projects have a finite existence; they start with some goal, and they end when the goal has been satisfactorily completed or when the team has been disbanded because of failure or because the project's objectives are no longer considered important. *Processes* are a set of tasks people repetitively perform to transform materials and information into something more valuable.[3] Projects and processes are completely different, and understanding their differences—and how they interrelate—is crucial to startup leadership. Table 3.1 summarizes the major differences and some important ways they relate to one another.

Table 3.1 Projects Versus Processes

Projects	Processes
Have never done this before.	Do the same thing repetitively.
Goals are about creating something new or about implementing a change.	Goal is to create value by repetitively performing a task.
Much less efficient than processes for transforming some inputs into an output (think of building a custom house versus houses built in a housing tract).	Processes are created by projects and therefore have an up-front cost of creation. This up-front cost is partially recovered each time the process is performed, as processes are much more efficient than projects.
Project status is monitored through achievement of milestones and the time and resources expended. The quality of project output is variable.	Process status is monitored through in-process measurements, often using statistical tools. The output quality of a process is typically greater and more uniform than the output quality of a project.
Projects are achieved by assembling people *temporarily* into a team with the skills and motivations required to achieve the project objective.	Processes are performed by people assigned *permanently* and who are trained in the required skills.
Project objectives and plans can be changed by whoever gives the project team its mandate and resources, provided the team also agrees.	Processes can be successfully changed only with significant planning and investment (a project is required to change a process).
Significant leadership is required to plan and execute a successful project.	Processes are managed, not led, unless they are to be changed.
Projects carry a greater risk of not achieving a successful outcome, relative to processes, because they do something new.	Process risks are well defined by statistics.
Projects create change.	Processes resist change.

Projects and processes must be used in balance in order for an enterprise to mature properly, and that balance shifts as the enterprise matures. Confusion between projects and processes stifles growth and destroys value, causing great frustration among many entrepreneurs.

All organizations have a *culture*, which is a shared understanding of how contributions are valued and rewards are given. The culture of an enterprise plays a critical role in its success, and once created it is extremely difficult to change. All groups of people who stay together for any period of time develop understandings about how they should behave in order to be tangibly or intangibly rewarded (for example, with improved status or special recognition such as bonuses). Culture exists irrespective of whether an organizational leader tried to consciously create it or not. It exists even in the least-mature enterprises—a culture is created as soon as founders start to make decisions that affect the status of their team. Each enterprise's culture develops through the reaction of people to the actions of managers and leaders with status high enough that they can give meaningful recognition and rewards. Founders have very high status and therefore have a disproportionate impact on how a culture develops.

Some aspects of culture are explicit or formal, but its most powerful aspects are implicit or informal. Formal aspects of a culture revolve around the written policies and rules that govern how the enterprise runs as well as the environment that the people work in. The informal aspects of a culture revolve around how people decide they will actually perform their work. Having a well-defined job with specific objectives does little to help employees understand how they should act to be rewarded, promoted, recognized, or given a more interesting assignment. Is it expected that an employee should make suggestions, take initiative in making improvements, always show up ten minutes early, or never question the boss? Even if the boss has a sign on his door stating "I love to answer questions," employees will have their own opinion on whether asking a question is a good idea or not. They will notice whether a questioning employee gets promoted or whether senior managers feel threatened by the act and give the questioning employee a hard time when the boss is not paying attention. ELs understand that informal expectations are more powerful in determining how employees, volunteers, suppliers, and others act than formal policies, directives, rules, or guidelines. ELs also understand that their actions play the most important role in creating the culture of their enterprises.

What about people? Don't they play a critical role in enterprises? Only the founder and the leader of the enterprise play a critical role, per se, which is what this book is about. Beyond the founder and the leader, what matters for people in enterprises is how well they can perform their assigned project and process tasks within the culture of the enterprise. The stark reality that the needs of enterprises are indifferent to virtually all the people that fulfill these needs creates a baseline feeling of alienation for many employees. People often feel they are "just a cog in a machine." Leaders must be sensitive to this by-product of enterprises. I discuss in Chapters Four and Five how leaders can develop personal bonds with their employees and teammates to mitigate this feeling of alienation.

SURVIVING THE FOUR STAGES OF ENTERPRISE MATURITY

Wendy Kopp did not understand the roles of projects, processes, or culture. This caused huge waste and inefficiency during the first two years of the organization. For example, Wendy's intuition was that it was best to get consensus agreements among all of her management for virtually every decision, which meant every decision was difficult to make and few reliable processes were in place. Just two years after founding TFA, Wendy Kopp seriously considered leaving. She was very lucky to have been introduced at that time to an accomplished business leader and consultant, Nick Glover, who explained the needs of enterprises to her, which gave her the confidence to fix TFA. Fixing TFA took another six years of significant emotional trauma.

To understand why TFA was ungovernable two years after it was founded, we need to understand how all enterprises mature. The growth of an idea into a value-producing and self-sustaining enterprise occurs in four distinct *stages*. These stages manifest themselves because projects, processes, and cultures do not just materialize; they must be created in a certain order subject to highly constrained resources. If they are not, a stunted, unproductive, and culturally problematic enterprise will ensue—analogous to what would happen if you were to raise an infant, child, or adolescent without sensitivity for the needs of each particular stage of the young person's life.

The four stages of enterprise maturity are[4]

- Customer validation
- Operational validation
- Financial validation
- Self-sustainability

Every enterprise must go through each stage in order to progress to the next. Attempting to jump past any stage results in an insecure foundation of projects, processes, and culture, which in turn leads to financial and cultural dysfunction. Enterprises cannot mature from one stage to another without their leadership maturing as well: entrepreneurs often stunt the growth and maturity of their enterprise by selfishly refusing to change their leadership style as required and wanting to leap over stages to work on innovative ideas that should necessarily wait for the final stage. Wendy had to spend several years backtracking through the stages she tried to skip, significantly changing the way she led to finally make TFA the socially valuable and self-sustaining enterprise it is today.

Stage One: From Idea to Real Customer

Your enterprise starts with your personal commitment to investigate turning your idea into something tangible. This commitment marks the start of *stage one*, which I call the *customer validation stage*. A *real* idea must identify some product or service you are thinking about delivering that some potential customers might be willing to pay for. Your idea must be exciting enough that you want to do it. Having an idea that you want somebody else to do for you without your involvement is just a dream. Stage one is entirely about validating your idea by finding out whether it can be morphed into something actual customers will give you money to achieve. Stage one ends when you have found enough committed potential customers that you can economically afford to start producing and delivering the product or service they are willing to buy.

Wendy Kopp got her idea for Teach For America when she was in charge of holding a conference on educational reform for a Princeton student organization she led. Listening to some speakers at her conference lament that top students did not go into teaching, Wendy was hit with the notion that there should be a way to attract accomplished students to teaching by creating a Peace Corps–like experience. Wendy became passionate about this idea. She convinced a professor to let her work out this idea in the form of a senior thesis, which all Princeton seniors must write in order to graduate. Researching the idea and writing the thesis enabled her to make a detailed plan on how to create a teacher corps, convincing herself the idea was doable. Wendy modified her senior thesis into a proposal for funding, which she sent to thirty business leaders in hopes that they would help her fund a teacher corps. This solicitation marked the start of stage one. From Wendy's thirty letters to business leaders, she found two corporate executives who were willing to give her some office space and $26,000 to start her project.

Stage one is all project and no process. It is all about doing something for the first time. Wendy had developed a decent project plan for creating TFA from her senior thesis work, which, as with all entrepreneurial plans, was later modified extensively. In her book *One Day, All Children*, Wendy admits to making up some of the plan on the spot. She would come up with answers whenever someone asked her how something would work that she had not considered. Changing the idea on the fly is what all entrepreneurs do as they talk with the potential customers, investors, employees, volunteers, or suppliers whose support they need. Every decision in stage one is just a best guess until a real customer says they want to pay for it. If Wendy had answered questions by saying, "I never thought of that! Let me figure out a process for doing that, and I will get back to you in a few weeks with an answer," she would have needed to raise more money than would have been possible while also losing the confidence of many people potentially interested in her idea.

Wendy Kopp and her team completed stage one in April 1990, just about one year after she had finished her senior thesis. Stage one ended when she received firm commitments from six school districts to hire TFA's teachers and Wendy had raised the $2.5 million she estimated would be needed to fund the first full year of operation.[5] The year had been full of crises, ending only when $2 million was raised just in time to fulfill commitments to 489 graduating college seniors to send them to teach in low-income school districts around the country. Wendy's leadership in stage one was instinctual and brilliant relative to what we now understand are best practices (you can find full descriptions of all the stages in Appendix D):

• She had done her research and scoped out, as best she could, the challenges she would face. Her senior thesis was a great vehicle for making what we will describe in Chapter Eight as an *entrepreneurial strategy*.

• She had talked with hundreds of potential customers, donors, employees, and advisors to get as much input and help as possible. She had not been afraid to call anyone she thought could help, even if she did not know that person.

• She had hired enthusiastic people who were passionate about her idea and were practical, rather than idealistic, about getting a wide range of tasks accomplished. She had hired talented jacks-of-all-trades who wanted to help her turn her idea into reality rather than hiring experienced experts who might have fought her for control.

• She had led stage one as a project and adjusted the project plan according to actual inputs from the customers, donors, and her new team members.

• She had delegated to others responsibility for key parts of her plan, such as recruiting graduates, finding school districts, and setting up a teacher training boot camp, thereby using everyone's ability to the fullest extent possible.

Stage Two: From Real Customer to Functioning Enterprise

Kopp's major problems, however, started in stage two, *operational validation*, which requires developing the ability to

- Deliver the product that customers actually want to pay money for
- Satisfy customers once the product has been delivered
- Confirm that you know how to find and capture new customers

Wendy had promised her customers (the school districts) that TFA would be operational and able to deliver the first corps of inspired and trained teachers within months of getting the school districts' commitments. Wendy knew this would be an enormous challenge and had started projects to develop the operational processes she would need even before stage one ended, including assigning someone to work out how to quickly recruit and select talented students. Under huge time pressure, the project was underplanned, underresourced, and chaotically executed, leaving many applicants angry. Wendy had even sent out employment offers to 488 students before she had enough money to pay their salaries.

Wendy asked one of her new recruits to quickly develop an innovative eight-week boot camp to turn new college graduates into inspired teachers of low-income students. Her team executed their projects as best they could with limited time and resources. This underplanned and underresourced boot camp created more chaos and anger among the recruits. The chaos disillusioned many, but fortunately not so many as to prevent the newly minted teacher corps being deployed to school districts in time to start the 1990–91 school year.

One objective of stage two is to deliver the product and make adjustments to the product to the point where you know it can satisfy existing customers and attract new ones. Stage two, operational validation, starts out by initially delivering products and capturing new customers as a series of one-off projects and then, using what has been learned from these experiences, develops very basic product delivery, sales, and administrative processes. Stage two does not end until the customer value proposition is well understood and basic processes to run the enterprise, satisfy the customers, and find new customers are in place and consistently producing happy customers.

Unfortunately, Wendy Kopp led stage two at TFA just as she had led stage one, as one big project where every decision would be discussed in a weekly huddle with everyone participating. Decisions about what to do next were made by consensus, except the twenty-five people who participated in the weekly meeting that ran from 9 PM till past midnight felt that consensus really meant that Wendy held veto power over any decision made.

As soon as an enterprise has a real customer, the enterprise becomes more complex overnight. Real customers give real feedback, and effectively digesting all that new information is critical for deciding what to do. Once past stage one, acting weekly by consensus is a disastrous leadership decision. At TFA, problems presented themselves faster than any group consensus could solve them, and performance suffered to the point where applications to TFA actually declined. The troops became demoralized, and the entire team threatened to quit unless Wendy agreed to be bound by a majority vote at these marathon meetings. She refused. The team did not quit; they just became more demoralized.

Wendy was also demoralized and completely exhausted, because at that point her approach was to try to fix her leadership problems by working harder and hiring more people. This actually made it more difficult for any of her team to find time to talk with her, and they spent more money while not actually fixing real problems.

Fortunately, at a time when she was depressed enough to consider leaving TFA, she was introduced to Nick Glover, an experienced executive and consultant. Nick arranged to listen to Wendy and her three most trusted lieutenants talk about their troubles for three days. He told them they needed to change. He explained to Wendy that she could not make all the decisions, and she needed to split the company into functional teams that had the leadership and responsibility to identify and fix problems themselves. The weekly meeting now would include only the heads of the functional areas: fundraising, program (that is, supporting the teacher corps), and staffing, plus a representative of the teacher corps.

Morale and decision making improved immediately. Once TFA's functional areas could implement their processes and solve their problems without waiting for the rest of the enterprise to agree with them, then stage two could be quickly completed. TFA then solidified its ability to recruit, select, train, and deploy a yearly corps of about five hundred teachers, delivered to a set of school districts that wanted them. Stage two was finally completed.

Stage Three: From Functionality to Effectiveness

Stage three starts when stage two finally has put into place critical processes to deliver the product, find and maintain happy customers, and keep the enterprise operating. The objective of stage three, *financial validation*, is to make the enterprise financially secure by making sure it can produce value under changing market and competitive conditions.[6] To complete this stage, the entrepreneur must put in place a new set of processes, flexible enough to handle significant growth and changes in demand, while not depending on any specific person(s).

Many entrepreneurs dislike this stage because it is not fun. It is all about making things work better, measuring performance to figure out where to make improvements, and ultimately making sure nobody needs you around to operate successfully. Stage three is about putting in place processes that are effective and flexible enough to meet any foreseen changes in demand. Stage three requires the enterprise to introduce new product and service variations to keep new and existing customers satisfied—the customer can never be ignored. The enterprise must create a strong foundation of processes that enable it to routinely deliver high-quality, cost-effective products. If the enterprise does not develop these capabilities at this time, then all future growth and development will be built on ineffective, unscalable processes, resulting in the loss of customers, a bad reputation, and wasted resources. In a competitive marketplace, stage three determines an enterprise's long-term competitiveness. Stage three is about introducing the myriad of product variations required by an ever-growing list of customers; it is *not* about developing innovative and risky new products, technologies, or business models—that is the focus of stage four.

Stage three ends when the enterprise is able to operate independently of any specific people, and its processes are proven scalable and efficient enough to produce significant value in the form of profit or surplus. Many founders hate to think that they are making their enterprise capable of effectively operating without them—in fact, many entrepreneurs even selfishly act up to get attention when their teams get close to establishing their ability to operate independently. Most entrepreneurs never finish stage three.

Wendy Kopp came perilously close to not finishing stage three. The relief brought on by the organizational improvements suggested by Nick Glover emboldened Wendy into thinking that she could once again focus on her personal mission of reforming education in America. She did not feel she needed to spend her time making sure her enterprise was on a firm financial foundation, producing consistent educational outcomes while operating effectively without her hands-on involvement. She felt that she needed to raise more money so she could enact more educational reforms. Wendy wanted even more from her team and her supporters, and over their objections Wendy insisted that TFA start two entirely new innovative educational reform programs, TEACH! and The Learning Project.

For any enterprise to become self-sustaining, it must create new, innovative products and services—but this can happen only after the enterprise has robust, scalable high-quality processes in place and is financially able to support the added costs. Innovative projects cannot be developed until an enterprise is financially stable enough to endure the extra costs and risks, which occurs only at the end of stage three. These two new programs drained TFA's financial resources, spread its leadership too thin once again, and again made Wendy frantic about raising enough money to make weekly payroll. Two years after

Glover's help and after having finished stage two, TFA had slipped back into crisis mode, requiring more money just as donors were frustrated and offering less. Morale was again terrible, and Wendy even found employees falsifying reports in order to cover up problems. The culture had become corrupt because Wendy had gone and done what she wanted without regard to the needs of the enterprise.

In 1995, after months of ongoing financial crisis, Wendy found herself having to deal with another equally dangerous crisis: an article in an established educational journal by a professor of education at Columbia questioned whether TFA added any educational value at all. This is the equivalent of the local newspaper saying your restaurant has roaches. The allegations were poorly documented and anecdotal, but they still had a detrimental impact on donations and morale. Wendy despaired. She didn't know whether TFA should go on, and she asked her team what they thought. They told her that TFA had been best when it had just started and was focused on a single goal, and that it was important to refocus on that singular mission.

In her depressed state, Wendy finally came to understand that major changes were necessary if TFA was to have any chance of achieving its original mission. She and her organization needed to focus on improving their essential processes and operating within their means. They needed to hold themselves accountable to achieving their original goals. She needed to fire poor performers and promote the people who were good at inspiring their teams. She needed to shut down TEACH! and let The Learning Project sink or swim as an independent organization on its own. To keep the original teacher corps concept alive and well supported—rather than always being poorly resourced and in crisis—Wendy needed to cut 25 percent of her TFA expenses and staff, leaving only the essential people and expenses.

When Wendy Kopp came to these realizations and committed herself to these changes, she became an entrepreneurial leader. These were selfless decisions, involving her giving up some dreams for the sake of TFA. After four years of detours and poor leadership, Wendy finally knew what she had to do to complete stage three.

She brought in a new team—including, as chief operating officer, a former TFA corps member and McKinsey consultant focused on improving processes and performance. Morale soared despite the layoffs. These changes brought a new culture to TFA to replace the old corrupted one. It would have been virtually impossible to change it otherwise, as the previous team had never known what an effective enterprise culture felt like. After two years of dedication to measuring and improving the effectiveness of all of TFA's processes, including fundraising and teacher training, the enterprise was producing consistent financial surpluses while once again growing the size of its corps and the number of communities it served. Stage three was finally completed.

Stage Four: From Effectiveness to Self-Sustainability

The objective of stage four, the *self-sustainability* stage, is to create a process for innovation that can enable an enterprise to finally become self-sustaining. Without the ability to innovate, an enterprise will eventually die because customers' spending priorities always change. Because it takes time for these shifts to occur, many entrepreneurs and stage three top executives feel no pressure to undertake the often contentious changes required to start and complete stage four. The result is their enterprise's slow demise.

Stage four is often contentious for these reasons:

• The resources required to support the innovation efforts typically decrease the resources available for other areas, setting up an apparent competition about who is doing more important work. Many erstwhile leaders let this competition fester to the point where key talent takes sides, setting up the culture to unproductively pick winners and losers.

• The enterprise's most successful managers have abilities that made them good at continuously improving complex processes (a stage three task), not at running open-ended, risky innovation projects. These successful managers can feel threatened when somebody with project leadership skills, working independently, is appointed to lead innovation. These managers have many opportunities to make the innovation leader look as if he is struggling.

The chapters that follow on building relationships (Four) and leading change (Six) give some essential insights on how to prevent these problems from derailing the completion of stage four, but many profitable enterprises complete stage three and never start stage four. The feeling is, why make risky changes when the enterprise is working and producing value? Entrepreneurs who are motivated to be rich have a particularly hard time justifying to themselves the need to work even harder to make their company self-sustaining once their firm achieves financial success. If the entrepreneur is not motivated to lead change, then clearly it will be difficult for him to motivate his team to do so. Some enterprises can survive for a long time just harvesting value from a single large market: think of Xerox and photocopiers, as well as many fine restaurants and fashion designers. I note only one exception to enterprises needing to complete stage four in order to become self-sustaining: enterprises that have been granted legal monopolies for essential services, like utilities or schools—their customers have no choice.

The stories of the many enterprises that are named each year to *Inc.* magazine's *Inc.* 500 | 5000 are telling. The *Inc.* 500 | 5000 is a listing of the fastest-growing enterprises in the United States, and virtually all of the companies on the list are in stage three—otherwise they would not be able to grow so quickly. The Kauffman Foundation, which is dedicated to promoting entrepreneurship, studied 1,300 of the companies that appeared on the list from 2000 to 2006. By 2010, almost half of the companies studied were smaller; most were *much* smaller. Five percent had gone out of business. About one-third of the firms had merged or been sold, but this was not necessarily a satisfactory outcome for many of the founders, as over 40 percent of the entrepreneurs that had sold their companies felt the need to start another enterprise, while another fraction had stayed working for the larger firm, thereby giving up on their motivations to be their own boss or to become extremely wealthy.[7] These statistics underscore the fact that most of the businesses that make it successfully to stage three do not make it through stage four.

In 1997, once Wendy felt secure that TFA was operating on a solid foundation of processes, she once again looked to expand the scope of TFA's capabilities. This time she was doing what the enterprise needed. Stage three had been successfully completed; now the enterprise needed to demonstrate that it could be innovative again. Having made difficult, selfless decisions multiple times to save her enterprise, Wendy was supported by her team, donors, and advisors when she revived TEACH! as The New Teacher Project. Now that TFA was on a solid financial and operational foundation, Wendy knew exactly what to do to make The New Teacher Project successful. Having led the efforts to put into place high-quality processes for each of TFA's core capabilities, everyone involved, from funders to employees, finally had complete confidence in Wendy's ability to take innovative education reform ideas and turn them into self-sustaining enterprises, inside or outside of TFA.

An entrepreneurial leader completing stage three has major advantages in being the leader of stage four. Having seen someone successfully lead the enterprise through three arduous stages, the employees and top executives will be much more likely support their leader when she says they all must change again to complete yet another stage. This is a major benefit of helping entrepreneurs to become ELs that some venture capitalists and boards of directors do not appreciate. Under the leadership of an EL, an enterprise will change as it will for no other, just as a caring and successful parent who has provided continuous selfless emotional support can best support their young adult as they become an independent adult.

I should mention that big companies that try to foster entrepreneurial thinking inside their organizations often screw up because they disregard these stages. The stages are required, in the order described here, to create a secure foundation from which an idea can change into a self-sustaining, value-producing entity. It makes no difference whether the entity being created is a new division within a larger corporation. Big companies often require their "innovation leaders" to document that they have capable processes in place before they are even allowed to talk to customers to see if they could be interested in the resulting products. Process development in stage one both wastes money and makes for mediocre products compared to designs that entrepreneurs develop directly from customer input. Processes must wait until stage two. Furthermore, large companies have many interlinked complex processes, and it is costly, time consuming, and risky to add or modify processes to accommodate new products that are too innovative. Many big companies stifle innovation because they don't want to deal with developing the completely new processes many new products require. This phenomenon has a name: the "innovator's dilemma."[8]

Big companies are challenged in another way to be as innovative as a startup. Big companies typically change leaders at every stage of a new product's evolution. R&D managers hand off to NPI (new product introduction) managers, who then hand off to production managers and sustaining engineering managers. Constantly changing leaders does not matter much when a new product does not require significantly different processes, organization, and subcultures. Products that naturally fit into what a company already does are really just extensions of the products the company offers. But nonincremental new products cannot be effectively developed, introduced, and nurtured to maturity without going through all these four stages. Changing leaders at each stage creates two problems. First, the handoff from one department to another always takes (that is, *wastes*) time. Secondly, an appropriately innovative subculture cannot be sustained through multiple different leaders with different leadership styles. I have seen this problem doom many large company's attempts to introduce otherwise worthy products and services. Big companies limit the scope of their innovativeness by changing leaders at each stage.

Building Relationships

Changing the world based on your idea requires that you get other people to help you. This chapter is about how you can create new relationships and strengthen existing relationships that you will need to launch and grow any enterprise. The relationship-building concepts I introduce here are simple yet extremely powerful. To illustrate the potency of these concepts, I use two different real cases, with the first one involving a new company initiated by a family. I have chosen to use a small family business case to start the discussion of relationship building because the simplicity of the enterprise focuses the attention of the case on the dynamics of the relationships involved and creates a solid foundation from which we can consider more sophisticated applications of the concepts in the rest of the chapter.

Michael was very disappointed with his job. Growing up, he thought that being a reporter would be a cool job, and he worked diligently toward that goal: top journalism student, editor of the school newspaper, local correspondent for news services, and so on. Now that he had achieved his goal and secured a job as a reporter at a major newspaper, he hated it. He was both uninterested in the stories he covered and ashamed that he had to sensationalize them in order to please his editors. He felt like he was making the world a nastier place, not the better world he had hoped good reporting might help create. He also felt that his reporter's salary would not allow him to give his family the comfortable life he wanted for them.

Michael's wife, Laura, was the daughter of a very successful entrepreneur, Larry, who founded and ran a retail appliance chain.

Larry had been very generous in giving the couple a nice house in a very good neighborhood as a wedding gift. Michael's salary barely paid for food and clothing for himself, his wife, and their five-year-old son, Jimmy, let alone the real estate taxes and utility bills on a bigger house than they really needed. Michael felt uncomfortable being so beholden to Larry.[1]

Larry knew Michael disliked being a reporter, as it was a topic at family dinners. Larry had invited Michael many times to join him at LL Appliances, but Michael didn't see himself as a salesman, or as his father-in-law's employee. Both Michael and Laura were shocked and intrigued when one night Larry suggested that he become an investor in a company that Michael and Laura could start and run together.

"You could make a lot of money, you could be your own bosses, you could be independent, and there is no good reason not to take my offer. It'll be your own show; I won't even give you advice if you don't want." Larry proposed to financially invest in his daughter and son-in-law's starting a chain of bathroom design stores. Larry knew from his appliance business that such businesses were growing fast and making their owners a great return.

Michael and Laura talked about the offer for a week before deciding to accept. They were very excited about the prospect of running their own business without the risk of having to borrow the money to do it. Michael worried about being even more beholden to Larry, but after a week of discussions with Laura he felt could take Larry at his word that he wouldn't give advice unless it was asked for.

The most common investor in all entrepreneurial ventures is a family member. In any given year, family members, other than the founder, invest twice as much money in startups as do venture capitalists. This fact should not be surprising because family members already share many feelings and common experiences such that a foundational relationship already exists from which to build a related business relationship. Chipotle, Dell, Microsoft, and Turner/CNN are examples of big companies that started with family support. Family businesses rely on customers, going through the four stages, and dealing with competitors and changing market conditions the same as any other business. The major fundamental difference between a family and non-family business is that there are pre-existing relationships between key stakeholders, which make the businesses easier to start but harder to mature. Relationship building is a critical skill for all entrepreneurial leaders whether or not they are working with a family member or have family members as investors.

Larry was thrilled that Michael and Laura would finally be their own bosses and that he was in a position to make sure they would be successful. Larry was self-made. He had grown up in a poor part of Brooklyn with poor immigrant parents. He had had to start holding down a job to help the family pay for food when he was ten years old. Larry had been an apprentice truck mechanic when he graduated from high school at seventeen, and he was proud of the fact he was good at both fixing a truck and selling a truck. After ten years of working as a mechanic, Larry had convinced the owner of a dealership to let him work the sales floor on weekends. He was soon making more money as a salesman than as a mechanic. After eight years of sales success, Larry had a house, $20,000 in the bank, and a fiancée. He was full of confidence, and he wanted more than anything to be his own boss. With the blessing of his fiancée, Larry opened his appliance store, taking out a second mortgage on the house to pay for the inventory. Thirty-two years later, Larry was a widower with a chain of twelve appliance stores, two houses, no mortgages, two children, one grandchild, and a 12 handicap at golf. One thing Larry didn't get enough of was time with his grandson, Jimmy, now that the little boy was so busy with after-school activities and playing with his friends.

Nine months later, after the bathroom store had been opened for two months, Larry felt frustrated that Michael and Laura were not asking for his advice. They had become avid readers of *Inc.* magazine instead. Reading *Inc.*, however, did not prevent them from making mistakes that Larry felt could have been avoided. They had hired and fired two receptionists while Larry had a great person he would have been glad to recommend to them if they had just asked. Another mistake he observed was that Michael and Laura were not wearing tailored clothing to work, not realizing they were sending a signal to their customers that they were not very successful. Discussions at family dinners had become stilted, as Michael and Laura brushed aside Larry's questions about what was happening at work. When Larry tried to make a suggestion as diplomatically as he could, Michael and Laura would respond, "This is a different business than appliances, and we need to run it differently." Larry felt they were purposely making him feel very uncomfortable any time he visited their store, even he was there just to offer to pick up lunch for them because they were working so hard.

It was plain that the situation had become tense and was heading in the wrong direction. The vast majority of the time, situations like this will spiral out of control, destroying family bonds and a business. But once those involved are armed with relationship-building skills, relationships do not have to spiral out of control. Unfortunately, most entrepreneurs, not just in family businesses, have underdeveloped relationship skills. Most businesses are founded by a person who is fixated on either money, a particular product, an idea, or an aversion to working for other people—all selfish fixations independent of strong relationships with other people. Fortunately, it is possible—and fairly straightforward—to foster powerful relationship-building skills to help grow enterprises and avert most people problems.

SHARED OBJECTIVES: THE FOUNDATION OF ALL RELATIONSHIPS

All relationships are formed when you have at least one shared objective with another person. No shared objective, no relationship. Some shared objectives stimulate a great deal of emotion; others are almost trivial. At work you share important objectives with your boss about completing your assigned tasks as he expects. On the subway platform you may share with a stranger a fleeting objective of squeezing into a packed subway car. A shared objective is any change that two people care about, but they do not have to agree how the change should be accomplished. *The shared objective exists whether the people realize it or* not; *all that matters is that at least one party takes some action to make the change happen.*

Here are some classic shared objectives:

- Anytime we want something, it has to come from somebody else with whom we have a shared objective of possessing that "something." That something may be tangible, like a book, or it could be emotional, like being acknowledged for being a good student.
- Anytime we want to achieve something that someone else also cares about, be it tangible or not, that achievement is a shared objective. The achievement may be intangible, like the passage of a new law limiting the sale of candy to children, in which case anyone who cares about the passage or defeat of that law has a shared objective.
- Many times when we want to change how we feel, it requires another person to stimulate that emotion. The action that must be performed by one person to change the feeling of another person is a shared objective.
- Similarly, when we want to change the emotional state of another person, whether they want the change or not, the emotional state of the targeted person becomes a shared objective.

Any potential change that has been consciously or unconsciously set in motion by the action of one person leads to the creation of a shared objective with any other person who cares about the change. The actions resulting from a single shared objective constitute a relationship and can fall into one of three categories: *cooperative, competitive,* or *retreating.*[2]

- A cooperative shared objective arises when you and the other person in the relationship agree how you will split the benefits and costs of trying to achieve the shared objective; for example, "I will get the book you want and give it to you."
- A competitive shared objective is one where you and the other person in the relationship do not agree how you will split the benefits and costs of trying to achieve the shared objective; for example, "I will not let you have that book."

- A retreating shared objective is one where either person in the relationship does not care how you will split the benefits and costs of trying to achieve the shared objective; for example, "I don't care if you get the book" or "I don't know where the book is."

We can have many relationships with the same person at the same time. People can be confused into thinking that there is a one person–one relationship rule. The people whom we feel are important to us are people with whom we have multiple shared objectives. Intense relationships—whether from work, family, or play—have many shared objectives that are some combination of cooperative, competitive, and retreating. Even your most intimate and powerful relationships are a mix of all three. As we will discuss, you actually need all three categories to create balanced and mutually satisfying relationships with anyone else—yes, all strong relationships need a mix of competitive and retreating shared objectives to be balanced with cooperative shared objectives in order to be emotionally satisfying.[3]

It is important for ELs to realize that anything they want to accomplish will require forming relationships, typically many different relationships with each of many different people, with relationship falling into one of the three categories: cooperative, competing, or retreating. *Being able to control or influence the category in which a relationship is formed will have a major impact on how easy or difficult it is to get people to help the EL accomplish what he wants.* ELs must be able to identify the myriad of relationships they have with people important to their success. Being able to identify each relationship with another person as a separate shared objective enables ELs to understand which specific steps they can take to improve the expected benefits of each shared objective. A related third insight is that by understanding the shared objectives between other people, ELs can then take concrete steps to improve the relationship outcomes of those around them.

There is a natural and fundamental precedence among the three categories of relationships.[4] Competition always takes precedence over the other two: you cannot retreat from or cooperate with someone who insists on competing with you. If you cannot agree on how to split the costs and benefits associated with achieving something you both want, then you will have to compete to see who gets to determine the split. Even if you want to retreat from a competitive situation, the other person may not let you. "Escaping" is a competitive act that requires you to be capable enough to elude your competitor. Retreat always takes precedence over cooperation because you cannot cooperate with someone who is disinterested in cooperating with you. Cooperation occurs only when both parties want it.

The skill of *relationship building* derives from understanding when to use each category of relationship and how to change a shared objective from one category to another. *ELs avoid the misconception that cooperation is always good, competitive relationships are bad, and retreat is something you want to avoid.*

UNDERSTANDING COOPERATION

Cooperation occurs when two people agree on how to share the costs and benefits of achieving some shared objective. You cooperate constantly; whenever you buy something, when you do your assigned work, and when you listen to a friend tell you a funny story.

Cooperation has its benefits. Cooperation is the most effective way for two or more people to create something new that neither party could do on their own. The reward and risk of cooperative shared objectives lies in whether the cooperating parties can achieve their shared objective. Cooperation is therefore the least risky way to achieve a difficult outcome (unlike competitive shared objectives, for which there is additional risk in determining how benefits and costs will be split), which is why many people feel cooperation is always good.

Cooperation requires a big investment of resources and emotional energy. This investment of energy is required to set up and constantly test whether the other party(ies) that share the objective remain committed to sharing the costs and benefits as expected. Not only do cooperating parties have to invest the resources and energy to achieve their shared objective, but they also have to invest in setting up the expectation for sharing, along with some form of monitoring to make sure nobody is going to get more than what was agreed to. You can see this clearly with commerce, which is a cooperative act that can occur effectively only with the enactment of many laws along with costly enforcement systems that everyone feels confident will catch cheaters. An important corollary to this insight is that you cannot cooperate with somebody you do not trust!

Cooperation has other challenges. Cooperation achieves mediocre—also called "lowest common denominator"—results because it requires achieving a consensus of how costs and benefits will be shared. We often feel disappointed in the results of cooperation that takes place with people with whom we do not know well enough to either compete with or retreat from, because you can only agree to do what nobody in the group objects to. As we will discuss, without competition and, very often, retreat, a top-quality result cannot be achieved.

Cooperation presents yet another big challenge: it resists change. Any time a part of the shared objective is changed, some or all of the energy and resources invested in setting up the mechanisms for sharing costs and benefits must be thrown away, requiring costly new investments. As a simple example, if you and your cooperating partner are going to bake an apple pie together but there are only blueberries at the market, the entire cooperation must be reevaluated to make sure all parties like blueberries. If blueberries cost more than apples, that leads to other resets in the cooperation: Who will pay for the extra cost? And if one person contributes more, will that person get to eat more of the pie? Cooperative relationships are fragile; that is why most of them do not last very long before becoming either competitive or retreating.

Because cooperative relationships require a heavy investment of energy and resources, you cannot have many of them. As we shall soon see, most relationships that people think are cooperative are actually retreats. ELs need to be very thoughtful and discerning about the relationships they start and maintain, because even the most energetic people have limited energy and resources available to invest in their cooperative relationships. Fortunately, hope is not lost for ELs who need the support of large numbers of people. In the next chapter we talk about how ELs can motivate large groups of people to help them achieve their objectives.

A final note on cooperation: not only is it costly, fragile, and inflexible, but it also can distract you from noticing other more productive and valuable uses of your energy and resources. *Cooperation is very costly to maintain and therefore should be used sparingly and only where it can achieve a very high return on the expended effort.*

A summary of the costs and benefits of each relationship category can be found in Appendix E.

UNDERSTANDING COMPETITION

Competition is much more common than cooperation; indeed, it permeates our lives. We are all inherently selfish and want the same things that others want. We all want some amount of status, attention, money, sex, comfort, fun, security, and feeling good about ourselves. We usually do not agree on how to share these things we want, in the quantities we want, with even our closest friends and family.

Competition is also commonly misunderstood as something to be avoided, when in actuality it is required in order to achieve high-quality results. Competition occurs when two or more people want to achieve the same objective but do not agree on how they will share the benefits and costs of achieving that objective. If two people decide to pursue an objective, in spite of not agreeing how to split the costs and the benefits, then each must expend additional energy and resources to force the other party to accept the split they want. That investment of energy and resources to determine an outcome constitutes a test of ability. "What" is being tested is determined by the two parties. It could be a test of who is stronger, but it will more likely be a test of who can convince some third person with power over all parties to choose between the competing proposed activities; for example, brothers competing for the attention of their mother, or peers at work competing over who will be promoted by their boss.

Competition adds significant value if it provides a meaningful test, such as gaining understanding of which strategy is better or which product is more appealing. The EL wants to create competitions in order to create high quality results and efficient operations. The challenge is to formulate competitions such that each competing person understands the benefit of achieving an overall better result by putting forward their best solutions to be judged in the harsh light of competition.

Competition can deliver benefits beyond performing a test: it can make some people feel exhilarated and other people more creative than usual. Many amazing performances and ideas have been generated under the pressures of a test. Competition does not bring out the best in everyone, and some major talents have also been crushed under the pressure of competition. Fortunately, the EL has a great deal of power and influence over how competitions occur within his enterprise and can control when and how he wants to compete with anyone he works with and also how and when employees are expected to compete with one another. We will discuss how to set up competitions in greater depth shortly.

Beyond emotional strain, there are other costs associated with competing over shared objectives. Achieving objectives through a competition is the most expensive way to accomplish a task, because the resources, energy, and time invested in the solutions ultimately judged as inferior are wasted. For all competitors who have had their solutions judged as inferior, the competition has destroyed value—not just the tangible value of the wasted resources, energy, and time, but also the intangible value lost in the degradation of their status.

One final point about competitive relationships: they can be either overt or covert. An *overt* competition is one in which both parties are conscious that they are competing. For example, any competition in which one person tells another of their intention to prevent something from happening is overt. A *covert* competition is one in which one party or the other does not realize that the competition exists. A common type of covert competition occurs when one person tries to create an emotional trap for another in order to get that competitor to act in a way that may not be in his best interest. We call this manipulation.

The EL wants to make sure that the competitive relationships within the enterprise result in meaningful tests of the quality of the projects and processes; without such competition, an enterprise cannot achieve high levels of productivity or value creation. For all other purposes, using competition is needlessly destructive.

UNDERSTANDING RETREAT

Retreat is an essential, extremely strategic, yet poorly understood form of relationship. A retreating relationship occurs whenever two people share an objective and one party does not care to receive the benefits of achieving the objective, while still sharing some part of the costs. We all retreat naturally when we daydream at work or find a place to be alone when family life gets too hectic. Retreats occur consciously any-time someone decides not to vote in an election or someone chooses to stay silent in a meeting when given a chance to contribute.

Retreat does not mean a person is indifferent to achieving the shared objective. Even if a person does not vote, that does not mean that she plans to stop paying taxes. Not voting is usually a conscious decision by a person that she will be content to live with whatever outcome occurs. Not caring about the outcome of an election frees up emotional and physical energy that can be invested in something the person considers more strategically important—maybe spending extra time at work or playing golf. In essence, a retreat is forgoing the potential benefit that comes from achieving the shared objective in return for not having to bear some of the costs, a savings that can in turn be invested in something more strategically important.

Retreating is essential because it reduces stress and improves overall emotional and physical balance. The act of "not wanting" is emotionally liberating; many people find that it stimulates their creativity. Many famous flashes of insight have taken place during thoughtful retreats such as sitting by a pond or taking a bath. Those who feel compelled to be ever active and engaged would be well advised to retreat more often. Indeed, ELs want to encourage retreating relationships, which help people to perform to the best of their abilities when it counts most.

Retreating has costs. Everyone has to pay to retreat by passing up potential benefits from achieving the shared objective while having already contributed some of the costs. Retreating can also be emotionally stressful when it induces a feeling of loneliness or isolation.

Retreating is often covert—you sneak it in rather than declare, "I am going to take a break from contributing ideas about how to help the team reduce travel expenses." Retreating has a bad reputation. ELs can improve their relationships and gain others' respect by acknowledging that everyone occasionally feels the need to retreat. If acknowledging retreats makes these relationships less covert and ad hoc, then the entire team is better off.

BUILDING POWERFUL RELATIONSHIPS

The more challenging and complex the tasks the EL wants accomplished, the more cooperative, competitive, and retreating relationships must be formed. There is a direct correlation. Each task requires some balance of cooperative relationships focused on creation activities, competitive relationships focused on testing the quality of the solutions, all interspersed with retreating relationships that enable participants to restore their emotional and physical energy levels as well as personal commitment to the overall shared objective.

Once the EL understands and can identify the cooperative, competitive, and retreating relationships that exist, he can build stronger relationships whenever he needs to. The straightforward strategy to build relationships is as follows:

- Ensure that all competitive shared objectives create valid performance tests. Each competition should yield valuable new insights into how to improve the performance of the enterprise.
- Shift other competitions into retreating or cooperation by offering to modify shared objectives, as described shortly.
- Shift some retreats, when the potential benefits are high enough, to cooperation by offering to modify the shared objectives.

All attempts to shift competitions into another category must start by acknowledging the shared objective that made it competitive. Any party can make a unilateral change in their expectations and behavior in an attempt to retreat from the shared objective or to make it cooperative. The least risky way to change the category of the relationship is to talk about it and negotiate a cooperative outcome. Without acknowledging the source of the competition, the default is that the shared objective remains competitive.

Shifting your shared objectives to achieve a better outcome is a very powerful tool because it is something you can control. You can often shift the category of a relationship by enlarging the scope of the shared objectives to increase the expected benefits to some minimum acceptable level. "You and I both want this promotion [a competition], but we might want it for different reasons; if you were to appoint me in charge of the next strategic planning project [cooperation], then I will say I am not interested in getting the promotion [retreat]." Enlarging the scope of a shared objective to make it less competitive is often referred to as "horse-trading." An offer to horse-trade can be done unilaterally or as a negotiation; for instance, "Let's see if we can figure out how to . . ."

A lack of understanding of the minimum expected benefits another person wants in order to cooperate in achieving a shared objective is the single biggest reason that relationships lapse into competition or retreat. Too often, competitors just do not bother to ask. That said, sometimes competition cannot be avoided: no enlarging of the shared objective can satisfy the wants of all parties, in which case it will come down to some test of who or what is "best." In order to stay in control, ELs always want to ask for and understand everyone's needs and wants, particularly their strongest sources of motivation.

In the context of relationship building we can also now understand the critical importance of self-awareness—it's a prerequisite for being able to understand and control the various modes of relationships. Once you understand your primary motivation, you can figure out how to modify your shared objectives to achieve what you want. If you don't understand your primary motivation, then your relationship building naturally defaults to focusing on short-term outcomes, which may not yield enough long-term results to justify changing yourself in order to change others. Once the EL understands her primary motivation and gains a mastery in relationship building, then she is transformed into an extremely powerful and effective partner.

One reason that relationship building is particularly poorly practiced among many entrepreneurs is that the selfish motives associated with wanting to be an entrepreneur result in a propensity to create an imbalance of competitive shared objectives at the expense of cooperative and retreating ones. Most entrepreneurs do not have a clue that they need to create a balance among relationship categories, nor do they realize when to use each type. Entrepreneurs are particularly resistant to changing their shared objectives, viewing it as a loss of control when in fact it is their primary control mechanism.

Getting back to Larry, Michael, and Laura, they didn't feel good about the tensions that were growing in their relationships nor with the progress of the new bathroom design business. They felt, but were not conscious of, the ramifications of new shared objectives that had been created with Michael leaving his job, Larry investing in the new business, and Laura working with Michael. Their most important new shared objectives are summarized in Table 4.1; let's take a more detailed look at these.

Larry wanted to feel acknowledged as the best businessman in the family, a title that Michael now also aspired to. Michael was very competitive; when he first wanted to be a reporter, he wanted to be the best reporter. Now that he was a businessman, he wanted

Table 4.1 Larry, Michael, and Laura's New Important Shared Objectives

Cooperative	Competitive	Retreating
Providing Michael and Laura a comfortable living from the new company Making the new company valuable	Time spent together with Larry Attaining status as "best" business person, thereby setting expectations on which business practices to follow	Communicating feelings Deciding on roles at work

to be the best businessman. He didn't want to be Larry's apprentice businessman, which is how he felt that Larry perceived him. This title was emotionally important to both Michael and Larry, because they associated it with their status within the family. This struggle for status was a competitive shared objective.

Larry wanted to feel appreciated for his strong financial and emotional support. He made this into a test. He wanted Michael and Laura to spend more time with him as a demonstration of their appreciation. Michael and Laura felt they already spent enough time with Larry. They thought that because they were both working longer hours than before, then Larry should understand that they wanted to spend less time with him so they could rest or be by themselves. How much time they spent together was another competitive shared objective.

Laura retreated from figuring out what would be her and Michael's formal roles in their new enterprise. She thought she would be good at sales, but Michael never asked her to do that, and she retreated into doing the jobs Michael didn't do. Michael subconsciously competed for the roles he wanted; Laura retreated, and Michael let it happen.

All three retreated from the shared objective of communicating their feelings to one another and then deciding how to work and live with one another.

The new shared objectives created by starting a new business are typically not very difficult to ascertain, but they can be hard to talk about. Laura could tell what was going on between her husband and her father. Michael actually asked her what she thought about her dad's unsolicited advice, and she told him, "You are too much like my dad; you have a hard time not being the star." If she had thought about it, Laura also would have figured out how she felt about the roles they were taking on in the new business. The biggest challenge is often just discussing everyone's shared objectives, because people inherently feel uncomfortable admitting that they are competing or retreating. If asked, Larry would talk about how he feels about spending more time with the family, and Laura would say that she wants to try her hand at sales. Laura could tell her father and husband that they had a problem in both wanting to be the star. Once someone asks others to think about what objectives they share and gives a few examples, then the others start contributing to the list and it grows quickly. A short discussion is usually required to figure out which shared objectives are the most important to the group.

Given the situation at hand with Larry and Laura, it is up to Michael whether or not he is willing to modify his desire for status and acknowledgment. Is his motivation to be an EL strong enough to override his need to be acknowledged as best? Does he need to dominate Laura at work? Is the relationship with Larry important enough to Michael and Laura that they can make more time for him in their lives? I have encountered this situation many times, and most of the people involved followed the trajectory of just letting the situation fester. Most real-life Michaels were not motivated strongly enough to change themselves—they did not even want to seek advice as they selfishly felt that would be a sign of weakness. Their businesses ultimately failed, and these Michaels suffered major emotional trauma, had their marriages fall apart, and lost the respect of their children. I know other Michaels who wanted to build relationships that worked better and who changed themselves accordingly. Most of these Michaels were ultimately successful.

If Michael could identify the motivations that were causing him to compete with his father-in-law, then he could realize he had several options to shift out of the destructive competitive mode:

- He could make Larry feel like he is acknowledged as a good businessperson, saying, "Larry, I aspire to be as successful in business as you are." This will shift one of the competitions into cooperation.

- He could explain to Larry how it was important to him that Larry keep his word and not give him business advice. This option would be most likely to succeed if Michael also told Larry why this was important to him: "Larry, I am a very competitive person, and I don't want to compete with you over who is the best at business; that is why I hesitated in accepting your generous offer to invest until you said you would not give any advice unless asked for." This is a retreat for Michael from feeling judged by Larry. If Michael cannot bring himself to acknowledge his father-in-law as a good businessperson, then this is his only alternative, short of competition. As with all retreats, this may not work if Larry wishes to pursue the competition.

• He could prepare to conclusively win this competition. He would have to step up his pace of learning how to operate a retail design business so that everyone around him would be astounded at how well it was doing. This would likely take years to accomplish, and the emotional toll would be great—maybe too great for his relationships to survive unscathed. This is a very risky option, as competitive options always are. Many entrepreneurs in similar situations just fantasize about how good they are and never try to get an objective third-party opinion, nor do they try to get third-party help in improving. In essence, many entrepreneurs never commit to actually improving their business skills to the point where they deserve the acknowledgment they so desperately seek.

Michael must also figure out his options for how to deal with Laura's retreat on business roles. He may choose to let it remain a retreat, which commonly happens, at least until the retreating party makes it into an explicit issue. Depending on Laura's personality, her retreat on this shared objective may show up as a new competitive shared objective at home, perhaps causing heightened tension in their relationship. Michael can turn this into cooperation and ask Laura what roles she thinks she should fill. Most Michaels I've known who failed with their business failed to make any adjustments with how they worked with their wives, in all cases resulting in divorce.

The shared objective about how much time Laura, Michael, and her dad spend together was an old one and was cooperative up until the new business started. The inherent challenge in all cooperative relationships is that they must be reformulated any time any aspect of the shared objective changes. If you are cooperating by agreeing to share an apple pie but find the pie is smaller than either party expected, then the cooperation may no longer hold. Because Laura and Michael's spare time is no longer as plentiful as in the past, this cooperative shared objective has become a competitive one, because none of the three involved parties have agreed on how much of their limited time to spend together. And because there are three people involved, there are more options to consider (for example, Laura and Michael could each spend time independently with Larry in addition to the three of them spending time together). Michael and Laura had created the competition by changing how they spent their free time. Larry also made spending time together covertly competitive by claiming that he did not want anything in return for his help. Larry competed by amplifying his display of disappointment each time Michael and Laura turned down his request to get together.

The well-intentioned cooperative shared objectives created by forming this company created competitions that were not well understood. These competitions eventually led to a divorce, as well as a rift between Laura and her dad. But it didn't have to end this badly.

As I previously discussed, all attempts to shift competitions into another category must start with acknowledging the shared objective and what has made it competitive. All the failed Michaels I have known understood that their relationships were creating undesirable feelings but still let competitive situations fester to the point where it destroyed their relationships with their previously very supportive family members.

Virtually all of the successful Michaels I have known focused on opening up the lines of communication with their spouses and partner family members. Sometimes they have needed a neutral and trained third party to mediate. These ELs made it a priority to have a cooperative shared objective of communicating their most important shared objectives openly, including sharing the expectations each party had about how the benefits and costs of the shared objective would be split. Simply communicating their shared objectives reduced tensions and enabled shared objectives to be openly, not covertly, negotiated.

There is no single "right" way for an EL to create any specific shared objective, but some ways are better and others worse. Every EL is unique, as is every situation. Without the ability to discern which category a relationship falls into, most entrepreneurs feel themselves trapped in their status quo, feeling a great deal of tension caused by their undeclared competitions, compounded by their frustration with the lack of emotional support from people who have retreated.

ELS AND THE SKILL OF RELATIONSHIP BUILDING

Relationship building is the practice of identifying shared objectives and discerning whether they are cooperative, competitive, or retreating, as well as modifying shared objectives to change relationships, when possible, into strategically more advantageous categories. Every one of us has a multitude of relationships going at any given time, so the ability to improve the benefits of some relationships, or to reduce the cost or risk of other relationships, is very useful and powerful. ELs want to apply their relationship-building skill to how they manage their own relationships as well as to how they help facilitate the relationships among people on their team. Enterprises can be brought down by the competition and retreat of key employees, stakeholders, or even volunteers. When two key employees are locked into such a competitive battle that their contest destroys the enterprise's ability to perform effectively, then the impact is far-reaching. ELs are judged by how effectively they defuse these competitions. Entrepreneurial enterprises cannot afford to have significant energy expended on unproductive internal competitions, thereby imperiling potential success. Employees do not respect leaders who allow that to happen.

Recall the problem of Adam, our protagonist in Chapter One: his head of sales was competing with the head of product management. Adam's investor cited this competition as one of the reasons he insisted that Adam step aside as CEO. Sales and product management personnel often argue because they both share responsibility for increasing business. There is an inherent competition to claim credit for successes in creating business—and potentially to blame the other for any problems in finding business. Fostering a cooperative relationship between these areas is a big challenge many ELs face. The entrepreneur's action will determine how much trust and respect the employees close to the situation have in their leader. It will also determine how they act relative to their peers. A great deal hinges on how well entrepreneurs can lead their teammates to create strong productive relationships amongst themselves.

Adam, like most inexperienced entrepreneurs, did not take the time to define his shared objectives with his heads of sales and product management. Without clear shared objectives, each person will define her own set, and unproductive competition is inevitable. Someone as inexperienced in sales and marketing as Adam will be challenged to know what expectation he should and could set. He will not necessarily get a good result by just asking his heads of sales and product management to set their own objectives. Adam did not even do that; he just expected them to do whatever they needed to do to make his firm successful, and his enterprise suffered accordingly. He lost his job partly as a result of his inaction.

Yet by simply understanding the basics of relationship building, Adam can empower himself to create a rational interdependent set of shared objectives with his heads of sales and product management. He could start by listing his objectives for his company over the next three, six, and twelve months. He could then sit down with both teammates and ask them what objectives he should share with each of them individually and what objectives they need to share between themselves to accomplish the company's objectives. As each shared objective is listed, Adam should ask, "So what outcome do you expect for yourself if we accomplish this objective?" Adam cannot be afraid to ask the hard follow-up questions when his teammates try to retreat from setting their shared objectives as a team; for example, if they respond, "I don't expect anything for myself, because this is for the good of the company, and it is my job to make the company successful." Adam could make his position clear by saying, "Our success will depend upon how well we work individually *and as a team*, so we *must* be willing to set our objectives as a team and to define our rewards as a team. Some of our objectives must involve competing with one another to test what is the best way forward. It is OK if you retreat from some of our objectives if that will enable you to focus on something *I* feel is more important instead." The "I" is important here because Adam, as EL, must be the person who finally accepts or rejects all shared objectives with their associated expected outcomes. He can ask someone more experienced and expert than he is to sit in and make the decision on his behalf, but ELs are ultimately responsible for the effectiveness of whatever is decided *and* for the results.

The discussions on setting their shared objectives and defining their expected outcomes will be contentious at times, but at least they can create a set of well-understood shared objectives that each person openly commits to accomplishing. Adam can undermine this entire process if he permits either the head of sales or of product management to qualify his commitment to accomplish the shared objective, given how he expects to contribute to, and benefit from, its achievement. This equivocation can happen in the meeting: "I will try . . ." (*trying* is not a commitment) or, more insidiously, by one individual coming to Adam separately and attempting to modify the shared objective "privately." Adam can expect to be tested by attempts to make side deals, such as, "In the meeting with Joe I didn't want to bring up my personal expectation to be promoted to executive vice president of sales once we hit our goal, but I have assumed all along that you support that." Adam's stance must be unequivocal: all team members must feel confident that they understand one another's expectations. He must therefore ask that this department head share his expectation with his counterpart, or Adam must disavow it: for example, "I understand that you aspire to that title, and I certainly look forward to giving you that promotion when it is appropriate, but nothing we agreed to accomplish in today's meeting directly relates to triggering that promotion." As you can probably start to sense, bringing up this point outside of the meeting is an attempt to compete with Adam over the shared objective of who controls the EVP of sales title.

Someone experienced in dealing with heads of sales and product management may not need to invest all the time and emotion necessary to set shared objectives as a team. He may be skilled enough to understand the best metrics to use, under what conditions, as well as the associated pros and cons of different ways to partition objectives to avoid mutually competitive situations. Few entrepreneurs I have encountered have this level of experience.

Sometimes an EL faces the challenge of having two employees who do not respect one another. This lack of respect may be transactional or it may be fundamental. A transactional lack of respect is caused by when one or both parties do not understand a shared objective. Transactional relationship issues can typically be solved with improved communication. Most people are unaware of how their traits bias them against certain other personality types that process information and emotions differently. As I described in Chapter Three, businesses often use MBTI personality classifications to help employees understand how to better deliver information and emotion to their colleagues. I will describe shortly how ELs make sure that their teams understand, as the EL does, the need to respect each person's personality type relative to how they want to receive and process information. This understanding can alleviate disrespect between two otherwise very productive teammates.

Fundamental disrespect comes from differences in core motivational values that transcend the enterprise and cannot be resolved by any changes an EL can enact. For example, one team member may feel that another member's insistence that he will never work past 5 PM is unacceptable for anyone he works with, because he works best at night and so do many other members of the team. If the two people with fundamental disrespect for one another must work together, then the EL must choose which of the two different value systems he wants in his enterprise. I have had to fire people for openly disrespecting a teammate; one time it was over a fundamental difference on how to motivate the sales force (there are some very strongly held beliefs about this subject). If I hadn't removed the person, then the competition would have been unresolved and ultimately would have required everyone to take sides, leading to an even more destructive competition within my company.

ELs AND THE SKILL OF COMMUNICATION

The most basic and fundamental of all relationships is formed when two parties communicate.[5] No powerful and productive relationships can form without communication. Whether people realize it or not, communicating always has the shared objective of accurately transferring information and emotion between two people. Understanding the strategies that can improve these fundamental relationships is an important EL priority, because accurately transferring information and emotion is essential to the effectiveness of people working together.

Some behaviors look like communication but aren't. For example, we often confuse communication with broadcasting. Broadcasting is when you send a message but you do not follow up to see if it has been received accurately. Broadcasting is not caring if a shared objective has actually been created. Writing an email and sending it to a large distribution list and then assuming that it has been read and accurately understood is not communicating; it is broadcasting (despite many managers protesting that their employees read and understand everything they send to them).

Communication means both parties participate—but it is not a symmetrical relationship, because the sender and receiver play different roles. The sender has the information and/or emotion that she wants to share with the receiver, whether the receiver wants it or not. Clearly, communication can be cooperative, competing, or retreating based on whether the information and/or emotion being sent is something the other person wants to receive.

Anyone who really wants to make sure information or emotion has been accurately transferred to someone else needs to ask for feedback. Most people who are interested to know whether their message has been received accurately look for visual clues to get the feedback they need. Some people are more adept at reading visual clues; this ability is a trait that is measured as part of EQ. Of course, many communications are not done face-to-face or are done between people who are not good at reading visual clues about whether the transmitted information and/or emotion has been accurately understood. It's easy for an EL to make sure the communications he sends are accurately received; he just has to ask, "Did that make sense?" "What did you hear?" or even better, "What else would you like to know about this?"

People receiving information and/or emotion from a sender also want to make sure they have accurately received the message. Those people whom we think of as "good listeners" naturally give us feedback on whether they understand the information or emotion we are sending to them. Good listeners are people with whom we know we have done a good job of communicating; they make it easy. Indeed, good listeners can play the lead role in improving an otherwise poorly constructed communication. These three techniques are hallmarks of good listeners:

- Nodding or saying "Uh-huh," is an indication that the listener is not confused by the consistency of the information and/or emotion being sent. This is not a true positive confirmation, but it indicates that the message makes sense.
- Paraphrasing what the listener has heard is a positive confirmation of the accuracy of the communication and precludes the sender from having to ask the follow-up question. The most basic form of paraphrasing is, "I understood what you just said to mean . . ."
- Communicating back an implication of the information or emotion that was transferred—for example, "What you said means that you must be very unhappy"—is the most powerful form of good listening because it leads to the most accurate *and* timely exchange of information and emotion.

Being a good listener always makes a communication cooperative, even if the receiver does not agree with the information or emotion being communicated. Cooperative communications are always best, because both parties know the information and/or emotion has been accurately received, so there are no misunderstandings, and each party can independently decide what to do about it. Accurately receiving even threatening information and/or emotions does not preclude a person from responding to the communication as they want or need to.

We often assume our communication is cooperative, despite the fact that we sometimes engage in behavior that makes our communication retreating or competing. Communication becomes retreating when the receiver of the information ignores the transmission. Not responding to an email asking you a question is a retreat. So is changing the subject. ELs should never leave an email from a teammate, customer, or other stakeholder unread for any extended period. Even when she goes on vacation, the EL needs to delegate someone to read and respond to all of her relevant emails unless she plans to do that herself while lying on the beach in Hawaii. ELs should never change the subject. You can always say, "I understand that you do not like the new coffee we've chosen, so let Bill know your opinion, and he may decide to change it," or the EL could say, "I promise to return to hear whatever it is you want to tell me, but I must run now to meet an important commitment."

Communication can easily turn competitive. For example, the sender may try to get the receiver to tacitly agree to something as part of receiving the message. Aggressive senders can try to establish their dominant status by intimidating their receiver with strong negative emotions, judgmental phrases, or name calling. An opposite tactic can also be employed, wherein the sender tries to lure the receiver into reciprocating their agreeableness or effusive praise with an acceptance of their position. The sender may try to manipulate the receiver's feedback as to the information or emotion that was sent. Asking a closed-ended question is often competitive. "Do you prefer X or Y?" seeks to constrain the receiver to make a choice the receiver may not wish to make.

The receiver may compete by refusing to acknowledge receipt of the information and/or emotion. For example, the receiver can attempt to take over the communication by immediately forcing the sender to respond to an onslaught of accusations (for example, "What you are saying makes no sense at all!"), unrelated information ("What you are saying is a waste of my time to even listen to"), or aggressive emotions ("It infuriates me that you even waste my time with that nonsense!" with the implication that *my emotions are more important than whatever is in your message*). Finally, the receiver of the information may try to change the message he has received to gain advantage over the sender. The receiver may purposely say he understood a different message: "So . . . you are not going to prevent me from taking your car to Las Vegas tonight."

Competitive communication is often not openly declared as such, and one party may not realize what is at stake. These covertly competitive forms of communication are often referred to as "manipulation."

There is an important distinction between a communication being competitive and the information and/or emotion being transmitted relating to a competition. It is not competitive to communicate, "I do not agree with what you said" or even "I will fight your proposal."

It is not competitive, communication-wise, for the receiver to demonstrate that she accurately received the information by saying, "I look forward to your fighting my proposal." These examples accurately convey information important to both parties and are good examples of cooperative communication.

Unfortunately, we sometimes do not even realize we are being manipulative with our communication. Who doesn't sometimes ask a very direct yes-or-no question to cut off further discussion? When effective communication is important, then the EL wants to make sure that his communication is clearly cooperative; the EL can ensure the cooperative intent of any communication by asking an open-ended question and then demonstrating good listening skills when the receiver responds to the question. An open-ended question is one that does not presuppose a particular answer; for example, "How would you suggest that I solve this problem?" Open-ended questions invite the receiver to be in the position of controlling the information and/or emotion being transferred and puts the sender in the position of being a listener. The cost of asking open-ended questions is that the communication often takes longer and some or all of the information and emotion received may not be relevant to the sender. In spite of your good intentions, the receiver still could give a competitive or retreating response. Even though open-ended questions require more time and patience, they are a good strategy for defusing competitive communication and competitive emotions.

Identifying competitive and retreating communication helps the EL do a better job of conveying critical information and/or emotions while also helping others do it. Because communication is the starting point for all relationships, being able to identify cooperative, competing, and retreating communication helps create more effective relationships everywhere within an enterprise.

OVERCOMING COMMUNICATION BIASES

We all have traits that predispose us to compete with people who do not think the same way we do. Biases can stand in the way of a person's forming effective relationships and communicating with large groups of people. An EL must become aware of his biases in order to overcome them.

As an example, early in my career I was shocked to find that I was considered a poor communicator by a significant fraction of the people I worked with. As a brash young engineering manager, I thought people were dumb when they started to tell me about their feelings when the issue was something I felt was a technical problem. I thought they were trying to change the subject because they were not capable of properly analyzing the situation. It was not until my Myers-Briggs training that I understood that many people need to express themselves through their feelings, irrespective of how well they understand technical issues. These Feeling "F" types are naturally more empathetic than my Thinking "T" type, which means they often communicate more effectively because most communication conveys emotions along with information. I had no idea that I needed F types on my team in order to properly implement *any* changes to processes that the T types like myself had mapped out. F types are critically important to figuring out the best solution to a problem, because all solutions require people to understand the changes being asked of them.

My coming to appreciate the potential of F types was only a first step in being able to work effectively with them, because they did not feel comfortable working with me. F types tended to view me as insensitive and hard to deal with because I never acknowledged either their feelings or my own. It was only once I started using a different vocabulary in the presence of F types that I could start effectively communicating with them. I started saying things like, "This feels right to me, how does it feel to you?" and F types would light up and feel that I was now a much more effective communicator. With T types I would ask a different open-ended question: "How did you come up with your recommendation?"

I never could have built powerful relationships and never could have led large groups without understanding how to communicate. Before I gained this understanding, I was ineffective at communicating and creating powerful relationships with anyone who wasn't a T. Every trait has its strengths and weaknesses, and every trait affects a leader's ability to master critical skills. If nobody had explained this to me and pointed me in the right direction for becoming an effective communicator and for understanding how to create and build relationships, I would have become a very unhappy, frustrated engineer unable to effect any changes in the world.

BUILDING POWERFUL COMPLEMENTARY RELATIONSHIPS FOR THE LONG TERM

I would like to end this chapter with an example of how to build powerful complementary relationships with people the EL must rely on in order for his enterprise to succeed. Every EL has several people who are particularly critical to his success and with whom he wants to create as powerful and complementary a relationship as he knows how. Armed with an understanding of the relationship-building toolkit, we can now understand how to construct these critical relationships.

My success as an entrepreneur would not have been possible without a deep and productive relationship with my second-in-command. My longtime chief operating officer (COO), Lloyd, the person who ran day-to-day operations at iSuppli, was somebody with whom I had a powerful, successful, and mutually supportive partnership based on a spectrum of specific relationships. These shared objectives influenced how we worked to create from scratch a very valuable global market intelligence company.

Lloyd and I cooperated on an overriding shared objective: to build the valuation of the company. I made sure I understood Lloyd's core motivations for joining iSuppli even before I extended the offer to work together. This shared objective became the primary one, to which all other shared objectives were subservient.

- We competed on the shared objective of how value would be created in order to test the quality of our ideas.
- I often retreated on many shared objectives relating to how we set pay levels or commission structures (in business you call this "deferring" rather than retreating). To make sure Lloyd felt autonomous and motivated, I needed to share objectives but retreat from making decisions that involved Lloyd's areas of expertise.

- We cooperated on the overall shared objective of ensuring the well-being of his family. This was another fundamental shared objective of Lloyd's, and meeting this objective was sometimes a struggle when our business was under financial stress. The fact that I demonstrated how critical this objective was to me by doing whatever I could to meet it built enormous trust between us.
- We competed on the shared objective of setting a reasonable compensation plan for Lloyd. We always had our different opinions, and we always had to find ways of adjudicating between us so we both felt the outcome was good for the company.
- We cooperated on the shared objective of creating a specific corporate culture. We both understood the importance of having a coherent culture at iSuppli; that meant we had to have similar visions of the culture we were working to create. We always coordinated the important actions we took so everyone at iSuppli could see we acted consistently with our vision.
- Lloyd and I often competed with how to deal with specific employee issues, to set up a test on the best way to handle each issue for the company and the employee.
- We cooperated on setting shared social objectives, with each of us doing the social tasks with which we felt most comfortable.
- We cooperated in keeping our board of directors informed, because we both understood the importance of effectively sharing information and emotions with this critical group.

This is not a complete list, but it is representative of the shared objectives we felt were important.

The list of distinct relationships that formed our general CEO-COO relationship grew in complexity as the company grew in size and scope. I was thoughtful, although not always successful, in creating specific new shared objectives with Lloyd. I wanted the competitions to be confined to areas where we did not agree but were important to increasing the value of iSuppli. The competitions were structured to be tests for which of our proposed solutions would be best for the company. We competed frequently, as we had very different perspectives on how to market our services and how much time and money we needed to invest in expanding our product offering. These disagreements always resulted in getting other people or groups to choose between our alternative visions. If I had simply mandated my solution, then if it wasn't considered best for the company by either Lloyd or others with better perspectives than mine, that could call into question the trust we had that we all were working toward building the biggest valuation for the company. As you would expect of unbiased competitions, Lloyd would sometimes win, as his desired outcome was judged better than mine. Because the rules I set were judged subjectively "fair" and objectively "effective" by all those affected, the results were well accepted. The company benefitted from these competitive tests, and I learned through the judgments of others more expert than me. Ultimately you want to construct your competitive relationships such that the competition filters out inferior outcomes, leaving the superior shared objective outcome as a benefit to others and as a learning experience for yourself.

Setting up fair tests of our ideas did not mean handing over control to Lloyd or some committee of judges. I retained full responsibility for the outcome of whichever solution we implemented. I exercised that responsibility by understanding the alternate proposals from Lloyd (and others) while using the judgments of experts whom I respected to help choose better solutions than I alone could have proposed.

In many cases I acted selfishly with Lloyd by retreating on objectives that we absolutely shared but that I didn't want to spend time doing. As part of the important requirement of maintaining trust, we let each other retreat from activities if it would help keep us refreshed for more critical ones. We never retreated when either of us asked the other for help in achieving any specific shared objective.

The evolution of our relationship was consciously implemented but was not planned—it evolved as required by the exigencies of the moment. I kept close tabs on Lloyd's objectives and desired outcomes and made sure he knew where we were in making progress toward achieving our objectives and realizing the expected benefits. To have withheld information would have harmed the cooperative relationship. Sometimes the news was bad, which led Lloyd to question his commitment to achieving the shared objective—that is natural and to be expected and is not traitorous; fortunately he never did retreat. Changes or additions to specific shared objectives were always made on an as-required basis, in a way consistent with improving the chances of achieving our most important shared objective. If at any time either of us had felt the other was no longer committed to doing everything possible to maximize the value of the company, the web of interrelated relationships would have begun to unravel, which in turn would have led to a crisis in our ability to work together.

We had to survive many crises over the twelve years we worked together: two economic meltdowns of the technology market, the September 11 attacks, unforeseen rapid changes to our end markets, intense competition, completely unreasonable requests from clients, and so on. Only a web of thoughtfully constructed cooperative, competitive, and retreating relationships could have taken us through a dozen years of value creation.

My partnership with Lloyd serves as a good example of relationship building. By using these methods of identifying shared objectives and forming relationships using the right category of cooperation, compete, or retreat, I have been able to create many equally productive, caring, and supportive relationships.

I also needed to practice shifting relationship categories many times during my iSuppli years. Many classic business disagreements had the potential to create deeply adverse emotions that could have led to mistrust or disrespect between critical members of the iSuppli team. Because mistrust and disrespect preclude the formation of cooperative relationships needed for any team, it is critical for the EL to understand how to shape shared objectives to resolve competitive tests. My CFO, Joe, and Lloyd were often unable to agree on how much of our company's services we could expect to sell over the following year. Dealing with this properly could help grow our company even faster, whereas making a mistake would have imperiled trust within the company and negatively impacted performance and corporate value. Understanding the options for breaking this classically dangerous competitive stalemate required understanding

the varied objectives shared by Joe and Lloyd. They had the overriding shared objective of building the value of the company, but in
this instance there was a competition over how that would be accomplished. Understanding this, I as CEO had the following options:

- I could let them compete on their own terms, because it was
  "their job" to jointly propose a budget to me (I knew they
  wouldn't physically fight, but a stalemate would build stress
  and could have created hard-to-control feelings about one
  another).
- I could define how the decision would be reached, by dictating
  the rules of their competition.
- I could just dictate the end result, taking them out of the final
  decision-making process altogether.
- I could offer counsel about the rules they could apply, so they
  could then possibly resolve their stalemated competition.

I could have mandated decision rules ahead of time, but I didn't.
Every year there were different issues that caused the competition over
setting annual plan targets. Because market conditions, competitive
pressures, or the reception of new products changed dramatically from
year to year, setting the rules ahead of time was not effective and could
have led to bad results. When annual plan competitions came up, I
would offer advice on how to achieve better outcomes to both Joe and
Lloyd, often giving them perspectives that they had not considered
themselves. The ability of a CEO to see potential opportunities and
solutions when stalemates occur is useful for turning competitions into
cooperation and adds value to the enterprise. Armed with my observa-
tions and suggestions, Lloyd and Joe always came up with a decision.

If they had not been able to decide, or if either Joe or Lloyd felt
my advice was biased and not worthy of consideration, then I would
have just dictated the result (after making sure I had fully understood
both of their positions). This backup plan was significantly less
desirable to Joe, Lloyd, and me, because if I dictated then I would
be making both Joe and Lloyd into advisors, disempowering them
from performing some of their basic responsibilities. In essence,

I would have had to shift a previously cooperative shared objective of decision-making autonomy with Lloyd and Joe to make it competitive. The new competition with me would have defused the potentially destructive competition between them. I could then work with each of them to turn the decision-making autonomy shared objective cooperative again. This multistep defusing of a highly charged competitive situation would have required a significant investment of time and attention on my part. Fortunately, I never had to use the backup plan.

Relationship building requires practice to be able to dissect real world relationships into their constituent shared objectives, but its wide applicability makes it well worth the effort. The most challenging part of practicing the skill is overcoming the fear of figuring out real shared objectives. Just asking will take you a long way toward proficiency. Entrepreneurial leaders need this skill to enlist and maintain the dedicated support of highly capable individuals. This skill is also essential for ELs because it helps them redirect and defuse potentially destructive relationships between key employees and other critical stakeholders.

Relationship building is a skill practiced with only a few people at a time. Because the number of interconnected shared objectives in any one group grows exponentially with the number of people in the group, a different skill is required to motivate large numbers of people to passionately help the EL with his vision. Motivating people is the subject of the next chapter.

Motivating Others

Motivating other people to do what you want has long been considered a rare talent—and unless you had it, the only way to get people to do what you wanted was to pay them or force them. Research into the sources of people's motivations now enables businesspeople and entrepreneurs to understand that motivating others is a skill they can master—charisma and other innate personality traits have nothing to do with it.[1] Motivating others is a different skill from relationship building. You build relationships one shared objective at a time;[2] you motivate groups of people to all share a single objective.

Dean Kamen is a brilliant engineer; all his peers and even his competitors agree on that.[3] He started his first company in high school, making special effects lighting for rock bands and groups that wanted to dazzle large audiences. When Kamen was twenty, his innovative engineering solutions caught the attention of a top executive at a major medical products company, who challenged him to solve a vexing medical instrumentation problem. Before 1971 there was no way to automatically and reliably set the dosage of drugs administered intravenously, which meant IV drugs had to be administered by nurses in hospitals. Dean thought about the problem, learned some machining techniques he would need to make a prototype, and invented the drug infusion pump. His new company, AutoSyringe, operating at first out of the basement of his parents' home, quickly grew to a couple of dozen employees, including even his college professors. AutoSyringe subsequently invented the portable insulin pump and grew even faster. The business was extremely profitable. Dean never finished college.

After eleven years, Dean sold AutoSyringe for what was widely understood to be a substantial sum. Based on his fondness for New Hampshire's state motto, "Live Free or Die," Dean moved there, bought an old mill, and started a company dedicated to inventing new things. He named the new company after himself, DEKA (DEan KAmen). His first product was an improved heating and air-conditioning system for large open spaces like the old mill he bought. His system now controls temperature at NASA's Mission Control in Houston, among other places.

Soon after its founding, DEKA was asked by another medical instrument company to improve dialysis machines, which then weighed 180 pounds and required special technicians to operate. They didn't do what they were asked to. Instead Dean and his engineers, over the course of five years, completely rethought how dialysis could be done. DEKA designed a dialysis machine that weighed only 22 pounds and could be operated and maintained by the patient. Licensing his portable dialysis machine to the major medical instrument company added significantly to Dean's already considerable fortune.

Working for DEKA and Dean Kamen is many engineers' dream job. They get to work on cool projects, and there is little bureaucracy beyond asking Dean. You are supported in trying otherwise outlandish designs; you even get awards for outlandish failures. Dean is very particular about the people he hires. He likes engineers who are impatient and rebellious, engineers who love to make things work. In spite of the fact that engineers at DEKA get paid less than they would receive at large industrial or technology companies, engineers stay at DEKA because they like it. Dean Kamen viscerally understands how to motivate the type of engineer he hires. He hires engineers with similar values and interests and with whom he enjoys working. Not surprisingly, the engineers whom Dean respects also enjoy working in the environment that Dean finds fun and mentally invigorating. As far as engineers are concerned, Kamen has what it takes, but we need to know what it is that engineers really find so motivating about working for Dean if we are going to be able to reproduce it.

MOTIVATION AND SELF-ACTUALIZATION

Researchers have advanced our understanding of what motivates people to perform tasks, which in turn has informed leaders on what they can do to excite others to help them achieve their vision. Such an understanding is particularly useful to entrepreneurial leaders. ELs now shape their workers' environments to filter out demotivating distractions while satisfying the basic needs everyone has to feel safe, to be warm and fed, to be accepted as a member of a mutually supportive group, and to be recognized for their particular contributions. When work environments satisfy these needs, then the leader is in position to take actions that help workers feel that their work is intrinsically motivated[4] and self-actualizing[5]—allowing them to reach the ultimate state of human well-being as defined by Abraham Maslow. When entrepreneurs ignore these needs, they risk being constantly distracted from achieving their objectives, because many people around them are unhappy and unproductive. ELs and other leaders know how to make their teams feel self-actualized; such teams can perform innovatively and productively over long periods of time, even under stressful conditions.

People feel and perform at their best when they feel autonomous, masterful, and purposeful. ELs therefore create environments and task objectives so that their employees

- Feel in control of their environment and their destiny
- Feel as if they are performing to the best of their abilities
- Feel they are doing something that is meaningful to them

Work environments and task objectives that foster autonomy, mastery, and a sense of purpose do not create motivations that supersede a person's core motivations; rather, they create motivations that are complementary to a person's core motivations. These inner drives to self-actualize inspire people to work hard and long to accomplish the goals of the enterprise and the goals of their EL. ELs foster in people the feeling that they are personally successful—the hallmark of leadership.

Dean Kamen worked diligently to create an environment at DEKA that

- Challenged engineers to propose their own solutions to the big picture problems that interested Dean Kamen
- Challenged engineers to master new skills that could be applied to solving these big picture problems
- Devised solutions that would make people's lives better

Dean gives awards for the best failures, so no engineer is afraid of failing. He consistently supports any engineer's desire to acquire a new skill that could unlock a solution. DEKA's lore includes stories of Dean whisking an engineer off in his helicopter to learn a new skill. DEKA holds periodic Frog Days on which everyone must create something new that has nothing to do with his or her normal work. For engineers, who love to make new things, DEKA is close to heaven. It is both DEKA's culture and Dean's actions that together are motivating. It wouldn't matter what Dean said if the culture at DEKA made someone feel threatened for coming up with innovative ideas that didn't work and wasted money. Workers, at DEKA and elsewhere, are not excited about performing tasks that result in less autonomy, set them up to be judged as a failure, or make their world a worse place to live.

Dean's particular style of motivating, while perfect for most employees at DEKA, could cause problems in a different organizational context. Dean Kamen is a great example to study because he can also *de-motivate* talented *nonengineers*. His failure to properly motivate highly talented and experienced manufacturing and marketing executives played a key role in the failure of the Segway, one of the most innovative inventions to ever come out of Dean's engineering company.

MOTIVATIONAL ISSUES WITH THE SEGWAY

DEKA's business model is to get paid by big companies to develop new technologies, which DEKA then licenses to the big company to use; they are perpetually in stage one. DEKA has never dealt directly with consumers, nor has it manufactured or sold the products it produces—with the exception of one attempt. The tale of Dean Kamen and the Segway illustrates how motivating engineers to work at a company whose value comes from new inventions is very different from motivating people to work for a consumer products company, a company that manufactures things, or any company past stage one.

DEKA's work on a wheelchair that could climb stairs led Dean and his engineering team to realize they could make a self-balancing, all-electric two-wheeled device—what the world now knows as a Segway. Dean felt that "his" two-wheeled device would revolutionize how people travel in urban environments. Dean did not want to license it to someone else to manufacture and market and thereby lose control over the invention, because he felt this was a unique opportunity to create one of the largest and most profitable companies in the world; he envisioned a company producing tens of millions of Segways a year.

Dean was afraid that some large automotive company would copy his idea, so he wanted to ramp up manufacturing as rapidly as possible. He insisted that the company develop the capability to manufacture large numbers of Segways before the first production prototype was built or the first Segway had even been shown to any potential customer. Essentially, Dean wanted stages one, two, and three to happen in unison. Such an accomplishment would have been unprecedented, but Dean was never scared to do things that had not been done before. Dean was and is a fabulous leader of innovation, which is to say that he is great at leading projects, especially those supported with ample resources and time. Dean had no experience leading projects that create complex low-cost supply chains, manufacturing processes, or processes for selling and marketing products to consumers, but that did not stop Dean from thinking that he could figure out how to reinvent these tasks, as he had reinvented so many other things.

Dean understood that he would need help. He hired several experienced automotive executives and a few marketing executives from large consumer products companies. He then proceeded to ignore their advice and overrule their decisions, calling them bureaucrats or "Mouseketeers" when he didn't like what they were telling him.

When told that critical expertise was missing from the team, he often refused to hire or refused to make any decision about how to resolve the problem. This was particularly problematic in the design and programming of the specialized microprocessors that are essential to keeping the Segway safely under control. This vetoing and ignoring the needs of experienced design and production experts, without pointing out a better alternative, made these experts and others feel out of control and demoralized, because they could not accomplish the objectives that had been set for them. Other no-win situations occurred because Dean made it known to everyone that he wanted to be involved in almost every decision. Many critical decisions on hiring, space, and part selection ground to a halt, in spite of Dean's insistence on an aggressive launch date. Most people on the Segway project felt terrible. When Dean refused to take responsibility for slips in the schedule caused by his management style, blaming the delays instead on the incompetency of the team, his team felt Dean was no longer committed to making them feel they would be successful.

DIFFERENT STAGES, DIFFERENT MOTIVATORS

Dean knows how to motivate teams of engineers engaged in stage one, a purely project stage, but he is not skilled at motivating teams in stages two, three, and four, when processes are essential for success. It is demotivating to skilled and successful people working to create processes to be mocked for being bureaucrats, have their requests for critical resources ignored, and have their decisions overruled by someone who does not understand or appreciate their skills. Dean's love of challenging open-ended projects is directly related to his aversion to processes. This aversion led him to overtly and covertly compete with anyone on his team responsible for setting up processes critical to the timely launch and successful marketing of the Segway. Many entrepreneurs with creative talent—think of chefs, fashion designers, architects, inventive techies—wind up in the same situation as Dean. They motivate those who can help them innovate, but they demotivate anyone who tries to help their enterprise mature beyond being purely project-based.

It is always challenging to motivate growing numbers of people as work becomes more process oriented, even when the leader is not personally averse to the needs of his maturing enterprise. Hiring project-loving, talented, and adventurous (even rebellious) employees in stage one presents a problem to any leader in stage two as they try to fit these people into more defined process roles. The EL sees this coming and works to mitigate the mismatch by letting his stage one hires know that their jobs may change for a while but that more adventurous projects lie ahead. Dean instead fought this stage, lost the support of his team, and lost both his company and control over his great invention.

The EL hires different types of people in stage two, and she motivates them differently from the people she hired in stage one. Stage two enterprises are naturally motivating to people who like to figure out how to make things work better. The EL should understand that "making things work better" is something she wants her stage two hires to feel they can be masters at doing. She must recognize and reward them for this mastery—for actually improving on the ideas so lovingly brought to life in stage one by the entrepreneur and her stage one team. It is difficult for any entrepreneur to praise people for improving on her work and ideas. The inverse problem can also happen: the entrepreneur may become so infatuated with the universe of possible improvements that she can constantly delay and interfere with her stage two team's attempt to freeze developments to the point where they can build required processes.

The EL can make people or teams feel autonomous in stage two by setting clear expectations about what improvements he wants in place and what he uses as criteria to judge improvement. He then needs to let the person or team work autonomously to meet these expectations. If the criteria are still ambiguous, then the EL can let employees feel in control of the improvement by asking them to suggest criteria.

Employees working in a stage two enterprise feel a sense of purpose because they can see their improvements become embedded into the fabric of how the enterprise operates. They also feel purpose in being associated with the mission of the enterprise. Employees feel highly motivated and prideful when the EL tells them she can recognize their specific contribution in the design of how the enterprise operates. A simple recognition that can be overheard by others—such as "Your idea on how to sort invoices by time zone will really make a difference to our ability to support overseas business, which is going to allow more people to buy our product"—will make the employee feel motivated to make more improvements and feel fulfilled by his job.

Stage three focuses intensely on creating new processes and improving existing ones. Because every action is tied directly to many other people and the actions they perform, change is hard and can be accomplished only by working deliberately in teams. Employees hired in stages one and two often feel demotivated in stage three because the enterprise feels bureaucratic and set in its ways. You may hear statements like, "This place isn't fun anymore" or "I don't feel like I have an impact anymore." Many entrepreneurs feel just like those employees, and they selfishly prevent their enterprises from ever maturing too far into stage three.

Although entrepreneurs may not understand how working at a stage three enterprise can make an employee feel autonomous, masterful, and purposeful, the EL does. The feeling of autonomy in stage three comes from pride in perfecting your skills and from working with other people on autonomous teams. Stage two hires, who have been chosen because they like to make things "better," can feel motivated in stage three by working on projects that design new processes required for the enterprise to expand or by improving existing processes. The adventurous people hired in stage one can be motivated by creating new product variations or opening up new markets. Employees newly hired in stage three should be chosen because they are proud of their ability to perform tasks at a high level of mastery, and they derive purpose from helping others improve. Stage three is when you hire people that are proud of their specific expertise. It may be janitorial expertise, baking, bookkeeping, call center supervision, strategy, computer controlled machining—whatever. In stage three it is important for the EL to create opportunities and support for career advancement by clearly answering the question, "How can I improve my skills and my value?" ELs in stage three wants to fill the enterprise with expertise and support these experts in the performance of their tasks.

Hiring people for their expertise can be threatening to an entrepreneur who selfishly insists on control. Because stage three cannot be completed until the enterprise can run apart from the involvement of any specific person, the personal ego challenges to the entrepreneur can be massive—many entrepreneurs can't make the transition. Unless the entrepreneur understands why his enterprise is imperiled by his insistence that the enterprise's well-being depends on his continued performance of some repetitive process tasks, then he will not do what it takes to train others to take his place. No matter how brilliantly the entrepreneur performs his task, his insistence on remaining critical to the operational well-being of the enterprise will demotivate his team. The team will feel insecure about the sustainability of their firm, and they will feel that the entrepreneur puts his own success ahead of theirs.

Stage four is tricky to lead because the EL must create a balance in the enterprise between innovation and efficiency. Once stage three has been completed, the enterprise is interconnected with hard-to-change, sophisticated processes. The enterprise relies on many people working together rather than any one person with a vision. And yet the future success of the enterprise now depends on the enterprise's reinstituting innovative, stage one–type projects. Without appropriate leadership, a successful stage three enterprise—which is complex and interdependent—tends to fear innovation and its implicit inefficiencies, unknown costs, and disruptive changes.

The EL's biggest motivational challenge in stage four is to ensure that the enterprise's culture is equally supportive of innovators and those who want to improve efficiency. Cultures derive from the way members perceive they must act in order to be rewarded and recognized by those in charge. It is very tricky to make two very different types of people feel equally valuable in the eyes of all managers with the power to give rewards and recognition. In stage four, career tracks must be modified to provide equally motivating autonomy and mastery opportunities for those innovative people who want to change everything and those enormously productive people who want to improve how they do what they already do. Some enterprises cordon off their innovators into special departments, like research and development (R&D). Some companies with extremely profitable businesses take a more general approach of stimulating and rewarding innovative activities in their operation by asking all employees to spend a set portion of their time at work investigating and proposing potential new products and services—3M and Google are famous for this. There are other successful solutions. Although entrepreneurs who have successfully completed the first three stages typically have built a great deal of trust and respect with their teams, making their employees want to complete the entrepreneur's vision, the efficiency-versus-innovativeness dichotomy is always challenging to resolve. There is no one best solution without downsides or risks. The essence of motivating key successful stage three employees to change once again, willingly accepting more risk, is to make sure they remain passionate about the greater purpose of the enterprise. The EL keeps her vision alive through all four stages and makes it the centerpiece of stage four.

Wendy Kopp is an excellent example of an EL who managed the transition from stage three to stage four very well—albeit on her second attempt. Wendy always kept Teach For America's stakeholders' expectations aligned with the broader vision of leading educational reform. Stage three was about putting TFA on a solid foundation on which the enterprise could grow and prosper. No manager or board member could object to Wendy's new educational reform projects once the organization was financially stable and had the means to do so. Because a stage three enterprise is no longer reliant on the supervision or expertise of any one person, Wendy could, in stage four, spend her time on new projects without anyone worrying about TFA's future. She had proven to everyone connected to her, through her very public sharing of what she learned to keep TFA alive, that she now valued those who could run and lead a very effective TFA while also appreciating those who could help her create new educational reform programs.

ELs enjoy leading their enterprises through stage four, because it revolves around their vision, and their joy is infectious and motivating. Stage four enterprises can enable a wide variety of people—with a wide variety of skills, core motivations, and personalities—to feel like they have opportunities for personal success while directly contributing to the success of the enterprise.

Leading Change

An enterprise is always changing. It changes in order to mature through the four stages. It changes in order to respond to customers and other stakeholders. It changes because environments, conditions, and competitors change. Enterprises change when the people who form the enterprise change. Successfully leading change is an essential skill of all entrepreneurial leaders (and a generally useful skill for all of us).

Many people, including ELs, consider change scary. Change easily triggers our fear of the unknown, because we can never know all aspects of any change with certainty. Many of us have a heightened fear of risk as well, and this adds to our fear of change whenever someone asks us to change something we feel has been successful for us—something that has not been anxiety provoking and perhaps has even produced some reward. As we will see, the skill of leading change revolves around creating the conditions that make everyone participating in the change feels secure that the change will be successful. Leading change is a special case of a leader's ability to make those around him feel they will be successful.

"Why do I need to change? I am already the happiest man alive." Jon liked saying those words because they always made him feel happy—and they muted that anxious feeling he had when he got up most mornings.[1] Jon was founder and CEO of Excellence in Training (EIT), a firm that offered training courses to governmental, industrial, and commercial enterprises in Southern California. Jon had founded the firm in 2000 when he was laid off from his position as the director of training at a major hotel chain. He had profitably grown EIT to revenues of over $4 million a year, delivering over 250 different courses a year. He had a permanent staff of 10 and over two dozen part time trainers whom he could call upon to give some of the courses EIT offered. Jon had contracts with a dozen medium-sized Southern California–based companies for whom he provided all of their training needs. He also offered 100 "open" classes a year in subjects such as time management and how to master PowerPoint. EIT was profitable and efficiently managed, with robust processes in place for selling and delivering courses, within a low overhead structure. Jon's expertise had not been necessary for the delivery of any classes, or for maintaining any clients, since 2005 when EIT had completed stage three.

Jon was satisfied with EIT, his family, and his ability to enjoy life. Founding EIT was the best decision he had ever made. Jon didn't need to make more money than he was already making, so he saw no need to stress himself by expanding or seeking dramatic change—hiring more people, finding customers outside of SoCal, or adopting technologies and methods that would allow EIT to deliver its classes over the Internet.

To ensure EIT's continuing relevance and growth, in 2004 Jon had set an objective: EIT would license and learn to deliver two new courses every year. Although licensing courses from other people or firms limited Jon's profits, it also reduced the risk inherent in having to invest in creating courses from scratch. His reticence to invest in creating new courses also reflected an early major failure in course creation that had almost sunk EIT. Jon didn't want to make that mistake again. Jon also didn't want to invest in the new technologies that would allow him to compete in the business of remotely delivering classes over the Internet. That would be costly and risky; besides, he loved to tell his customers that nothing could ever improve on a class where the teacher was in the classroom paying personal attention to each student.

In 2009 Jon's doctor told him that his blood pressure was creeping up and was probably the result of stresses in his life. Even though Jon protested emphatically to the doctor that he had no major stresses, he knew that he worried about EIT. Jon's typically anxious mornings stemmed from his sense that the training business was finally changing in a way that would make firms such as EIT obsolete. Training was becoming a commodity, and prices for online training were a fraction of what EIT charged. Specialized classes such as computer security were much more valuable, but the people who created these classes were now licensing them exclusively to national firms and not to regional ones like EIT. EIT's ability to remain viable without changing was not looking good.

THE ANXIETY OF CHANGE

As far back as 2003 Jon had anticipated these changes in the market. He had considered his options back then, and each had presented challenges that made him feel uneasy. The options Jon considered included:

- *Become aggressive in sales and marketing in order to compete with national training companies.* To make this option work, Jon would have to bring in a full-time salesperson and probably a marketing person too. If EIT was going to compete with much larger training companies, it could no longer be the laid-back environment he loved.
- *Bring in a partner who had technical skills and could spearhead efforts to expand EIT's online course offerings.* Jon shivered, wondering how he could determine who was good technically and who was not. Having a partner would mean his no longer making every decision; it would mean changing the culture of EIT.
- *Milk profits out of the existing firm to prepare for its gradual decline and eventual closure.* Regional training firms such as EIT could not be sold for a great deal of money, so the best way to get the most financial value from the firm could be to just milk it. Jon found the thought of milking his firm until it died depressing.
- *Grow by licensing specialized classes from experts.* The profitability of this option was mediocre because revenues were shared with the expert who created and owned the class.

- *Start creating valuable classes to replace classes that were quickly becoming commoditized.* This option would involve finding specialists who were also interested in training others. Jon's experience was that specialists required a great deal of effort to find, train, and nurture and could not be relied on. Specialists often would leave without any notice to accept more lucrative work.

Back in 2003 Jon had decided to be proactive about changing EIT and tried to create more valuable classes by working with specialists. This attempt ended badly. Jon worked with some experts in the field of computer security to create what, even in retrospect, would have been a blockbuster set of classes. But the team charged with creating the class had produced unusable material; the effort had taken twice as long as expected, caused significant negative cash flow, and required Jon to quickly get a second mortgage on his house to keep his then three-year-old (early stage three) company alive. No book that Jon had read clearly explained what he had done wrong. He had correctly used all the project management techniques that EIT's class on the subject taught, but these techniques had not prevented the disaster. Jon's conclusion at the time was that he needed to be more technical if he were to lead a firm that offered valuable technical classes and that his real expertise was teaching people how to train others and to sell training services.

After that 2003 disaster, Jon decided that he should stick to doing what he felt he was good at. Shortly afterward, Jon decided to license classes created by other people rather than develop them within EIT. Although Jon sensed then that this was a stopgap solution, it nonetheless helped EIT grow steadily from 2004 through 2008. In spite of the major recession, the company still showed a profit in 2009, but rather than feeling satisfied by that result, Jon sensed that the turning point in the training marketplace that he had anticipated back in 2003 had finally arrived.

As I have already mentioned, many entrepreneurs are reluctant to go beyond the point where their enterprise is financially stable—why change what is already working? Jon's fear of change and fear of risk had been strongly reinforced by his disastrous failed attempt at creating sophisticated new classes. A combination of losing a medium-sized client that decided to switch to lower cost online training and the appearance of several well-financed online training startups rekindled Jon's fear of the future. He woke up most mornings thinking about potentially losing everything he had created for himself and his family.

LEARNING TO CHANGE

After getting the news about his blood pressure, Jon decided to act. Again he drew up a list of his options, which was virtually the same as the list made in 2003. He thought long and hard about what to do. He asked his wife. He asked his friends. He even asked everyone at work. There was a common theme in what Jon heard: "Your work is an important part of your life, you have many people who rely on you, you can't let EIT die an agonizing death, you need to figure out how to change."

In 2009 Jon again came to the conclusion that his best option was to figure out how EIT could develop its own sophisticated classes—provided he could figure out what he had done wrong in the previous attempt. This time Jon decided to seek the advice of experts and advisors. He started by writing down what he wanted to accomplish as well as the next steps he planned to take.

Five-Year Objective
1. > $4 million/year of revenues from advanced courses
2. Advanced courses profits ≫ mainstream course profits
3. Great COO in place, so lifestyle can return to something similar to today

Next Steps
- → Ask at least twelve "change experts" for advice on how to make EIT capable of developing and delivering sophisticated classes.
- → Discuss with top ten clients what will be desirable classes for next five years.
- → Ask retired chairman of US Training for advice.
- → Develop speech for team on why this change is exciting and explain the path forward.

Jon framed this list and put it on his desk. Shortly after composing the list, Jon told his employees that he was working on a new strategic plan and that he would tell them about it as soon as it was finished. He said he would ask for each employee's input as part of putting together the plan.

LINING UP THE DUCKS

Over the next month Jon talked to more than a dozen "change experts." A few were college professors who told him things he couldn't understand, and a few were consultants he felt only cared about selling him a quarter million dollars' worth of consulting, but overall he got advice that he boiled down to a list of five prerequisites he needed to put into place for himself and the people he worked with. He labeled his five fundamental prerequisites: comprehension, motivation, skills, resources, and communications.[2]

1. *Comprehension:* Everyone responsible for designing and implementing the change must share the same understanding of the change objectives. This prerequisite makes sure all team members have the same shared objective relative to the mission of the team. Creating an alignment of comprehension is difficult even among a few team members, and it must start, of course, with the EL's comprehending why the change is necessary.

2. *Motivation:* All members of the team implementing the change must be motivated to see that the change is successfully accomplished. As we have seen, motivation drives actions, so we must make sure that each team member is motivated to achieve the shared objective of the team. Aligning motivations of team members toward a common goal can be challenging. Without aligned motivations, some team members will cooperate with their team members, but others may compete or retreat.

3. *Skills:* The project team must possess or control the skills necessary to design and implement the change. Missing skills will cause a team to fail at their mission.

4. *Resources:* All the resources required to perform the project must be made available to the team. Missing resources will cause a project team to fail.

5. *Communication:* Everyone impacted by the change must understand its importance. This prerequisite creates an overarching shared objective with everyone who will be called on to change their customary work activities—which presumably they have been completing somewhat successfully, or they wouldn't be in their current position. A great deal of communication is required to implement and maintain this prerequisite.

Once these prerequisites are in place and remain in place, then it is hard to screw up. Not only do you have the skills and resources lined up to implement and support the desired change, but you also have assembled a team of people who are aligned on what needs to be done and personally excited to do it.

Deploying an appropriate communication plan is an equally critical prerequisite. This requires communicating, not broadcasting, with the many people who could have their routines, responsibilities, and status altered as part of the desired changes. These communications focus on why the desired change is important to the enterprise, to the EL, and to all stakeholders—including customers and suppliers. Because all communications are two-way, these communications generate the feedback that confirms everyone understands why the change is important. These communications make it clear that you are offering to cooperate on an important shared objective with all of those you are asking to change their routine.

Even after all have been offered the chance to cooperate on the proposed change, they can choose to compete or retreat instead. In essence, when properly deployed, this communications prerequisite enables the EL and his implementation team to understand who they can count on to help implement the change, who will fight it, and who will neither resist nor help. This is critical information the implementation team needs in order to decide how to proceed. Yes, some people may need to be removed or replaced; change is not a consensus exercise. Nonetheless, if the implementation team and the EL do a good job of explaining why the change is important, then the people who plan to resist the change are not the people the enterprise can count on anyway.

When this communication prerequisite is ignored, chaos often reigns. Without these communications, you send the message that no one who is expected to change their routine is important enough to even be offered the chance to cooperate—each of these people will accordingly feel left out and alienated, becoming resistant to the leadership rather than supportive of it. Without being able to understand the cooperative support that can be expected, the implementation team is completely in the dark about what they need to do to really get people to change—hence the chaos. This communication prerequisite, with its offer of cooperation, typically results in plenty of feedback and suggestions relative to local issues that the implementation team would otherwise have naïvely overlooked.

I call the process of putting these prerequisites in place "lining up your comprehension, motivation, skills, resources, and communications ducks" or "lining up the five ducks"—it's a phrase I've used to make the concept memorable. It's a compelling way of describing and tracking this set of change prerequisites.

Even though Jon understood what he needed to do, he knew he was not yet in the position to start transforming EIT into a provider of sophisticated training. He needed some specific information in order to create a credible plan. He needed to understand the skills and resources that EIT would need to design and implement these new capabilities. He also needed to be able to clearly articulate why this change would actually be a good thing for each of EIT's employees. He knew that he could not just say that these changes would be good for everyone because they would reduce his blood pressure.

Jon decided he would get his team to help him craft the right message. He made another list:

Things to Figure Out

- Why is this good for every employee?
- Talk with five people who have developed successful technical classes.
- Talk with five people who have successfully sold technical classes.

It took another eight weeks for Jon to feel like he really understood what skills and resources he would need to be sure this major transformation of EIT would be successful. Jon's strategy of soliciting the advice of established heads of training departments at high-tech companies paid off in several ways. They told Jon how they created their unique classes; they told him of their frustration in not being able to get good classes from training companies; they told him what skills EIT would need and where to find some technical experts he could use as consultants to help him prepare materials. This strategy had another big payoff when Jon felt impressed, yet comfortable with Robert, one of the heads of in-house training. Robert gave great advice, and Jon visited with him several times. During a dinner session, Robert confided that it was his dream to some day do what Jon had done and start a successful training company. Jon responded, "Why not see if you can make your dreams come true by working with me? I suspect we could someday be partners." Two weeks later, Robert gave his company two weeks' notice that he would be leaving to join EIT as its new research director.

EXPLAINING THE IMPORTANCE OF CHANGE

Almost three months after his "wake-up call" at his doctor's office, Jon assembled the EIT staff together to tell them his new vision for EIT. Jon was excited about the prospect of change, which came through as he told his employees:

"We have a great company and a great team, but we need to change. We need to change in order to survive the changes that are sweeping our market, but we also need to change in order to create compelling opportunities for each of us to grow in our professions and our ability to excel."

Jon then explained the inevitability of the changes he wanted to make. This was a simple way to make the point that the changes were important. Jon continued by giving some facts that supported the credibility of his plan.

"As you know I have spent the last three months constructing a vision of our future together. I'm now extremely excited about EIT's opportunities. I have spoken to all of our major customers, I have spoken to each of you, I have spoken to other successful people in our field, and I know we are capable of making our company uniquely valuable to our existing clients and, just as important, uniquely valuable enough to attract new clients from around the country."

Jon ended the opening portion of his speech by reiterating the personal importance of these changes. These changes would create more rewarding careers and add to each employee's existing skills. He tried to make it clear that the transformation would make EIT a better company, ending this section by sincerely committing to help each employee successfully make this transition.

"I think of the next level we can take our company to as 'EIT+,' and I think each of you can play key roles at EIT+. You may have to change what you are doing, but I promise you'll get whatever training you need to develop any and all new skills you'll be asked to perform. I promise to ask each of you, over and over again, 'How can I make these changes easy for you?'"

Jon then proceeded to sketch out his plan to develop three new courses over the next twelve months for clients who already indicated they wanted to buy these courses if they met their expectations. Jon outlined how he would be working closely with the clients along the way to ensure that the new courses would make them happy. Jon then introduced Robert, EIT's new research director, and described how he had successfully developed highly technical in-house courses for a major computer company. Jon went on to explain how he had formed an advisory board that would help and to whom he would feel accountable for the success of this change. He had successfully recruited the shrewd and well-known founder of US Training onto this advisory board, along with one of the change experts with whom he felt most comfortable. Jon ended by saying that he would meet with his director of training, director of accounting, new research director, and HR manager every Monday morning to review progress and make sure everyone had the resources they needed to be successful. Over the following forty-eight hours Jon met face-to-face with each employee and several of his best part-time trainers to answer their questions and make an inventory of their concerns.

The speech Jon gave was fairly generic and could apply equally to most any change effort. But Jon was sincere, and his employees felt that. Transmitting that sincerity is an important objective, as it makes the communications personal. EIT employees now believed this change was important to Jon and important to their careers, and some, though not all, felt that it was important to expanding their opportunities. By talking with clients, Jon had already aligned the other major part of the communications prerequisite, as key clients now believed that EIT+ would deliver to them important new courses.

WORKING WITH THE TEAM

The plan Jon developed, committed to, communicated, and began to execute was one in which the change prerequisites—the five ducks—were aligned to the point where the effort to change EIT into EIT+ was credible and the change project could proceed. Jon explained to his implementation team that he believed the team would transform EIT into EIT+ by developing the capability to create and deliver very advanced and profitable courses while infusing the culture with a pride of teaching others advanced concepts. These courses would make EIT+ more profitable and would expand the professional opportunities of the trainers. Each of the other members of the implementation team described their understanding of the project to one another as follows:

• Robert, the new research director, saw this project as something that would transform EIT and make it into an exciting place for him to work. He felt the market needed a training company with leading-edge courses and that EIT+ could be the leader. It was a bold plan, but Robert felt that Jon had prepared extremely well, was capable, and had the financial resources to pull it off. He made it clear to everyone that he had left his secure job to join Jon because this project was important and would impact a big market.

- Dotty, the director of training, described how this project would transform EIT into a very different place. It would make EIT's course material much more valuable—but also much more demanding to deliver. Dotty did not know exactly how these changes would impact her career or the career opportunities of her training corps. She knew that neither Jon nor anyone else had that answer. Dotty said that without this capability EIT would slowly die. Dotty said she respected Jon for making sure EIT would not die.

- Viola, the accounting director, felt that this project would make EIT into a much stronger enterprise and make her job more important. She added that Jon was wealthy enough to hire the people he needed to make this successful.

- Molly, the HR manager, said this was an exciting project and would make EIT into a more secure place to work. This project also would mean that she would get to spend some more time with Jon, and she thought that would help her know more about EIT's business.

The core team's understandings about what they would do together and what their efforts would accomplish were tightly aligned with the change Jon wanted to implement, which meant that the first prerequisite of change was in place. Dotty had some legitimate questions relative to how the materials would be delivered by her trainers, but she understood and supported the validity of the mission, and she was willing to help the change effort and work hard to develop the support EIT would give its trainers to instill the confidence that they could deliver more sophisticated classes.

Prerequisite two, motivation, was also now in much better shape than it had been during the bungled 2003 change effort. This duck had required thought and some discussion to get aligned. Whereas previously Jon's motivation had been to personally make more money, now he realized his motivation was to lead a very profitable leading-edge training company, EIT+. His motivation was now about transforming EIT into a stronger company and a more satisfying place to work. He loved this project and felt that his legacy rested on its success; he would do everything in his power to see that it was successful. His wife was supportive of the effort, and that laid to rest a major fear that he no longer worried might constrain his efforts. Jon put a great deal of effort into making sure his team felt equally emotionally tied to the success of this transformation project.

Jon knew from his previous disaster that his trainers would be concerned about their jobs. He knew Dotty would be key to figuring out how to utilize existing trainers and finding and motivating new trainers with technical degrees. Because Jon knew Dotty would have questions, he met with her first after giving his speech. He told Dotty that he did not expect her to give any of these advanced classes, but he thought she would still be able to lead the training corps. He sensed from the meeting he had with her that she definitely did not want to see the project fail because it would likely be viewed as her fault. Jon believed Dotty when she said that if she did not feel she could do a good job finding and training technically astute trainers, she would ask him to put her in charge of the nontechnical training corps or she would go find another job. Dotty told Jon that she was ultimately motivated to see the project be successful because it could make her job more interesting and challenging.

Jon had hired Robert because he had a technical background, was already skilled at creating sophisticated classes, and had a burning desire to be an entrepreneur. Robert's motivation to be an entrepreneur would be satisfied by being a driving force in a very profitable and successful training company, one that he played a pivotal role in transforming. As part of the offer to join EIT, Jon had promised to make him a partner in EIT if all three of these new courses were well received by clients. This was a selfless move on Jon's part, as it meant that EIT would not be "his" but a partnership with others whom he respected.

Jon could tell that Viola, his accounting director, was motivated to see that the transformation was successful because it would mean more job security and also potentially higher pay when the company became bigger. After Jon told Viola he wanted her to help with this project because he relied on her good financial sense, Viola explicitly brought up the subject of the success of the new classes resulting in her responsibility growing along with the company. Jon was prepared for this comment and agreed that managing the accounts of a bigger enterprise was a more responsible position. Jon even said that he looked forward to paying Viola a bigger salary when EIT was bigger and more profitable. Viola was completely on board.

Molly, the HR manager, was a single mother, and this transformation would mean more job security. She told Jon that she believed him when he said that without this transformation EIT would slowly die. Molly was always influenced by what she heard the employees she looked after tell her, and she knew that the staff was anxious about the project because they also believed that the project was make-or-break for the future of EIT. Molly really wanted to do everything she could to help transform EIT into EIT+.

These motivations would stay aligned naturally, provided the team remained confident the transformation would be successful and no personality clashes put personal competitive objectives ahead of the team's cooperative ones. The biggest personality risk was how well Robert would integrate with the team. Jon and Robert had explicitly discussed the importance of his acceptance by the training staff and that Robert's success and the success of the project depended on it. Jon had made sure Dotty was part of his deliberation on hiring Robert, so she had spent considerable time with him before the offer was made. Jon understood that Dotty did not want Robert's position; she also felt that Robert was not interested in taking over her responsibility for hiring, training, and developing the training staff. Dotty expected Robert would one day run EIT if this project was a success.

Jon paid a great deal of attention to make sure he had all the required *skills* in place to succeed, having talked with many people in the industry who had successfully created challenging courses. Jon was confident he knew the skills he would need. Hiring Robert gave EIT the skills needed to design some excellent courses, but EIT would still need to develop skills to deliver these courses on the scale required to make EIT very profitable. Jon was confident that he, Robert, and Dotty had the skills to develop a process for training trainers to deliver each technically demanding course. To jump-start this process, Jon proposed finding and hiring a couple of recent engineering graduates who also had some acting or public speaking experience. Once they figured out how to train young recent engineering graduates, then they would know if it would be possible to train some of EIT's more successful existing instructors. Because they were planning that it would take six months to develop the first three courses, Jon and his team at EIT+ felt they had at least four months to align the skills duck for the delivery of the courses. They felt that the risk of not being able to train skilled trainers was small enough not to have to delay the start of class development.

ELs sometimes face the problem that a skill they need to implement a change does not exist or is not attainable. If a critical skill cannot be made available, then the EL has two options:

- Set up a stand-alone project to develop the skill and delay the overall project plan accordingly.
- Reduce the scope of the desired change so that substitute skills will work.

Jon's challenge was not that a required skill did not exist; rather, it was that he did not have enough of the skills required to deliver as many classes as he wanted—that is, not enough new classes to accelerate the growth of EIT.

The *resources* prerequisite was the most straightforward for Jon to put into place, because EIT had been consistently profitable and he had plenty of money in the bank. Jon set aside twice the budget he thought he would need to pay his new advisory board; hire Robert, two engineering grads, and some technical experts; and pay for new stationery with a plus sign after EIT. This project did not require any new equipment, offices, or specialized research space, as can be the case for other types of change efforts. If Jon had decided he wanted to deliver his new courses over the Internet, then he would have needed to acquire computer resources, but he decided early in his deliberations that he wanted to stay at the high end of the training business, with courses given in person, so computer system resources were not needed. The technical expertise needed to help put the materials together could have posed a problem if it was essential yet unafford-able. In the case of the three classes that Jon chose to develop in the first year, Robert already knew the technical experts that EIT+ would use to help put course materials together. Jon had done a good job lining up this duck.

The resources available to many ELs are more tightly constrained than in Jon's case. Required resources may not exist; essential resources may not be affordable. Even though many entrepreneurs are excited by the challenge of succeeding in spite of limited resources, the EL proceeds by either scaling down project objectives or breaking the larger project into subprojects and proceeding only on the subprojects that have been resourced up front. *Breaking larger, riskier, and expensive projects into less resource-intensive subprojects is something ELs do on a regular basis to reduce risks and costs.*

Although Jon had done an excellent job of explaining to all of his employees and his major customers why it was important for EIT to change, and then listening to their feedback to get their suggestions and see if they agreed, he did slip up a couple of times in soliciting feedback on the periodic project updates he gave to the staff. Jon updated the entire EIT staff once a month on project status. At that meeting he asked employees, "What do you think we need to pay more attention to?" or "What about this project update makes you feel uneasy?" Their answers, coupled with Molly's ongoing regular contact with every employee, constituted Jon's method for making sure his messages were accurately received. Nonetheless, on one occasion an unexpected crisis with an important client caused Jon to cancel the staff update, and he never got around to rescheduling it. This missed meeting came right after the training staff had heard that EIT was going to recruit two engineering grads to join the training team. Despite Molly's and Dotty's repeated urging that Jon reschedule the meeting, Jon insisted on prioritizing other activities that he felt were even more urgent. Two of Dotty's better trainers began searching for new jobs during that time and left soon afterward, because they felt they would not be as important or valuable to EIT once younger trainers were hired. Did they leave because of the gap in communications? Perhaps, but Jon felt extremely lucky that no more trainers had left at that time. More resignations would have impacted EIT ongoing business, which would have thrown the company into a crisis that would have diverted Jon's attention away from leading the transition—making the project fall farther behind schedule, making regular staff communications even harder to fit into his schedule, and perhaps even causing additional staff to lose confidence in the chances of the transformation succeeding.

Jon did a very good job of putting in place the five prerequisites for change. In the first place—crucially—he convinced himself that a change effort was needed, possible, and attractive. He was personally motivated to make the change succeed, and he built on a core of his own vision, motivation, experience, and capability mix to flesh out the plan for change. The vision coalesced for him in his draft of five-year objectives and next steps. In these next steps Jon diligently sought advice from more experienced people to feel comfortable that he knew how to lead the development of technically advanced courses. He constructed, from the advice of experts, the five prerequisites that he needed to put into place to enable the success of the project. He determined that there were things he still needed to know in order to line up his ducks, and he dedicated himself to discovering what resources and skills he would need and then went out and procured them. All this discovery, consulting, planning, and procuring, all the while keeping everyone around him informed about what he was doing, took three months. When the plan was ready to present and Jon's ducks were lined up, he made his speech outlining why this transformation would be important to each of them. Finally, he began to execute on the plan, taking care to keep communication open and to continuing to make sure the ducks stayed aligned.

NOTHING IS PERFECT

Of course not everything went as smoothly as desired in the months after Jon gave his speech. Jon, Dotty, and Robert took a year, not six months, to feel comfortable that they had a good process for training technically savvy people to deliver EIT's new courses. This delay caused several crises when the first two courses were to be delivered and there were no trainers certified to deliver either of them. Robert stepped in and delivered one of the courses himself, twice. Robert and Jon had to pay one of their technical experts a large sum to take a week out of her vacation to bail them out by teaching the other course. Dotty, Robert, and Jon recruited and fired three different trainers whom they thought could deliver the new courses but could not. They found out that recent college engineering grads were too inexperienced as practicing engineers to successfully answer practical follow-on questions from seasoned and savvy practitioners. After nine months of frustrating effort, they finally figured out that hiring people from the help desks of technology companies yielded successful and highly motivated trainers. One of these trainers proved so personally engaging that he was able to sell clients more EIT+ courses. He eventually became Jon's first full-time salesperson.

The delay in finding competent trainers meant that they could not sell the new courses as quickly as they wanted, which meant that it cost Jon more money than budgeted (but still slightly less than double the original budget that Jon had set aside). As mentioned, two of Dotty's best full-time trainers left EIT because they felt their careers would advance further in less technical training enterprises. Fortunately Dotty was able to replace them without too much trouble.

Jon's considerable deliberate and premeditated efforts saved his company (and possibly prevented major medical problems), opened up new opportunities for Jon and his employees, satisfied an unfilled need in the market, and created considerable value. A couple of years after deciding he needed to learn how to lead change, Jon's lifestyle was back to where it had so enthusiastically started. EIT+ had started 2009 as a late stage three company on the precipice of decline and emerged in 2011, having completed stage four, as a fully matured, truly valuable enterprise that was now actively sought after as an important acquisition candidate by larger business services companies. Bravo!

Most entrepreneurial stories like Jon's don't end so happily. As we have discussed, most entrepreneurs either choose not to change, because they don't want to, or fail at implementing change, because they insist they can do it all by themselves. Jon's motivation for making the change was a good balance between wanting to prevent a personal financial and entrepreneurial disappointment and wanting to fulfill his implicit promise to provide good careers for his employees. Once he was able to personally embrace change and put in place the necessary prerequisites, his clear dedication to making the change successful for the firm made those around him feel he would make them successful—the hallmark of leadership.

Creating a Personal Leadership Strategy

A t this point you have a good picture of what it takes to be an entrepreneurial leader. You are capable of growing an idea into a self-sustaining enterprise once you master five skills: self-awareness, the basics of enterprises, relationship building, motivation, and change leadership. Understanding these five skills is the prerequisite for success once you have a strong motivation to take an idea and turn it into a value-producing and self-sustaining enterprise—the kind of motivation that won't fade when challenges and crises arise. It only remains for you to decide whether you really want to take an enterprise through each of the four stages of development from inception to self-sustaining value—and are willing to do what it takes to achieve that goal.

This chapter pulls together the ideas of the previous chapters into a plan of action. The focus is now on creating and implementing a personal strategy to acquire and master the basic skills every EL needs—a strategy that you hold yourself accountable for achieving. Your *personal leadership strategy*, or PLS, leverages the motivations, traits, and existing skills that give you the desire and energy to succeed as an EL, while mitigating any of your traits and motivations that could impede your ability to master these skills.

At age thirty-six, Keri had worked in two different jobs since graduating from a big state university with a degree in English.[1] After college, Keri had first worked for a local PR agency but ultimately decided she did not like many of the clients that she was compelled to promote through her efforts. After leaving the PR agency, Keri worked for six years as the executive assistant to the General Manager at an auto parts factory that employed two thousand people. Keri liked the pay, liked the guy she worked for, liked many of the projects she was given, but did not care at all about auto parts. She married a manager in the purchasing department, and they had one child. Shortly after having her daughter, Keri left her full-time executive assistant job to start a business from home, designing and hand-decorating wrapping paper for local stores. Over the course of five years, Keri's wrapping paper business grew to $250,000 a year in revenue, with four full-time employees, and generated as much income for the family as her husband's job. When her daughter was seven and in school full time, Keri started to allow herself to get excited by the prospect of making her company as successful as possible. She set herself an objective of determining what it would take to succeed at growing a tiny part-time enterprise into a profitable, self-sustaining, and, she hoped, large company.

STEP ONE: TAPPING INTO CORE MOTIVATIONS

Keri started her process by examining who she was at that moment.[2] She made notes on her motivations, traits, and entrepreneurial skills. She asked herself whether she wanted to run a large successful company badly enough to sacrifice time with her family (not to mention sleep) and endure the stress she knew she would feel dealing with contentious issues and business matters.

Keri felt that she would need help and support if she was going to take on an enterprise-building project. She first sought emotional support from her husband and from her older sister, with whom she was very close and whose personal judgments she trusted on whether she could lead a substantial company (her sister was a marketing executive at a major mail order company). Whether Keri would aggressively dedicate herself to creating a valuable company or just keep it as an activity to produce supplemental income would depend heavily on her husband's support and on her older sister's opinion of her chances. The toughest question both her husband and sister asked was, "Why do you need to do this?" This question prompted Keri to reevaluate her core motivation—the one that needed to be strong enough for her to shoulder the pressures of being an EL. It took Keri three weeks to come back with her answer: "I need to feel that I am a great example of a woman who can raise a wonderful daughter and also be in charge of my own life. That will be expected of our daughter, and it needs to be expected of me. It would also be my fantasy to someday turn a successful business over to our daughter. I hate to think that I could not achieve these goals."

Keri started her personal leadership strategy with the right first step: determining her motivations and making sure they were credible to people who knew her well. It turns out that in Keri's case these motivations were not new to her; she had been aware of them for at least five years, since she and her husband had gone through a year of couples therapy to get their marriage back on track after their baby was born. It took three weeks for Keri to reconnect to these core motivations. The "What do you need, and why do you need it?" question focused Keri on how she would feel like a failure if she did not set a good example for her daughter—it made her tremble to think of not being someone her daughter respected. Once she reacknowledged this burning desire, Keri was able to passionately answer her sister's and husband's question and the many follow-on questions about what she would do under different difficult situations. It was obvious to them that Keri really wanted this, and they let her know that her feelings and reasoning had convinced them that she could succeed and that this quest was something they would help and support.

Keri had begun her process of making a personal leadership strategy (PLS) by acknowledging her strongest motivations, which, as we discussed in Chapter Two, include both the motivations driven by strong desires and the motivations driven by major fears. Your strongest motivations should make you feel excited and scared, or else you haven't been honest with yourself; Keri trembled at the thought of hers.

Motivations that count are scary because they define failure—when we acknowledge them, we also acknowledge that we may not get what we so badly want. Core motivations are always exciting because they give you permission to focus on being fulfilled.

STEP TWO: GETTING OBJECTIVE MENTORS

Once you've uncovered your deepest, scary/exciting motivations, the next step involves getting a mentor (if you do not already have one or more). For the purpose of creating a PLS, you'll need an objective, experienced person or group of people whom you respect to help test your ideas and your capabilities throughout your journey. You cannot accurately judge your level of skill and self-knowledge, and mentors classically act as judges for their mentees.

A mentor is not the same as a friend. Friends weigh their advice against the cost of hurting your relationship. The shared objective with a mentor—the basis of your relationship—is for the mentor to feel like a successful counselor in return for sharing his time, experience, and advice. Keri reached out to her old boss at the auto parts factory, explained what she wanted to do, and asked him if he would be willing to give her unfiltered feedback on her plans and ideas. He was flattered by her request, but he asked that in return Keri agree to make their time together as efficient as possible and to drive to his office for their meetings. Past bosses make good mentors, but finding someone who has been successful leading an enterprise such as yours is even better.

A board of advisors is another classic way to get this kind of objective judgment, but it takes much more effort than a one-on-one mentor relationship, because it involves finding at least three people, arranging for them to meet together, and usually offering some formal compensation. Jon, profiled in Chapter Six, created a board of advisors because he wanted them to have specific expertise and he planned to use them on an ongoing basis—he also agreed to pay them for their effort to meet formally together.

Virtually every EL has had one or more mentors. You cannot consider yourself competent, let alone a master, in relationship building if you cannot find a mentor, and you cannot build a viable PLS without this kind of experienced and impartial help.

STEP THREE: INVENTORYING YOUR TRAITS

Once your motivations and your mentor(s) are in place, the next step is to inventory your traits and consider how each trait will make it easier or harder to master EL skills. Listing your traits does not require any soul searching and should not stir up too much emotion (if you feel strong emotion while writing down your traits, then you need to look for some still undefined motivation or major unmet need that is driving you to feel uncomfortable with who you are). How your traits challenge you or help you acquire the skills of an EL is straightforward. The most important part of this step is in devising strategies for mitigating the challenges that your traits bring.

Keri had a good idea of her traits. She had taken a class on interpersonal relations when working for the auto-parts company, and the class included the MBTI. In college Keri had thought she might want to be a teacher, and her education classes had taught her about her own learning styles. She knew of her other traits from other tests she took, from her experience in couples therapy, and from listening to how other people talked about her. She wrote down what she knew about her traits in a matrix that accounted for how each trait would both help and hinder her work as an entrepreneurial leader (see Table 7.1).

As you can see, her traits could pose some major challenges for Keri in growing her business. Being an idealist tended to make her obsessive about getting things done in only the "right way," made her slower in getting things done, and made her potentially difficult for nonidealists to work with. Being easily distracted also could slow down her decision making to the point where she could not keep up with customer demands and market forces; it also irritated decisive people. A person who, like Keri, fears confrontation has a challenging time getting the best results from a team. Enterprises that are led by idealistic, indecisive, and nonconfrontational people typically have low productivity and mediocre products and cannot grow beyond being a small firm. Many aspiring ELs with this combination of traits have been improperly counseled to not even try founding the enterprise of their dreams. But all of these challenges can be mitigated with an appropriate personal strategy informed by self-awareness, which is

Table 7.1 Benefits and Challenges of Keri's Traits

Trait	Helps	Hinders
Myers-Briggs: INFP	Inspiring visions Sensitive to emotions of others Strong values Open minded, other than with core values	Scared of dealing with other people Idealistic Slow to trust
Auditory learner	Good at remembering what was said Good listener	Bored with reading Poor motor skills
Physically Large	Makes people feel secure People are naturally deferential	Can scare some people or make them feel uncomfortable Perceived as awkward
Easily Distracted	Excited by new possibilities	Challenge to be on time
Easily Excitable	Good at avoiding confrontation	Often later regrets emotional decisions Avoids emotionally charged issues
Intelligent	Can solve complex problems Can think strategically	Overcomplicates problems Can appear arrogant
Good Design Sense	Professional designers feel respected	Some customers do not care about or disagree with my design opinions

what Keri did, and what other actual ELs with these traits do. No combination of traits should make a person give up on the desire to become an EL—provided they create and implement an effective PLS.

STEP FOUR: ASSESS YOUR SKILLS

As an aspiring EL, you now need to assess your skills. You'll need input from your mentor, former coworkers, and bosses—people who have seen you do things. Your demonstrated skill levels can be determined using this crude scale:

- *Basic:* You can describe the skill, and you can explain how you would apply the skill in a situation that you have experienced or are familiar with to the satisfaction of the people you know who have this skill ("My boss ignored understanding the skills and resources he would need, which turned moving to new facilities into a costly nightmare" or "I admired the way my roommate in college motivated his singing club by offering to introduce them to a Broadway producer; this gave them an enormous sense of purpose"). Your skill level is basic if you have failed to perform a task or are afraid to perform a task in spite of having been trained to do so ("My fear of confrontation makes me reticent to create competitive situations, even if it is in the best interest of everyone involved"). ELs must honestly acknowledge if their skills are only basic in order to formulate an effective strategy for dealing with the lack of proficiency.

- *Competent:* You can describe how you actually used the skill successfully in a situation ("After I took Myers-Briggs I learned to productively work with 'F' types by describing the source of my feelings" or "I described to my boss how his project plan overlooked communicating to people whom he planned to move, and he put me in charge of doing that").

- *Master:* You can describe how you used the skill under different and varied stressful circumstances. Stressful circumstances could involve competitive or time pressure. It could also involve solving a long-standing problem that had resisted solution attempts by others. Jon's actions to lead successful transformation of EIT in spite of his previous failure make him a master at leading change. Wendy mastered understanding her enterprise's needs and putting them ahead of her dreams of expanding educational reform. Conversely, Dean Kamen was not a master motivator when he launched the Segway because he failed to motivate his marketing and manufacturing teams.

- *Best-in-Class:* If you are able to succeed where others with even master level skills have consistently failed, then you are best-in-class.

Brian O'Kelley's system networking skills are best-in-class, as are Keri's paper design skills.

If you are frustrated by your level of proficiency in performing a task, then there is some trait or motivation that you must acknowledge is causing the limitation. For skills that impact your ability to lead others, work with your mentor and others that know you to understand these skill limitations.

You need to be able to convince an objective third party (not yourself) of your proficiency—our brains are not wired to challenge ourselves on self-conceptions we believe are self-evident. ELs hold themselves accountable for their performance; this requires an objective appraisal of their skills. At this point it is best to concentrate on just the skills needed to be an entrepreneurial leader. Later, as part of making an entrepreneurial strategy (distinct from your PLS), you will figure out whether there are additional market-specific skills that may be required to lead a particular enterprise. Keri and her sister made an assessment of her proficiency of the five essential EL skills (see Table 7.2).

Keri, like most new entrepreneurs, is not very skilled. She has had some professional coaching in self-awareness, and that makes her a master in that area. She has also succeeded in motivating her current four employees, but she realizes that this has been a very limited test of her motivational skills. Her other EL skills—relationship building, leading change, and enterprise basics—are at a basic level.

Entrepreneurs often believe that their intelligence or common sense can substitute for any of these skills. Most entrepreneurs, no matter how smart they are, don't realize they need these skills until they have failed. Jon, after he had once failed at changing EIT, sought out and met with a dozen experts on leading change to learn about what he needed to do in order to be successful once the need for change again became apparent. Wendy and Brian also succeeded only after they had failed. But failure—with its wasted money, time, and destroyed relationships—is not the only way to learn these skills: prior awareness of how necessary the skills are and the use of mentors,

Table 7.2 Assessment of Keri's EL Skills

Skill	Proficiency
Self-Awareness	My mentor and therapist acknowledge good alignment between their view of my core motivations, traits, and skills and my own assessment. → master
Relationship Building	I can improve relationships with people I know well, but I cannot easily build new relationships. Fear of confrontation makes me incompetent to lead emotionally charged teams or relationships. → basic
Motivation	I can excite artistic women with my vision. I like telling people when they do a good job, which also motivates them. My team will do almost anything for me. I have no experience motivating men. → competent overall, but probably a master motivator with women
Leading Change	I cannot lead controversial change, which means I always default to a lowest common denominator result or I just do it myself. →basic
Enterprise Basics	I feel very comfortable with the concepts, as I like reading stories about entrepreneurs and picking out how they went through the stages and how they created their unique cultures. I have no experience. →basic

advisors, and others can allow you to develop them without enduring the crucible of failure.

STEP FIVE: DRAFTING A PERSONAL LEADERSHIP STRATEGY

The objective of a personal leadership strategy is to decide on what actions you need to take to achieve your ambition of succeeding as an entrepreneurial leader. It is a document you create in order to hold yourself accountable for your own development. The document affirms your motivations, traits, and skills and sets out a list of actions you plan to take to leverage some of your motivations and traits; mitigate other motivations and traits; and acquire, develop, and master the skills it takes to be a successful EL.

Based on her assessment of her motivations, traits, and skills, and with her mentor and sister providing advice and support, Keri wrote a summary of where she felt she was as she started her journey. She then described her intended actions—the forward-looking part of her PLS. Keri's strategy was straightforward, but it took four revisions to get to the point where her sister said she wasn't overcomplicating it. She started with a series of statements that captured her intentions to grow her company, to develop as an EL, and to overcome her fears and other obstacles to her success:

> I will inspire designers and people interested in crafts to create interesting and fun paper for all types of occasions. I will create a profitable and valuable company that I can turn over to my daughter. I will set a great example for my daughter and all women who aspire to be great mothers and good business people. I will surround myself with advisors I respect who have experience in running major successful companies. I will ask my mentors and advisors for their input as I hire new people, develop a sales force, and encounter challenging new situations.

Keri next focused on what mitigations she felt comfortable using to offset the personality traits that made her indecisive.

> I can no longer be afraid to make decisions. When confronted with an important, scary decision, I will ultimately decide by asking myself, "What are the best and worst things that can happen to me if I make the decision one way, and what are the best and worst things that can happen to me if I make the decision the other way?"

Then she wrote down the key actions she planned to take to cultivate the human resources she already had in place—both her existing employees and herself as a leader committed to her own development:

> I will develop both Karen and Yang to take more responsibility, which will allow me to spend the time I need for growing the business. Karen understands the paper decorating processes and can run production. Yang is fantastically creative and will do a great job overseeing design. I will seek out some good sales people to advise me and who will help me find and motivate a good salesperson to

join me. I will meet with Karen, Yang, and whomever is my new salesperson at least once a week to get their input on priorities.

Keri understood that she did not know how to deal with contentious issues without specific help.

I need to find someone that can coach me on how to lead through contentious situations. I will ask my old family therapist for some names.

Finally, Keri put in place a simple process for making sure she would update her PLS to maintain its value and relevance.

I will take a day off of work every six months to revisit my development plans.

Energized by the strength of her motivations and the clarity of her vision, Keri diligently followed through on her personal development plan. She visited the local Small Business Administration and found that they could introduce her to some experienced advisors. Keri didn't like or respect some of the people she was introduced to but she had great respect for two who were willing to advise her. Keri also reached out for advice to a cousin-once-removed who had a successful printing firm a thousand miles away on the East Coast. Keri visited her cousin and found she had a great EL skill set and was willing to coach her. She also hired a professor of business from the local state university to help her understand how company finances work. Finally, the family therapist she hadn't seen in five years did give her some names of people he knew who gave classes on assertiveness and other interpersonal skills that Keri, from her self-assessment, knew she needed to strengthen.

Over the years Keri grew her business into a substantial specialty paper products company. It wasn't easy for her, but she received important help and advice from the people she found. She and her cousin talked on the phone several times a week, sharing what was happening with their respective businesses. Keri formed a small board of directors made up of the advisors she respected the most, including her cousin.

The board did not have any formal fiduciary responsibilities, but they felt responsible for advising Keri on how to make her enterprise more successful. They met every three months, and Keri found it extremely productive and energizing to assemble a list of the things that had been accomplished and those things that had not gone as planned.

Keri still found it difficult to bring up contentious issues, even with her closest colleagues. She mitigated this trait by telling her team about her aversion, and her team responded by working hard to agree amongst themselves. When they could not, they brought decisions they could not resolve to Keri in writing, with the arguments for and against each of the proposed options clearly laid out so that the emotions were taken out of the analysis. When she had an issue with someone on her team, she would outline the issue in writing, always explaining that this would help her be objective about how to resolve the issue. The few times when this did not work and somebody insisted on debating points face-to-face, she accepted the meeting but made it a point to reiterate her position and say that she only felt comfortable reviewing rebuttals to her position that were put into writing. Keri loved her team for helping her not have to judge among them, and the adaptations they used allowed her to fulfill her executive role despite her aversion to confrontation.

Completing the PLS made her realize and remember what was really important to her. All decisions became part of getting the results she wanted, rather than taking on a life of their own.

Every EL's PLS is unique. However, as I mentioned earlier, the PLS must be a written document of some sort. Seeing your motivations, traits, and skills written down enables your brain to see more connections than it could if you kept the list in memory. That said, there is no right or wrong way to describe your starting point and map out your plan. Some people make bullet points; others write an essay. In working with many aspiring ELs, I find that the people who take the time to write detailed notes to themselves, by virtue of the extra investment of time and thought, often have deeper insight into their own abilities. A more terse and succinct Keri might not have written a short essay for her PLS; she might have just put the following note someplace where it would serve as a constant reminder.

Decide

Delegate

Assert

Feedback

"Keri the Terse" would know what these few words meant and to what actions she would hold herself accountable. Having written a PLS also means that as skills develop or don't develop, as previously hidden motivations surface, or as some trait proves more challenging to mitigate than planned, the PLS can be quickly and effectively modified. *You do not want to forget any of what you have invested so much to discover.*

Entrepreneurs who feel that asking for advice or modifying their behavior to improve relationships constitutes a personal failure typically think that they do not need a PLS. When the trait of being very closed-minded is coupled with a motivation of needing to feel dominant, the combination may be very difficult to mitigate. It is the hallmark of an extremely selfish individual and someone who is not willing to be tested or to act selflessly. It is also a combination that characterizes a percentage of entrepreneurs—individuals who feel that company founders do not have to take orders from anyone and want to dominate those they hire. In my experience, such entrepreneurs are incapable of growing into ELs who can produce a valuable, self-sustaining enterprise unless they can find a successful EL to be their mentor. Every EL I have known or studied has at some point had at least one other EL from whom they sought advice.

If a person is truly incapable of mastering one or more of the fundamental EL skills, then the person can adopt a strategy of finding a partner who has the appropriate mastery. Among such people may be highly introverted individuals, who can find it extremely uncomfortable, if not painful, to work for long periods of time with many people whom they do not know intimately. Many painfully shy individuals have ideas that they aspire to turn into some tangible reality, so they want to become entrepreneurial leaders. Some of their brethren have succeeded, so it is definitely possible. The best strategy for each painfully shy individual will be different. I have seen many extreme introverts take public speaking classes, which helped them feel they could act their way through well-defined situations. Another classic solution is to partner with a parent, sibling, mate, or someone else with whom the EL is extremely close, who acts as the "face" to the public while the shy entrepreneur focuses on perfecting processes and creating product enhancements. Washington Roebling, the builder of the Brooklyn Bridge, used his wife as his link to the outside world; Howard Hughes used a succession of personal assistants. Even extreme introverts can fulfill their ambition to change the world if they are willing to adopt a strategy of finding a small number of individuals with whom they can work and who are motivated to make their vision a reality.

APPLICATION OF ENTREPRENEURIAL LEADERSHIP SKILLS

Part One introduced a set of skills and key insights that can greatly enhance an entrepreneur's chances of being ultimately success-ful. Part Two focuses on how ELs apply these skills and insights to avoid five common mistakes that cause entrepreneurs to fail. Most entrepreneurs fail for multiple reasons, but it's likely the failure was in some way precipitated by one of the following mistakes:

- Creating unfocused, distracting, and wasteful strategies
- Implementing unleadable organizational structures
- Hiring people who don't fit and not firing ones who do not contribute
- Misusing teams and setting low expectations for their results
- Misunderstanding the nature of crises and what leadership is required to resolve them

Avoiding each of these pitfalls requires the use of several different skills and insights we have already discussed in Part One. No additional skills or insights are needed.

We start this second half of the book by considering how to put together a compelling strategy for turning your idea into a value-producing, self-sustaining enterprise. This step is not what most entrepreneurs think it is.

Strategizing Fragile Growth

This chapter naturally follows the discussion of the PLS, as entrepreneurial strategy outlines the specific skills and resources that will be required to take a particular idea and turn it into a real enterprise. Many entrepreneurs mistakenly fantasize that they add the most value to their enterprise when they are creating grand strategy and outsmarting the competition. There are three objectives of entrepreneurial strategy:

- Establish demand for an idea.
- Create an enterprise that can satisfy this demand.
- Make sure the enterprise creates enough value and innovation to sustain itself.

In other words, the objective is to get through the four stages. Because no entrepreneur or EL can forecast exactly how their enterprise will progress through the four stages, what customers will actually want to buy, and what people can be recruited to help, *entrepreneurial strategy* is therefore an exercise in determining which projects and processes will create the most value with the least risk, within the constrained resources available to the entrepreneur.

Before an enterprise is fully mature—that is, before having completed stage four—it is highly vulnerable. Entrepreneurial strategy focuses on getting enterprises through the four stages as diligently as possible: not so fast that critical processes have been poorly implemented, but not so slowly that competitors can capture your momentum or other forces trigger a premature decline. Immature enterprises have undeveloped processes and few resources, which means that entrepreneurial strategy must focus on highlighting which resources are essential and which are not at any point in any stage of development. As the cases in this chapter show, the entrepreneur must be strong enough to say "no" to all requests that would take *any* time, attention, resources, and focus away from activities essential to getting their enterprise to the next stage.

Not until stage two has been completed does an enterprise have any enduring and leveragable structure. In stages one and two, businesses shift their business models frequently as they try to find real customers (meaning real demand) for whatever they can offer. Max Levchin and Peter Thiel's various pivots in founding PayPal are legend.[1] In 1998 Max graduated from the University of Ilinois knowing he wanted to start a company. He had studied cryptography, the art of protecting information by encrypting it into an unreadable format. Max moved to Silicon Valley, where he met a hedge fund manager, Peter Thiel, who offered to partner with Max. At first their company, Confinity, produced software that turned handheld personal digital assistants (PDAs), the precursors to today's smart-phones, into encryption devices. Max's software design was brilliant, but virtually nobody wanted to write ultrasecure programs for PDAs. Max and Peter then tried leveraging their ability to make PDAs into highly secure devices by selling software that turned a PDA into a digital wallet. Money could be securely exchanged between PDAs with no apparent middleperson. Many of the techie elite thought this was a cool enhancement to a PDA, and Confinity generated significant interest and publicity. Peter and Max raised $4.5 million dollars from venture capitalists to grow the business.

The problem was, not many customers other than the techie elite wanted to transfer money via PDAs. Confinity put a functional demonstration of their PDA software on their website to allow potential users to try the software before downloading it. It was soon obvious that more people wanted to use the Internet demo than wanted to use their PDA software. People wanted to transfer money over the Internet securely, particularly the growing number of people using eBay. Peter and Max's third pivot was to make their website a secure internet payment site that they renamed PayPal. There were many other companies offering secure internet payments, but PayPal's founders felt their best chance of success rested in their ability to prevail in this market.

PayPal's internet payments were secure but not fraud resistant. Much of the company's early investment went towards refunding chargebacks for fraudulent transactions. It was not until Max and his team of programmers developed effective fraud detection software that PayPal became a valuable and profitable enterprise. PayPal's expertise in secure transactions was a critical prerequisite to succeeding in this business, but the real value they delivered proved to be their algorithms to detect fraud. Over the first two years of its life, Confinity twice made it to early stage two, only to regress back into stage one when the markets proved to be too small. PayPal had to restart stage two a third time because a fraud-detection process had to be developed and implemented in order to effectively deliver their service.

PayPal/Confinity successfully struggled to complete stages one and two. Max and Peter were single-minded in answering a specific set of questions:

1. What can we offer to attract real customers?
2. Are there enough customers?
3. How can we reliably serve all these customers?

For the enterprise to survive long enough to answer these questions required many different actions. Max had to find Peter, software had to be written over and over again, money had to be found, service and support agreements put into place, and so on. All these actions were taken in order to find customers, make sure there would be enough of them, and then put into place the basic infrastructure to reliably service the customer.

When you are dealing with a fragile, immature enterprise, your strategic possibilities are limited by your enterprise's stage of maturity. You make changes to your idea in stage one because you can't find a customer and in stage two because you can't satisfy enough customers or you can't reliably deliver your product. As in the case of Confinity/PayPal, it can make sense to repeat stages one and two if your product doesn't capture enough customers to satisfy you or it doesn't work reliably. Competitive advantage in the first two stages of enterprise maturity comes from finding a few real customers and determining that you understand how to satisfy the customers' actual needs. *In stages one and two, you develop competitive advantage naturally because you are figuring out how to satisfy a substantial group of real customers that others have not satisfied or could not satisfy!*

TWO TYPES OF ENTREPRENEURIAL STRATEGIES

The basics of how enterprises work and the stages they must go through to mature determines *what* you have to do and the order in which you have to do it. An entrepreneurial strategy suggests *how* you will do what you need to do to get your enterprise from an idea all the way through stage four. The strategy for developing the idea into an enterprise can proceed in either of two fashions:

• You visualize your path to success in order to test critical assumptions. Business plans and business model canvases are common ways of analyzing critical assumptions relative to the idea's potential to produce value. Planning a set of actions that you expect will cause your enterprise to be successful is referred to as a *causal* strategy.

• You can also feel your way step by step toward making your idea successful based upon what happens with each step. There is no set plan, just a general direction. This is referred to as an *effectual* strategy.[2] Effectual strategic processes set up experiments to test important next steps. You ultimately answer the same set of questions as with causal strategies, but you do so empirically and only as you need answers. Research shows that this is the most common type of strategic process among entrepreneurs and dominantly so with serial entrepreneurs.

ELs have successfully used both causal and effectual strategies. Wendy Kopp, our hero from Chapter Three, created a detailed visualization of how she would create Teach For America during her senior year at Princeton. Her plan gave her confidence that she knew what steps she would need to take to make TFA a reality. Many of the assumptions about how much money and resources she would need to get TFA up and running (that is, through stage two) were naïve, but that's true about most assumptions about doing anything completely new. Naïve assumptions do not cause enterprises to fail. Bad reactions to actual events cause entrepreneurs to fail, particularly if those reactions cause a loss in confidence in the entrepreneur's ability to lead. Because of her forethought and planning, Wendy had her first teacher corps of 489 top graduates trained within a year of graduation. Because of her plan, Wendy, an entrepreneurial rookie, was able to convince sophisticated business leaders to support her efforts. Armed with her plan, Wendy did a brilliant job leading TFA through stage one and some of stage two.

Max Levchin and Peter Thiel followed an effectual model in deciding what to do next with their venture. There was no way they could have conceived of a plan to create PayPal when they launched Confinity. A detailed business plan would have been a waste of time. Effectual strategies work best when the entrepreneur thinks about the next steps as an experiment, with a specific hypothesis that will be tested. Proving each hypothesis right or wrong generates the additional information that leads to a rational next step. For each experiment the entrepreneur needs to think about how much he is willing to invest to get this information. Not considering cost can lead to wasted time and money that could cause the enterprise to fail before it is financially self-supporting. Wasteful experiments that don't help move the entrepreneur toward a successful venture are easy to avoid by just writing down these factors:

- The hypothesis that you plan to test (say, "There are enough vegans to support a vegan food offering in the food court of my shopping mall")
- The experiment you plan to undertake (say, "I will pass out free vegan food samples at the Firemen's Fair and see how many people ask unprompted where they can find this food")
- The results that will cause you to take the next step in one direction rather than some other direction (say, "If I get at least two

hundred people over four days to tell me, unprompted, that they want me to open a permanent place, then I will rent space at the local mall")

BASIC STRATEGIC QUESTIONS

Based on what we know from Chapter Three about how an enterprise works, here is a set of questions every entrepreneur needs to answer, one way or another, in order to figure out how his idea can mature into a value-producing enterprise.

Who will want to buy your product?

You need to be able to describe the customers who will want to buy your product or service. The more you understand your customers—who they are, what they think, how they spend their time, and so on—the more comfortable you can make them feel with being your customer.

Why will they want to buy your product?

The EL must eventually understand what benefits the customer will get from buying her product. Benefits are those aspects of the product that make the customer feel better. This is called the "value proposition."

How can they know they want to buy your product?

You need to understand how you will find potential customers to tell them or show them what you have to offer. Will you be going to trade shows, or advertising, going door-to-door, or (using our example) giving out free samples at the Firemen's Fair?

Where will they want to buy your product?

Will customers buy your product on the Internet, in a store, directly from a salesperson who visits their office, or some other way?

How much will they be willing to pay?

Until you know how much customers are willing to pay, you cannot be sure your idea can ever produce value. Unless a similar product or service already exists, this is a hard question to answer definitively until real customers have had the opportunity to actually buy the product.

What process will you use to make and deliver the product?

You must understand how you can create your product. It is a waste of time to test a product idea that is impractical to produce and deliver.

Are any special skills required for the enterprise to succeed?

Most types of enterprises require some special skills to start and to lead. Many types of enterprises require licensing (such as real estate brokers) or certification of skill levels (such as CPAs). Starting certain tech companies can require a very specialized set of skills.

Are there any critical enablers to making and delivering the product?

ELs take the time to discover who could prevent them from making their product (for example, someone owns a patent to make the product, or a regulatory agency has to certify that the product as safe), and also who could be willing to help them as a partner.

How much will it cost to make and deliver the product?

The cost to make the product has three components: (1) the cost of the input materials or services, (2) the cost to operate the processes to make, test, and deliver the product, and (3) the overall costs associated with any waste or losses associated with the process.

How much money will it take to set up your rudimentary (stage two) processes for delivering the product, finding and satisfying customers, and administrating the enterprise?

You need to estimate how much investment you will need to set up your enterprise and its rudimentary processes in order to know how much money you will need to have on hand or be prepared to raise.

These questions must be answered completely by the end of stage two. The earlier in stage two you can answer them, the lower the risk that resources and time will be wasted creating processes that will not reliably satisfy customers or that cannot capture an adequate number of customers.

I often get asked why there is no specific consideration of the competition in any of these foundational questions. *Finding real customers is the same as finding out what you really need to know about the competition.* If a competitor is doing something relevant to what you want to do, then you will hear about it from your potential customers, and you will adjust your idea accordingly. Causal strategies explicitly consider what actions the entrepreneur can take to protect his idea from competition and how to make it through stage three successfully without having to compete directly with any dominant or powerful competitor. Experienced serial entrepreneurs understand the critical importance of sneaking up on powerful competitors, and their initial effectual actions typically focus on customers not directly served by powerful competitors.

There are other versions of these basic questions to determine business viability, and there are some excellent books on how to find the answers—essentially, on how to get through stage one and into stage two. I really like Steve Blank's *The Startup Owner's Manual*, Osterwalder and Pigney's *Business Model Generation*, and Eric Reiss's *The Lean Startup*.

Savvy ELs use a combination of causal and effectual processes to produce their entrepreneurial strategy. It is worth every effort to get whatever useful information you can about your potential customers, competitors, potential partners, and suppliers from experts, other entrepreneurs, investors, market participants, market observers, retirees—whoever may have direct knowledge about the market and how it operates. This information helps you set direction and be able to sort practical from impractical, and useful from useless potential actions. You will get plenty of valuable insights from thinking through the steps you must take to get your enterprise to the point where it produces value. For example, Wendy Kopp, in making her detailed plan for TFA, and realizing what caused analogous institutions to be highly influential, understood how critical it was to achieve a certain scale to create an enterprise that could have any social impact. Without this and other insights, Wendy would not have succeeded, and these insights could not have come from an effectual strategy. There is no excuse for not knowing all you can about the opportunities you see.

Furthermore, you need to establish a reasonable estimate of how much money you have versus how much you may need to get you into business. This estimate should be only as detailed as the information you have available—clearly labeling your estimates as guesses.

Before the end of stage two, you can estimate costs, expenses, and investments based only on similarities with other existing products and businesses. It is a complete waste of time to build detailed financial models based on a large set of speculative assumptions and information you know nothing about.

Effectual experimentation is essential when you have no good examples or information—which is true much of the time before you understand what products you will be selling to which customers and what price. Stage one is mostly a series of trial-and-error experiments. There are too many aspects of most potential products for there to be a simple way to determine how many customers will be willing to buy it—let alone how much they would be willing to pay. Even experienced chefs adjust their menus, recipes, and ingredients up to and after their restaurant's opening to improve reviews and attract more business. Each adjustment to the menu is an experiment that may generate more business—or less.

STAGES AS STRATEGIC BEACONS

The stages of the startup serve as your strategic beacons. Entrepreneurial strategy at any point is about doing what it takes to finish the stage you are in. Everything else is a waste of time and resources. Of course, deciding on the who-what-when-where-and-how of finishing the stage you are in, with the least risk, is what ELs must discover and decide. Your choices are nonetheless highly constrained by a lack of resources and capabilities. Successful ELs lead their enterprises through the four stages by methodically building capabilities, in a predetermined order, in the least amount of time, with the fewest people, while spending the least amount of money.

Stage One Strategy

The strategic imperative in stage one, the focus of all actions, is to find, as quickly as possible, potential customers who align with what you think you know how to deliver. Strategic thinking in stage one focuses on answering these higher-level versions of the ten strategic questions:

- *How can I "best" (that is, fastest with least effort) find real customers?* This will ultimately lead to understanding who will be your customers.
- *How can I make a very basic product (also known as the minimum viable product or MVP) attractive enough so some customer will actually agree to try it?* This will ultimately require you to understand your value proposition.
- *How can I deliver the MVP when I find a customer willing to try it?* This will ultimately lead to understanding the initial projects and processes required to make and deliver your product.

Throughout stage one the EL will relentlessly focus on nothing else other than solving these interrelated who-what-how puzzles as quickly and cheaply as possible. When you have answered these three questions, then you have found the first customer for a product you can actually produce. To make it worthwhile to take the enterprise to the next stage, the customer, MVP, and potential delivery method all must align. Doing anything else is a waste of time and money!

A very common strategic failure in stage one is to shift direction because of actions a competitor *might* take. The actions you take with potential customers in stage one will reveal to you all that you need to know about potential competitors. Long-term competitive advantage is created only in stage three and beyond, so unless you are trying to annoy a powerful competitor, you will not be important enough to them in stage one to merit a reaction. *Capturing any customer in stage one establishes a competitive advantage that is a beachhead for a long competitive war.* Not until you know you have satisfied your initial customers in early stage two can you understand why they actually wanted to deal with you rather than the competition. If you can exploit the customer's reasons for valuing your product, then you have a clear path forward.

Confinity pivoted in stage one because they couldn't find a customer, and they pivoted once again in stage two, returning to stage one because they couldn't find enough customers. When Max and Peter performed their last pivot back to early stage two, they chose to pursue a business with established competition, but they had found a large group of customers that they could service better than anyone else could. (Even then, they had to repeat much of stage two when they had to make major adjustments to their processes to include fraud detection.) Stage one is exhausting because you have to find real customers before your money and energy run out. But if you are motivated to not give up from the exhaustion or rejection, then you will feel exhilarated once you find your real customer.

Stage Two Strategy

The strategic imperative in stage two is to implement three core capabilities:

- Simply and reliably deliver the product to the customer.
- Simply and reliably capture new customers and ensure that these customers are satisfied.
- Simply and reliably administer the enterprise (paying salaries, ordering materials, paying bills).

Before the entrepreneur knows exactly how to implement these three capabilities, she must have answered all of the ten strategic questions. Because at least three of the ten questions have been answered in stage one, finding the answers to the remaining questions must be included as part of the projects to design core processes.

If the enterprise needs to find investors, then finding the answers to the ten strategic questions must be considered a stand-alone project. Most professional investors require that an equivalent of these ten questions be answered before they will seriously consider an invest-ment. I do not list raising funds from professional investors as part of stage one because it is almost always a mistake to attempt this before you know who your customer will be.

In a stage two enterprise there are many more activities going on in parallel than in stage one. Stage two is strategically perilous because entrepreneurs can become distracted by the significant amount of information being generated. The entrepreneur now receives customer feedback, feedback from other stakeholders such as employees and suppliers, and progress reports from the various project leaders, as well as projections of cash requirements. Some entrepreneurs are overwhelmed and abdicate leading critical activities, or worse, they shut critical projects down. Hiding from customers and/or employees is very common; Wendy did that, as do many introverts. Other entrepreneurs just ignore some or all of the information they receive because they consider it too detailed and distracting from an essential big picture—"It is not strategic, so I can't waste my time on it." Stage two is all about learning to satisfy your first real customers. Their ultimate satisfaction requires that the entrepreneur care about the details of their needs. All information coming from customers is strategically important in stage two.

Any entrepreneur who makes the projects in stage two any more complicated and challenging than they need to be just reduces her chances of success—and unavoidably wastes money. A good strategy makes effective use of the resources at hand, and entrepreneurs cannot afford to waste their money and resources in stage two on anything else but getting the enterprise up and running to satisfy their first customers. Adding projects such as evaluating competitors or creating a more effective forecasting process must wait until stage three. Similarly, any projects focused on developing new products, new technologies, sophisticated processes, *or strategic planning* serve only to siphon resources and support away from the actual activities that ensure that the enterprise can be successful. Adding complicating objectives to any of the existing projects is also wasteful. Offering more product variation can come *after* the initial product is reliably delivered and clearly satisfies its target customers. The mantra of the EL in stage two is "How can we make it simpler?"

Another stage two strategic mistake made by many entrepreneurs is ignoring the requirement that the product perform reliably enough to satisfy customers who buy it. If many customers are disappointed in the product, if the product cannot be delivered reliably, or if the product doesn't perform as expected, then the problem must be fixed.

PayPal succeeded where all their competitors failed because they stopped to solve the problem they found while others ignored it.

By understanding the strategic imperatives of stage two, the entrepreneur can choose how he wants to stay in control. The strategy can be to partner with someone with great organizing talents who will not be overcome with all the information and who can help critical projects in need of additional leadership. Another strategy could be to grow very deliberately, only as fast as you can fund your own growth.

Stage Three Strategy

By the successful conclusion of stage two, the enterprise has customers who are committed to the new product or service, and the enterprise must be committed to those customers. Without this commitment to customers, the customers will not be committed to the enterprise. With your commitment and your value proposition confirmed, the strategic imperative of stage three becomes creating a sustainable balance in the enterprise between effective processes that generate significant value yet are flexible enough to meet the expectations of existing and potential future customers. If processes are complex and expensive to accommodate a great deal of flexibility, then they may not generate enough value to enable the enterprise to grow or make improvements in the future. If the processes are inflexible but low cost, they make the enterprise vulnerable to competitors' taking customers away by offering the product variations they want. Determining the best strategic balance between cost and flexibility requires capturing accurate and relevant information on customer demand and costs. It also requires making forecasts on how revenues and costs can change with time, with economic conditions, with added investment, with competitive pressure, and under any number of other conditions that may be specific to the marketplace or regulatory environment. This information and these projections must be credible or else the resulting decisions will be flawed.

Furthermore these "improved" processes form the foundation from which the company operates profitably and grows. These processes must therefore operate without the direct involvement of the entrepreneur or any other unique person or supplier. An enterprise committed to its customers cannot risk not being able to deliver its product based on any person not showing up for work. The enterprise cannot risk having its financial well-being or its ability to survive compromised by unique parties—not even by the founder. There are very few truly "unique" individuals in the world, but entrepreneurs often make themselves "unique" by building incomplete processes around them. If you are the only person competent at performing a very specialized, hard-to-learn set of steps in a process, then you are unique. Fashion, design, and specialized consulting are examples of businesses that often create processes around unique individuals. Making yourself or somebody else essential to an enterprise makes it vulnerable and less valuable, which is inconsistent with the strategic objectives of stage three. It is OK to rely on "talent"; many businesses do. "Talent"—in industry parlance, a person with world-class skills—is nonetheless generic because talent can be replaced with somebody else with the same level of skills within an already existing process.

Strategic decisions in stage three are not sexy, but they are crucial to long-term value generation. Flawed decisions result in loss of the market to competitors or inadequate value generation. Either way, the future of the enterprise is compromised. ELs make sure these decisions are based on credible information.

When Wendy Kopp decided to launch two new programs to run in parallel to Teach For America—TEACH! and The Learning Project—she made a classic entrepreneurial strategic error. Wendy believed that her strategic imperative was to expand TFA's capability to reform education in America. Education in America was in critical condition, and Wendy felt she was in the best position to do something about it. Although TFA was struggling, Wendy saw critical unmet needs in how new teachers were recruited and trained that she now understood how to fix. These new programs were complementary to the mission of TFA. They made almost perfect strategic sense from the perspective of an institution that provided high-quality new teachers to public schools—but they almost caused the ruin of TFA.

They took focus away from building critical processes and systems that TFA needed to deliver its core service more effectively and with higher quality. These new programs took resources away, including the attention of Wendy and other key TFA leaders. This would have been a textbook great strategy for a mature TFA, but for a fragile enterprise it was a fatal strategy to pursue. It was only when Wendy shut down one of the programs and spun out the other that TFA was able to flourish.

When Wendy Kopp realized she absolutely needed to put TFA on a strong financial foundation, she focused herself and found skilled people to help design and implement robust processes for TFA. This attention, and the subsequent years of work to implement the improved processes, resulted in an enterprise that produced excellent results for its customers for TFA and for its staff.

Stage Four Strategy

The strategic imperative of stage four is for the enterprise to implement a process that serves to renew or rejuvenate the enterprise. This renewal can come in the form of introducing significant new types of products, making major leaps in existing capabilities that set new product or service benchmarks, creating new business models, or opening up entirely new markets. Without such a renewal process, the enterprise will atrophy through inevitable changes in customer demographics, technological advancement, and competitive pressures. The process of renewal is required to make an enterprise self-sustaining (with the exception of government-mandated monopolies).

At the beginning of stage four, the EL has a wide range of strategic options to consider—limited, however, by the skills and resources the enterprise can invest in the resulting transformation. At the beginning of stage four it makes sense for the EL to consider her possibilities. These possibilities can be considered either causally or effectually. Wendy Kopp transformed TFA from an enterprise that recruited and trained talented teachers for disadvantaged school districts to an enterprise that partnered with disadvantaged school districts to create transformational experiences that dramatically improved educational outcomes. She led this transformation of TFA, with the help of her top executives, after carefully considering data on the causes of major long-term improvement in educational outcomes.

Most enterprises do not make it to stage four, and many of those that do wind up not successfully completing it. Most entrepreneurs, or the professional managers they have brought in to replace them, fail to gain the support of the enterprise in shifting focus, funds, and skills onto activities that most employees, particularly influential process managers, consider highly speculative. Without the active involvement of the leader of the enterprise, preferably an EL, it is virtually impossible to put into place the five prerequisites for change—no matter how much "strategic opportunity" the project leader may see.

Making it successfully through stage four often requires transforming the culture of the enterprise. Without leadership, the culture of stage three defaults to a culture of efficiency and risk mitigation, which naturally resists supporting speculative transformational projects. Founders who can lead their enterprise through all four stages can, with foresight and continued reinforcement of a bigger vision, maintain a culture that embraces change and innovation throughout stage three. Wendy Kopp made it clear to TFA that they had to continue to innovate to lead educational reform. There was very little second-guessing of the stage four initiatives at Teach For America.

Many enterprises attempt to sidestep the need for rationalizing speculative projects of renewal by creating separate R&D departments. Unfortunately, many R&D departments develop only derivatives of existing products. Other R&D departments fail at getting the rest of the company to accept responsibility for promoting their truly innovative products or process breakthroughs, so innovative products never make it to market or are only ineffectively marketed. Many companies with R&D departments never complete stage four (Xerox is a good example).

Another stage four strategy is to buy innovation. Many companies use this strategy; Cisco is a notable example. The challenge with this strategy is that the cultural issues remain. If the culture of a successful stage three enterprise is incompatible with the culture of the company they acquire, then all the acquired talent will perform poorly and leave. Companies that are successful at buying innovation have cultures that continue to support the innovation of the people of the acquired company. Companies that complete stage four by acquiring and successfully integrating innovative teams have visionary leaders equal to those at companies that successfully created their own processes of renewal and innovation.

Entrepreneurial strategy is very different from business strategy as it is taught in business schools. Revisiting the analogy I used early in the book, what parents do with their infant to ensure that it grows into a healthy and happy child is very different than the actions the same parents will take to make sure their child matures into a healthy and happy teenager, and finally into a self-sufficient, happy adult. As an infant grows into a young adult, the parents' strategic choices are constrained by the developmental needs of their child. Parents instinctually know that they cannot ignore the developmental stages their child goes through. The child will not read well if you start teaching her reading when she is a teenager. The strategic decision parents must make is not whether to teach their child to read but what system or school to use for the instruction.

On the other hand, business strategy is about making best use of the assets of the enterprise relative to the projected needs of existing and potential markets. It is analogous to the considerations healthy adults make in deciding what to do with their life. Adults are free to choose their next steps, but in making their choices they are well advised to think strategically about how to best leverage their education, physical stamina, and so on—that is, their motivations, traits, and skills. Being in a position to create a PLS is exactly analogous to the point at which enterprise should consider putting together its grand strategy—when it has become an adult at the end of stage four.

Entrepreneurial strategy is highly constrained, but all good strategy is about focusing on what will yield the greatest long-term benefits with the least amount of risk. ELs use the stages of enterprise maturity as their strategic beacons to eliminate distractions and focus all efforts on productively growing their idea into a strong value-producing, self-sustaining enterprise, as quickly as possible, and with minimal resources.

9

Organizing to Succeed

Even the best entrepreneurial strategy can be so poorly executed that it fails. Many otherwise smart and charismatic entrepreneurs fail to execute because they have designed organizations that are impossible to lead and that make it difficult to execute the projects and processes essential to producing value. A well-conceived organization, in both its formal and informal structures, focuses the EL's ideas and actions coherently throughout the enterprise, helping everyone understand what he or she needs to do to help the enterprise succeed. A poorly conceived organization blurs the entrepreneur's ideas and actions, resulting in an indecisive and incoherent enterprise. ELs consciously design their enterprises, both the formal and informal structures. As the number of people that an enterprise comprises grows, the formal and informal organizations easily diverge, making it unleadable—as the next story illustrates.

Arun was extremely smart and well educated; he had a PhD from MIT in electrical engineering.[1] Arun was driven to succeed, to prove to his famous political father that he could meet his extraordinarily high expectations. Upon graduating from MIT, Arun went to work at Testor, a company that had been cofounded by his best friend's father, Dr. Patel. He had been Arun's mentor growing up and treated him as a full member of the family. Dr. Patel's only son, Arun's best friend, was not interested in going to work for Testor; he was set on becoming a successful brain surgeon. Dr. Patel had lobbied Arun all during his university years to come to work for Testor. He had even told Arun that he would be groomed to become the CEO when Dr. Patel retired.

Being groomed to become the CEO of a billion-dollar company by its founder was an offer that the twenty-six-year-old Arun could not turn down.

At Testor, Arun regularly put in sixty-hour workweeks in an apprenticeship program set up expressly for him. In the course of two years, Arun had three different assignments. For six months he served as assistant to the VP of marketing and learned about marketing promotions as part of the launch of a new line of portable generators. He then worked as the assistant to the president of Testor Asia. While living in China, Arun spent a great deal of time at the Testor factory, helping project manage a major capacity expansion that was nearing completion. After coming back to the United States, Arun, working in R&D, was put in charge of developing a battery charging unit that could be sold along with the new line of portable generators he had helped launch the previous year.

Even though these assignments made no use of his PhD, Arun loved learning how a major company operated. He also loved the encouragement he received from Dr. Patel, who said he was doing a great job and that he had impressed many of the top executives with whom he had worked. Arun sensed that his personalized managerial training program made many Testor top executives nervous, because he was being treated as the founder's son, but he was not sure what to do about their nervousness, so he ignored it.

At the end of two years, Arun was appointed to be the manager of business development of the $75 million portable generators business, a very responsible position for a twenty-eight-year-old. Unfortunately, three months later Dr. Patel died of a heart attack, and one of the other cofounders of Testor, who had retired from the company a year before Arun joined, replaced him. Six weeks later, Arun was called to meet the new CEO, who tersely fired Arun during a meeting that lasted two minutes. No reasons were given other than, "Testor no longer needs your services." By the time Arun got back to his office his belongings had already been packed into a box and he was escorted out of the building by a security guard.

This humiliation added to Arun's innate fear of his father's criticism. After spending two weeks hiding from everyone he knew, not knowing what to tell them about his "change in job status," he decide he would go to business school. After five days, nineteen phone calls, and a quick trip to Europe, Arun had talked himself into the next class at one of the top ten business schools in the world. Arun finally told his father that he had left Testor to go to business school because he didn't want to be limited to working on "mundane industrial products"—repeating a phrasing that his father used to describe Testor's business.

Two years later, at the age of thirty-one, Arun started working at a new private equity firm, Spring Market Ventures, founded by two partners who had recently split off from one of private equity's legendary firms. Over the next five years Arun did well; he was made a full partner and offered a small share of the profits of the firm in addition to a share of the profits of the three deals he had been personally responsible for bringing to Spring Market. Two of these deals were already yielding returns greater than five times the money invested, so Arun, after just five years in private equity, was already worth more than $5 million.

Shortly after making partner, Arun met Paul, the CEO of one of Testor's major competitors, at an MIT reunion. Although Paul was considerably older than Arun, they had much in common, and they continued to meet whenever Paul was in New York. Arun quickly became a close personal advisor to Paul, and over the next three years helped him buy a few companies as well as divest a division that no longer fit into the company's strategic plans.

Yet as Arun approached forty, he felt as if he had led a mundane life that was falling short of his father's expectations. He was also far short of where he would have been had Dr. Patel fulfilled his promise to make him the CEO of a major global corporation.

Shortly before Arun's fortieth birthday, he and Paul were invited to tour the laboratory of a professor who had developed a technology that could potentially reduce the power consumption of factories and commercial high-rise buildings by 2 percent. Arun and Paul both felt strongly that this technology would be game changing, as it would result in tens of billions of dollars of annual energy cost savings. Within a week of the demonstration, Paul and Arun had convinced the professor, Manuel, to accept funding from them to form a new startup.

A year later the new company, 3E, was still in stage one, and Arun decided that he would have to step in as full-time CEO if the company were to fulfill its potential for becoming a billion-dollar corporation. There were several reasons for Arun's decision to leave his position as partner of Spring Market:

- Two well-qualified candidates had left the position of CEO, each after only a few months on the job. Both candidates had left because they could not work well with Manuel, the CTO, or Arun, the chairman.
- Arun and Paul had each invested $3 million in the venture, and Arun felt their investment would not yield a big return unless an experienced executive such as himself was in charge.
- The technology had been well received by several major corporations, and 3E could not afford to risk losing momentum by searching for another CEO. Leadership continuity would be particularly important over the coming year, as they would build the equipment needed to demonstrate the technology on a commercial scale.
- Arun had come to believe that leading 3E was his opportunity to be accepted by his father and to be heralded as a major global business leader.

The day after Arun joined 3E as its full-time CEO, the enterprise transitioned from stage one to stage two, as Paul, Arun, and Manuel decided which customer they would work with to build their demonstration equipment. For the next twelve months Arun worked seventy-hour workweeks as he saw to every detail of the mechanical design of the equipment and all aspects of the relationship with the customer, raising another $6 million from venture capitalists, hiring twenty-five new employees, and recruiting and communicating with a new board of directors, as well as managing the PR to keep interest levels high but not give away too many details about the technology and the demonstration equipment.

At the point when 3E installed its demonstration equipment, seventeen of the forty employees reported directly to Arun. Arun justified a flat organizational hierarchy (with nobody more than two levels below the CEO) to himself and others, as it would enable faster decision making and attract a higher caliber of employee. Another unspoken problem the flat organization solved was that, considering that nobody wanted to work for Manuel, they could report to Arun instead. Running the day-to-day aspects of the engineering team meant that Arun just took on more responsibility himself. He particularly disliked having to facilitate the coordination meetings between Manuel and the people who should have been reporting to him. Nonetheless, Arun felt that his putting in more hours at work and supervising more people was a small price to pay to compensate for Manuel's brilliant but difficult personality.

Arun became visibly more anxious and impatient as unanticipated design problems surfaced with the first set of demonstration equipment, just as contracts with the second and third customers were being finalized. Several of Arun's more experienced managers offered to take on more responsibility to reduce his workload, allowing him to concentrate on solving the growing list of design problems, but their offers were ignored.

Frustration grew all around, as the technology staff could not work together effectively with the customer's project management team to solve the reported design problems. Decision making at 3E ground to a standstill as Arun spent all his time trying to work with each individual on the technology team to separate fact from conjecture and to decide on each small step forward. Decisions would often wind up being reversed when Manuel would later bring new facts to Arun's attention. Several key engineers retreated entirely from trying to solve either the technical or the Manuel problems, saying, "Just tell me what to do."

After tensions mounted with the customer, Paul and the board of directors got involved. When Paul called and said, "I think you need help; we need to talk." Arun's heart started to race. He feared a show-down with Paul, who had the power to fire him if supported by the new investors.

(UN)CONTROLLABLE BY DESIGN

Arun had successfully managed projects, and he had successfully advised growing enterprises, but he had fallen into a trap that captures even experienced entrepreneurs. Arun had established an uncontrollable organizational structure. Entrepreneurs can have great ideas, good traction with customers, as well as talented and dedicated team members yet still fail to execute their strategy because their organization can't respond to the needs of the enterprise and its customers.

Organizational structures delegate responsibility, authority, and social status within the enterprise. Organizational structures delegate the authority of the CEO throughout an enterprise in return for each authorized person's accepting some responsibility. Often this delegation is represented only by some box on an organization chart, and there is little other information, other than the accepted practices defined by the culture, to define exactly what authority has been delegated in return for what responsibility.

Culture plays an enormous role in how an organization actually operates. But organizations also play a role in shaping culture, as they are an important baseline in sending messages relative to who gets rewarded for what behaviors in the enterprise. At a minimum, irre-spective of how much actual authority has been delegated, the *super-visors* listed in the boxes on organization charts dictate some set of priorities to the people they supervise. The specifics of how responsi-bility, authority, and status are apportioned set de facto priorities and therefore are major determinants of culture.

Many entrepreneurs do not realize that they lead two different organizational structures: the formal and the informal. The formal organizational structure is usually written down in the form of a chart showing who reports to whom. Irrespective of whose name is in some box, absent direct instructions, people tend to naturally prioritize their actions with people they feel closest to physically and emotionally. Unless a person's actions are precisely dictated by their formal supervisor, the informal structure may actually set many of an enterprise's actual priorities. The informal organization is hard to describe because it operates based on who actually influences the decisions that will be made. In spite of what an organization chart says about how Jim is responsible for an activity, Jim may not actually make the decisions. Jim may always ask Mary for her opinion, and Jim may always render that opinion as his decision. Jim may be afraid to make a decision that Mary doesn't agree with—maybe out of fear but also, perhaps, out of respect.

Chaos reigns when there is a significant misalignment between the formal and informal organizations. Arun suffered from this problem in his inability to manage 3E's technology team. Influencers such as Manuel operated out of sight in getting decisions he did not agree with overturned or delayed. 3E's engineers knew that Manuel was the expert on the technology that he had invented; they also knew that Arun was a micromanaging boss. Engineers retreated from discussions on how to solve 3E's design problem because they felt doomed to fail in the eyes of either the formal or informal organization. Misaligned organizations cause inconsistent shared objectives. They are often the source of such comments as "This place is very political." On the other hand, when entrepreneurs focus on eliminating all informal structures, then employees feel nonautonomous and controlled. Enterprises with stunted informal organizational structures are often labeled as "bureaucratic."

Many entrepreneurs, like Arun, want to make it explicitly clear through the formal organization that they hold final decision-making authority over specific areas—in Arun's case, over seventeen areas! Other entrepreneurs are more comfortable operating through the informal structure because it allows them to go anywhere and talk to anybody, about any subject, whenever they want. They use the informal structure to retain an option about what they want to get involved with. Designing an entrepreneurial organization, both its formal and informal structures, gets very personal. The leader has enormous influence over the architecture of the organization, and he wants *his* organization to reflect how *he* wants to exert *his* authority and influence. The architecture of an enterprise is a major manifestation of how the entrepreneur has chosen to balance his selfishness with his selflessness.

Many leaders lose the trust of key supporters, inside and outside of the enterprise, by putting in place an organization that does not support their ability to perform their jobs. In the case of Arun, he sent a message to the enterprise that he had created a flat organizational structure so that decisions could be made quickly. When the enterprise had to deal with a complicated customer issue, then decision making within 3E's flat organization actually slowed down. The flat structure overloaded Arun with people requiring his attention about critical situations. 3E's employees experienced their inability to get Arun's attention as evidence of his abandoning them during a crucial time. They knew Arun was busy—they forgave him for that—but they did not forgive him for retaining full authority for making all final decisions when he was unavailable.

FORMAL AND INFORMAL

As it turns out, the informal organization *can* make decisions faster than the formal one. That is a major reason why enterprises with stunted informal organization feel bureaucratic; it frustrates people when there is no informal structure to use to speed decision making. On the other hand, as we saw with 3E, decision making can grind to a halt at an enterprise where the formal organization overloads while the informal organization is misaligned with it. Too many entrepreneurs have lamented, "Why doesn't anything get done in this place anymore?"

Arun would have been well advised to acknowledge 3E's informal structure by taking the time to understand how it actually worked. Many ELs take the time to go around their enterprise asking, "How do decisions really get made?" ELs ask their top executives to do the same. When the EL feels that an informal structure might not function in accordance with the enterprise's strategy, then he will intervene, using some combination of these classic techniques for aligning formal and informal organizations:

- *Assign tasks to teams that make the informal organization more visible and formal.* These teams can create alignment when they contain people with both formal and informal authority and responsibility. Without both formal and informal influencers on the team, the misalignment can be compounded, because it represents yet another organizational framework with incomplete authority. If the EL gives these teams his support and uses them to pursue his priorities, particularly those that do not naturally align with established processes, then these teams become very powerful alignment tools. Arun never asked Manuel and his engineers to form a formal team (Arun was afraid of dealing with Manuel in front of other people), so this alignment never occurred.

- *Merge portions of the informal structure into the formal structure.* This happens when "dotted-line" reporting relationships are inserted into the formal organization chart. A dotted-line reporting relationship implies that the three people connected by the dashed and solid lines should be consulting with one another on decisions that impact their groups. This can work in very specific instances where you need the person with formal decision-making authority to acknowledge the need to consult with his informal organizational counterpart.

- *Establish a formal matrix organization, in which a person can have more than one official boss; these acknowledge that some employees in the organizations may be expected to formally consult with multiple supervisors before making certain types of decisions.* Matrix organizations tend to be employed by extremely large mature enterprises where all decision making follows very prescribed processes.

Unfortunately, Arun did none of these things to mitigate the chaos at 3E. In times of crisis, entrepreneurs often assume they are the only person who understands the enterprise well enough to solve the problem, which only makes the situation worse. It turned out that Paul had not called Arun to fire him; he and the other investors felt that changing a leader during a time of crisis would have amplified the problems at hand. Paul had actually called to offer to send in some consultants he respected. Arun told Paul he felt he was close to solving the problem and that bringing in new players would just delay implementation of a solution. The situation at 3E was perilous because Arun was so afraid of failing. He felt that because he was smarter and could work harder than anyone else, he had to be the best person to lead 3E out of the crisis. It took two more months of chaos, an angry customer that demanded their $250,000 back, and plenty of bad publicity for Arun to admit defeat and ask Paul for his advice. Because Arun had lost the confidence of 3E's board, top managers, and engineers, he resigned after helping to bring in a new CEO. Arun went back to being a partner at Spring Market Ventures.

ORGANIZATIONS HELP ENTERPRISES MATURE

New technologies, new processes, and new systems are always tricky to put into operation in the real world because nobody has yet encountered the precise problems they cause, nor do people yet understand the subtleties of their implementation. Arun's challenge was classic. The organizational structures implemented by most entrepreneurs, both formal and informal, create inefficiencies or, worse (as in the case of 3E), destroy value. Informal organizational structures are constantly changing based on the people, projects, and processes that define how the enterprise creates its value. Formal organizational structures change only occasionally, because it is very hard work and very distracting to make the change—usually when the entrepreneur is frustrated by his inability to get some result he wants. Organizational structures, both formal and informal, need to change according to the needs of the enterprise, not the needs of the entrepreneur. As with the case of entrepreneurial strategy, entrepreneurial organizational options are stage dependent and highly constrained.

ORGANIZING STAGE ONE

Stage one has a single objective and a single focus: get a customer to commit to use the product. No complex structures are required, and communication between everyone in the fledgling enterprise is the top operational priority. Huddles are the best way to organize stage one. The EL calls a huddle anytime there is new important information to share and react to. Each huddle is called to discuss only one thing, so no agenda needs to be composed other than telling everyone why the huddle was called. Everyone who needs to hear the information is invited, and everyone assembles as quickly as possible. In the huddle the new situation is discussed, and everyone has the opportunity to give his or her idea on how to react. Once the EL feels that an appropriate response has been decided on, the huddle is ended and the EL or someone else summarizes all agreements the group made in terms of how to react to the new information.

Structure is constantly reaffirmed or adjusted in each huddle, based on who is assigned what task. Obviously, task assignments will flow mainly to those with the most appropriate skills. Whenever there is work overload, which does happen, the huddle can assign additional support to help the overloaded person.

The ad hoc informal huddle works very effectively when the entrepreneurial leader is good at communicating issues and everyone with a relevant perspective can give their input. The EL also must be willing to steer the discussion to a conclusion and make sure all concerned understand their role in effecting the agreed-to changes. This is de facto real-time duck alignment. Arun was great at leading the 3E stage one huddles.

The challenge comes when the group gets too large to all huddle together. This normally happens in stage two but can happen in stage one for large and complex undertakings. The EL needs to see that project teams are formed for the larger or more complex parts of stage one. The leader and appropriate members of the project team can attend the huddle and report any duck alignment issues they may have. The project leaders can then work with their project teams to make any adjustments as decided in the huddle.

ORGANIZING STAGE TWO

By the end of stage one, the huddle feels like a great way to lead, but it is time to change. Many entrepreneurs, like Arun, Wendy, and Dean Kamen, get hung up here because they like the huddle so much.

Stage two is about creating the rudimentary core processes required to actually deliver products, to capture customers, and to perform critical administrative tasks like managing the cash, raising money, and hiring and firing people. The informality and ad hoc nature of the huddle is inconsistent with the requirement to create structure in stage two. Structure requires structure.

Stage two structure starts with changing the huddle into a recurring meeting, with an agenda and a fixed set of attendees. The mission for this meeting of key people is to jointly coordinate all activities, resources, recruitments, and so on that are required to satisfy customers and find new customers. The EL must use this meeting to check if the ducks are lined up to successfully accomplish the critical project-to-process transitions that define this stage. Note that you will need a name for the meeting, because it is a constant reference point for discussions. I will refer to this meeting as "the leadership team." Arun was afraid of having a leadership team. He was afraid that his inability to control Manuel's emotional outbursts would cause the rest of the team to question his leadership abilities.

One of the first things the leadership team will do is to create and resource the teams responsible for designing and implementing the rudimentary core processes, while keeping the enterprise running. Setting up three teams—customer, product, admin—is typical, but it can be any other small number depending on the exact nature of the business. For example, a fourth team may be required for creating a process that applies for and maintains official licenses necessary to participate in a regulated market. Another team could be required to raise money. Each team can be small or large depending on their task. In each case the ducks must be aligned, and that will be challenging.

Throughout stage two, valuable information is being captured about what the customers really find valuable as well as better ways to deliver the product. All this information needs to be digested and turned into insights that will inform each of the teams how to best design and implement their processes. The constant stream of new information will challenge the teams to go faster or slower, to shift their goals, to capture new skills and to find new resources. Ducks will be constantly scattering. This flow of information was critical to the success of 3E. Arun's insistence on tightly controlling the dispersal of customer information added to 3E's inability to satisfy their customer.

Too much formal structure in stage two slows down decision making. A structure based on several teams is the best all-around solution because it keeps a simple formal hierarchy aligned with the informal structure that is created based on how the teams actually operate.

I need to make a comment about computer software at this point. Software can potentially define yet a third dimension of organizations: the formal, the informal, and the "systematized" as defined by the needs of software. Processes do not exist to any extent in an enterprise before the end of stage two, and entrepreneurs who install any type of "enterprise" software (software that controls enterprise-wide processes, such as human resources, manufacturing, and accounting) in stages one and two must recognize that they have added extra constraints to the enterprise architecture without adding any operational advantage. Enterprise software adds value when it facilitates the flow of information, particularly between processes, as well as the creation of summary metrics that aid decision making. Before stage two is completed, there is rarely a need for management software more complicated than a spreadsheet. You will be able to understand what type of software will add value to the organization only after processes have been designed, not before.

ORGANIZING STAGE THREE

The objective of the organization in stage three is to facilitate the creation and control of efficient, scalable, and competitive processes for all repetitive work. Structures get complex in stage three with the implementation of more processes, many of which are interrelated. Complexity may reach the point where no one person may understand how the enterprise really works and who is actually responsible for any specific result. This is dangerous territory, where control and leadership can be lost in spite of success in growth and profits. Arun never made it this far. The data show that many Inc. 5000 entrepreneurs fail at this point.

Enterprises in stage three get structured from both the top down and the bottom up. As an enterprise grows, top managers and leaders must formally share more and more responsibility with others in the enterprise because they no longer have the time to make every decision within their span of control. Stage three represents the point where the formal organization chart should appear. At the same time, every member of the enterprise is becoming more experienced in performing his or her formal and informal duties. Most employees are continually making changes, consciously and unconsciously, in how they perform their work. Each member of the enterprise is assessing who is most likely to help the enterprise succeed. Informal networks of influence therefore become very important to stage three continuous improvement efforts, empowerment, and also in the maturation of the enterprise's culture. Many entrepreneurs lose control over how their enterprise actually operates early in stage three because they naïvely assume that things work the way they want them to.

Some leaders like and encourage every employee to experiment with how to improve the work they do. Other leaders hate the constant shifting in actual responsibilities and feel a loss of control that comes with this empowerment. An important part of the culture of an enterprise coalesces at this stage based on how much attention the leader pays to the alignment of the formal and informal organizational structures. The coalesced culture will impact future organizational decisions, making it easier or harder for anyone to change how work is managed and improved. Informal networks of influence may be more or less prevalent depending on how the culture perceives that independence is rewarded or punished. The directives of a manager may be taken as a suggestion or as words to act upon without question, depending on how the enterprise's first formal structures were formed, how well they worked, and how much the leader was involved in the alignment of the formal and informal structures. These were challenges Arun faced at 3E because he had naïvely implemented more organizational structure in stage two than he actually needed.

By having so many people report to him, working in three distinct areas, Arun had created a formal organization that made it unclear who was ultimately responsible for the product, the customer, or running the company. Arun was the only one who had a complete overview of what was happening at 3E. When problems arose, he basically lost control of his enterprise.

In general, the EL cares passionately about how her enterprise operates and wants to tightly align formal and informal decision making. The larger the organization becomes, the more complex the projects and processes become, and the harder it becomes to align. This means that the larger the enterprise gets, the more time the EL must spend making sure the formal and informal structures are working effectively.

There are no "right" or "wrong" formal organizational structures, although they generate a great deal of debate and emotion. All organizational structures are compromises between cost, flexibility, responsiveness to the customer, empowerment, governance and regulation, and risk. Many entrepreneurs hate compromises and therefore create for themselves informal structures so that they adjust responsibilities at any time with little notice—with resulting confusion and loss of accountability. Their actions create trade-offs that have not been considered by many and therefore appear irresponsible to some. There are nevertheless "better" and "worse" structures for specific missions and strategies, and choosing better structures greatly reduces the need and pressure to generate confusing new informal structures in order to focus on top priorities.

Every reporting relationship, whether formal or informal, corresponds to sets of shared objectives. The EL wants his enterprise to create shared objectives that dictate organizational structure based on these basic tenets:

- *People should be asked to do only those things that they can succeed at doing.* Asking people to do things they are not capable of doing properly is an abdication of responsibility for achieving a shared organizational objective. Failure is never anyone's desired outcome. In other words, depending on how the leader plans to make those around her feel they can succeed, she should design the organization around either the capabilities of specific people or generic skills.

- *The success of a working relationship is always the responsibility of the supervisor.* The supervisor's success depends on how clearly he constructs cooperative shared objectives with those who work for him and with those who work with everyone he supervises. An organization is immediately viewed as corrupted if someone of higher authority blames someone of lower authority for a failure to execute.

- *People who do not trust one another should not work for one another.* Cooperation requires trust.

- *How the EL delegates responsibilities to others, how she asks others to delegate, and how she holds them accountable for their results determines whether the culture expects responsibility to be shared with mutual trust and respect.* When responsibility is shared with trust and respect, this creates structures that adjust smoothly to support the EL's objectives. Such cultures positively affect enterprise performance.

Enterprise structures that appear in stage three strongly influence an enterprise's ability to focus on its most important performance objectives. Research tends to support common sense relative to how structure affects performance.[2]

- *Decision making is faster the fewer people share a responsibility.* The more organizational layers between the final decision maker and the lowest level consulted in the decision, the more slowly decisions will be made. Fewer layers create more responsive processes—*provided* they do not overload any person in the hierarchy. Arun failed to anticipate the intense simultaneous demands on his attention required to fix problems.

- *Responsibilities for processes shared between peer organizations require trade-offs and compromises in process performance.* These trade-offs can be cooperative, competitive, or retreating. Optimizing the performance of a specific process requires a structure that eliminates the sharing of responsibility between peer organizations. A direct line of control creates improved performance, but at the cost of a loss of flexibility.

- *Effective communication, often implemented through software, can speed decision making between layers of an organization and across different groups reporting to different supervisors.* The challenge with implementing software to simplify and systemize communications is that organizations change much faster than software can be modified. In general, complex and highly integrated software can hijack control over organizational structure and reduce flexibility. This can be an acceptable price to pay in stage three once the EL and his team understand what they want to optimize and how they want to optimize it. Software will almost certainly be required to facilitate communication between different parts of a stage three enterprise, but committing to new software too soon, before the enterprise understands its customers and potential competitors, actually impedes growth. Everyone is always surprised by how much information can be analyzed and disseminated using good old-fashioned Excel spreadsheets rather than the latest dazzling innovation. I have seen three-hundred-person enterprises run on Excel!

In stage 3, using these simple tenets of how structure impacts performance and priorities, the EL will deploy an organizational structure to optimize enterprise performance in whichever parameters he judges most important: cost, flexibility, simplicity, low inventory, short manufacturing cycle time, variability, risk, and so on. He will be lauded if he chooses his parameters and supporting structure well—and derided if he chooses poorly. The EL always optimizes for a very small set (no more than three) of parameters in stage three. These few parameters should define how the enterprise creates value better than any competitor. When an entrepreneur optimizes for too many parameters, with a resulting complex organizational structure, then the enterprise risks producing mediocre results in all of them.

ORGANIZING STAGE FOUR

In stage four the EL wants to keep in place the core structures that made the enterprise successful at the conclusion of stage three. Innovation activities should take place in teams dedicated to innovation projects, formed by capable individuals from around the enterprise. Everyone working on these teams should be full time and have no other distractions or higher priorities. These teams should minimize interference with the existing flow of work; that means giving the team members their own resources (change cannot succeed without the necessary resources). They should report to the EL or a direct report to the EL who is also recognized as a great innovator. Putting people from the original stage one team on these innovation teams helps the team visualize how products are successfully developed and what successful innovation feels like.

An EL who can articulate her vision and her strategy for achieving the vision and then describe how she has structured the enterprise to make the strategy easy to implement will be seen as a very powerful leader by people both inside and outside the enterprise. The EL will have also succeeded in making her enterprise an inspiring and desirable place to work. In the next chapter we discuss how to find and recruit the best people to populate the enterprise and work diligently implementing the EL's vision.

10

Hiring and Firing

If your enterprise is going to grow, you are going to need to hire people to help you, as well as fire people that do not help you enough. Each hiring and firing impacts how much the enterprise's productivity is improved and whether its culture is reinforced or dissipated. An entrepreneur has everything at stake with getting this right.

Nate was thirty-two years old and someone whom everyone described as "gentle and brainy."[1] He seemed destined to be a successful engineer like his father and both of his grandfathers. Beginning when he was a teenager, Nate had loved to design and build things like radio-controlled gliders. Nate now had a PhD in electrical engineering and was working as a postdoc researcher at University of Illinois. There he had developed an improved open-air sensor for measuring a dozen dangerous gases. The key to Nate's device was a semiconductor device that responded differently to each pollutant. The research world was very impressed with Nate's device; this gave him the opportunity to either remain in the academic world or start his own company. After working two years as a postdoc, Nate felt he preferred designing things that people would actually use rather than designing things only professors would use. And after having applied for several patents, Nate knew his idea was protected enough that he could leave his research position and work full time to start a company making his gas sensor. He talked with his several of his father's successful engineering friends about what it would take to start a company. He estimated he could develop a prototype free-air gas sensor for about $200,000. With the encouragement of his parents, he decided to fund his company using money they loaned him as well as his modest savings. He called his company Twelfth Sense, and he set up in a very afford-able suburb south of Chicago, not too far away from where he grew up.

Nathan's first hire was Armand, a graduate student from another lab who had heard that Nate would be starting a company and had asked to join. Nobody else had asked if they could join the company, and Nate knew he would need someone to work full time on building a prototype device. Armand's graduate student background made Nate feel comfortable that he could do the work. He asked Armand why he was willing to leave graduate school without his PhD. Armand said that his biggest ambition was to be an entrepreneur, not a researcher, and he thought Nate's device was a winner. Nate was flattered that Armand knew about his device, and he said, "Sure, let's work together."

As soon as Nate made the offer, Armand fired back, "How much of the company are you willing to let me have for being your first employee and working for the same wages I am getting as a research assistant?" (Top graduate schools' electrical engineering research assistants are paid around half of what that person could get working for an estab-lished company.) Nate was not surprised by the question and already had his answer prepared: "Let's work together for six months and see how we like it. Let's figure out how much of the company to give you based on your actual contributions. Don't drop out of school; just take a leave, so if it doesn't work out you have a ready-made fallback."

The other person Nate hired was a friend of his mother. Nate had known Christina most of his life, and he admired how efficient she was in running her house and her family. Nate had heard from his mother that Christina had been laid off from her job at a local clothing store chain. Christina had managed the bookkeeping for the stores, and Nate felt that he could use somebody to run the finances and handle various other needs, such as having to prepare promotional materials (on a small startup team, employees must wear many hats). Nate's parents, who were loaning him the money to start the company, also thought hiring Christina was a great idea. Nate called Christina to offer her the job without even asking her whether she wanted it. His parents had already brokered the deal by telling him Christina was willing to accept a much lower salary in order to "work with the family."

Once on board, Nate, Armand, and Christina met every day to talk about what needed to be done next. When he wasn't supervising Armand or Christina, Nate spent his time visiting potential customers. Nate had envisioned that with Armand's graduate student background and Christina's experience bookkeeping and running a family, they would not need much supervision. He assigned Armand to fabricate a prototype device. Christina was assigned to find some small inexpensive space, set up phones, and help put together sales presentations.

At the end of two months Nate had concerns about both his teammates. Armand was smart, but he was more theoretical than practical in designing the prototype gas sensor. Armand was eager to learn and had a high IQ, but he had a below-average design sense. He could not tell a sexy-looking enclosure from a kludgy-looking enclosure. He couldn't understand how you could tell if the front panel looked cluttered and complicated. He also had no idea of—and no interest in knowing—which designs would cost less to produce. He didn't care whether a joint was welded or riveted.

Christina was an issue too. She didn't get along with Armand. Because Christina was a friend of Nate's parents, her opinion of Armand had become a discussion topic whenever he saw his parents. Furthermore, although Christina was an excellent bookkeeper, she had not used PowerPoint very much. It was less time-consuming for Nate to put together slides he wanted to show to potential customers than to ask Christina to do it. Worst of all, Christina was very set in her ways and often acted like she was his mother when Nate asked her to do something she disliked.

The first two months Twelfth Sense was in business felt like a roller coaster, with the excitement of each new potential customer interest turning into disappointment. Actually getting a customer to commit to using a new type of sensor meant convincing them to develop and introduce a new product line, and most companies were not willing to take such a risk. At the end of two exhausting months, Nate was ecstatic at first that he finally found a customer willing to commit. The customer was small, but it was someone willing to pay money to buy a hundred devices, provided five fully functional prototypes could be delivered within sixty days. Unless Twelfth Sense could deliver in that short a time, the customer would not be able to develop their new product in time for the major industry show. If the five prototypes could not be delivered in time, then the potential customer would instead use its own R&D team to develop another product.

Nate was more worried about the deadline than he was excited about finding a potential new customer. He knew it was conceptually possible to finish the prototype design and build five units within sixty days. But it was not possible if Nate had to do his job and Armand's job and if he could not utilize Christina to assemble the parts together and then test the units.

Nate's situation is classic. Entrepreneurs often hire people they know who "sort of fit." Entrepreneurs often prize availability over certainty that a person has the appropriate skills and is adaptable. Remember from Chapter Five on motivation that stage one is naturally motivating to people who like change and to do many different tasks rather than mastering just one or a few skills. A jack-of-all-trades is very valuable in stage one. Bringing in anyone who does not have any of the required skills and who requires significant supervision makes the enterprise much less productive—a high price to pay at a very critical time for the enterprise. When early employees do not get along and require their supervisor's attention to mediate issues between them, it is even more disruptive and costly. Nate fell into the trap of thinking that because Armand and Christina each had the ability to master one skill (electrical engineering research in the case of Armand, and bookkeeping in the case of Christina), both had the general ability to quickly master many skills. Neither Armand nor Christina was a jack-of-all-trades.

Many entrepreneurs hire friends, and even lovers, to reduce hiring risks associated with skill and cultural fit unknowns. This hiring strategy actually *adds* significant risks that are difficult to mitigate.

The shared objectives of friendship have nothing to do with the success of the company. An entrepreneur needs to ask himself, "Which is more important: my friendship or the success of the company?" If the answer is the friendship, then do not hire the friend.

Nate wound up losing his first real customer because he put together the wrong team and he did not spend time making sure the team he created worked together productively. He wound up telling both Armand and Christina that working together was not going to make any of them successful. Armand went back to graduate school, and Nate paid Christina for three weeks until she found another job. Nate had to start over, having wasted eight months and over half of the cash he had started with.

Nate's situation was actually better than some, because at least he had not given Armand an ownership percentage of the new company as he had asked for. Many entrepreneurs agree to give early employees, particularly those with very hard-to-find expertise, a percentage of the company to compensate them for accepting a low salary while making them more dedicated. If Armand had owned a piece of Twelfth Sense, then he would have felt entitled to have a say in whether or not he should leave, and he likely would feel he was leaving behind value that he should be compensated for giving up. It could have cost Nate more money. In the extreme, Armand, if he was angry at Nate, could have insisted that he have a say in how the business was run and put up roadblocks to its success. Putting off the conversation about becoming a partner until after Armand had demonstrated a real and lasting contribution to the success of Twelfth Sense had potentially saved the company. This is generally a good practice.

PRECIOUS LOST TIME

Shaken but not beaten, Nate was determined to do a better job of hiring on his next try. He did his research on good hiring practices. That wasn't hard, because there is plenty of advice on the Internet; you just need to sort the good from the bad. Nate's research led him to write down these points:

1. Create a description of my vision that is exciting to potential hires.

   → I need to tell a story that recruits can emotionally relate to and makes it clear to them why working with me "is such a big opportunity."

2. Figure out the skill sets needed to get the company to the point where it can produce real devices and then scale up to volume (that is, to stage two and beyond).

   → I need to research which skills I will need and ask people with experience for advice.

3. Describe the responsibilities of the position and how they will certainly evolve.

4. Figure out where to find people with the targeted skill sets.

   → This will involve more research and asking people outside the enterprise for advice.

   → I will then make as many phone calls as needed to find at least five target candidates.

5. Figure out how to contact people with the targeted skill sets.

   → This may involve the help of intermediaries.

   → I must have an interesting story to introduce myself to the target candidates.

6. Figure out how to test the people who have been contacted to see if their skills are at the right level and if they will be compatible with the team and the culture.

   → I must be ready to perform the tests.

7. Figure out what value to offer the people whom I want to hire.

   → I must involve labor lawyers to make sure my offer is legally responsible.

   → I want to present the offer in person.

8. Figure out how to orient and augment the skills of the people who accept their offers.

   → I must train and nurture the person I hire.

These essential project steps require a great deal of focused attention, dozens of phone calls, and many hours of work to implement. A reasonable estimate is that it will take at least forty hours of work, if not eighty or more, spread out over a couple of months, to find a potential employee with the right skills and cultural fit. And the potential candidates may not accept after investing all this time. Even after hiring a good candidate, there are more hours of direct involvement required to bring them up to speed with what they need to do and how they need to do it. Even then, after all this screening and indoctrination, the person still may not work out. Hiring is always risky, for these reasons among others:

- The differences between proficient, masterful, and best-in-class skill levels require testing under stressful conditions that are difficult to simulate in a hiring process.
- Cultural fit often cannot be verified until after the person has logged many hours of actual work and has made many independent decisions.
- Some personality traits cannot be determined accurately without prohibitively expensive testing.

The chances of a successful hire are greatly increased if you can be very specific about the skills you need and if you know how to test for the skills. Even better, if you have seen or are directly aware of the work of a given individual, then you can dramatically reduce the risk that the person's skills are not adequate. In the early stages of a startup you need your employees to perform many different tasks.

Unfortunately, Nate completely underestimated what it would take to hire the right people. Wanting to ensure he would make no more hiring mistakes, Nate became reticent to make an offer to anyone he thought was not a perfect fit. Thus indecisiveness meant that it took four months, double what it should have taken, to hire two people. To speed up hiring, Nate could have engaged qualified candidates as consultants or contract workers to check out their cultural fit. Using this strategy, Nate could have gotten work done while still assessing a person's subjective qualities and ability to perform in the Twelfth Sense work environment.

It was just a few weeks short of a year after he started his company before Nate felt comfortable soliciting potential customers again. By that time there was another sensor technology that potential customers were interested in trying, which ultimately became the one the market accepted.

Many entrepreneurs fail in the early stages of their enterprise because they didn't hire the right people or they took too long to hire. I, along with many other ELs I know, keep a list of everyone with whom I have come into contact who has impressed me, as well as people who have impressed other people I trust. I have made it a point of making contact and staying in contact with these people. Successful hiring is also about being always on the lookout for talent so that when you need it you know where to find it.

HIRING AS A PROCESS

Another important dimension of successful later stage hiring is illustrated by the case of two rivals, Jennifer and Burt. At one time Burt had been Jennifer's protégé, before he broke off to form his own firm. They both owned market research companies that offered similar analysis of internet usage—a very valuable set of information in what was at the time an explosively growing market. Both firms were similar in size, just under forty people, but for either firm to capture the market for internet data, they would need to grow quickly by hiring additional market analysts and sales people. To be successful in measuring something like internet usage, you have to develop significant scale in both gathering information and the ability to sell your information around the world. Both companies were very profitable, had significant positive cash balances, and knew what they needed to do. They nonetheless went about hiring the new people they needed in very different ways. Jennifer asked her operations manager to dedicate herself full time to hiring the twenty people needed and to come back in a week with a request for the resources and skills she would need. Jennifer realized she needed to turn hiring into a process. Hiring new people would be repeated at least twenty times over the next few months, and she felt that the investment required to make hiring as efficient and cost effective as possible would have a positive payback.

Burt was a perfectionist, and he approached the problem very differently. It was Burt's perfectionism that made it impossible for him to work for Jennifer. Burt felt that he needed to maintain the perfection of the team he had assembled. This meant Burt wanted to maintain hiring as a set of distinct one-at-a-time projects. He felt this would ensure the quality and fit of each new team member. Burt heard that Jennifer was hiring people for her project quickly, and he reasoned that this would lead to a poor-quality product. He was wrong; good processes produce higher-quality results than one-off projects do.

Processes are much more cost efficient in achieving repetitive results; they also produce higher-quality results relative to one-at-a-time projects. With a hiring process in place, Jennifer hired twenty analysts and sales people within four months. Although Jennifer dedicated one full-time person to running the hiring process, the total amount of time spent by all the people at her company in hiring the twenty people was less than it would have been if each person had been hired as a separate project. Burt hired five people within six months. With staff in place, supported by a good training program, Jennifer offered a high-quality global internet usage product a year before Burt. Her product also cost less than Burt's.

How did Jennifer accomplish this? She had identified the minimum analysts' skill set and developed methods to test for those skills. The specification of minimum skills, coupled with a good process for finding people, enabled Jennifer to hire more junior analysts with fewer years of experience. Jennifer's new hires fit into her company culture better and were more productive than Burt's. Jennifer ran Burt out of the market.

Entrepreneurs can set up hiring processes too soon. Hiring processes take time and money to set up—they require a project no less. A good hiring process calls for somebody skilled at recruiting or someone dedicated to learning and practicing recruiting skills. You need a hiring process when you know you will need to hire a steady stream of new employees, not just a couple of people a year. An alternative used by entrepreneurs with ample funding is to contract for a professional recruiter to hire hard-to-find people. The challenge with using a recruiting firm is that the shared objectives are inherently misaligned. The recruiting firm's mission is to *hire* somebody, whereas the entrepreneur wants the person she hires to successfully perform, support the culture, work well with colleagues, and ultimately like the job. Recruiters get paid in full when a person starts the job, not when the entrepreneur finally decides that the new hire is doing the job well.

FIRING EFFECTIVELY

Jennifer's hiring process was not perfect; she actually hired twenty-seven people to wind up with twenty she felt were properly skilled and a good cultural fit. Jennifer fired four people within six months of having hired them. Three other people resigned to accept positions at other companies (two of whom were hired by Burt!). Jennifer and her VP of internet products kept a watchful eye on each new analyst, giving each one formal training and informal coaching. Any new hire who did not develop their skills as expected was quickly and effectively counseled out of the company. Counseling a person to find a job with a better career and salary prospects is the cooperative way to fire someone. Helping the person find that job with better career and salary prospects is even more cooperative and rarely generates animosity or bitterness. Nate feared having to tell Armand and Christina that he would have to let them go. He procrastinated making the decision, which just meant that all efforts were delayed for months. Both parties benefit when you set up cooperative shared objectives between the boss and the person being fired.

The hardest people to fire are those who are losing their jobs through no fault of their own; that is, through a layoff, euphemistically referred among "professionals" as an "RIF" or "reduction in force." By the time Burt finally decided that he could not compete with Jennifer in the internet information market, he had hired eleven people whom he had to lay off. Burt may have been remiss in understanding when he needed to use processes rather than projects, but Burt handled his RIF well because he was not afraid to accept responsibility for his mistakes. Burt called together the eleven people he had personally hired and told them that he had made a major error in realizing what it would take to compete in the internet information business. He said he was responsible for each of their jobs going away and because he personally had lost a significant amount of money trying to build up this business he could only afford to give each person two weeks of severance. Burt offered to write each of them a great personalized recommendation that would make prospective employers realize they were dealing with a talented individual. Some people were angry, but Burt's accepting responsibility tempered much of that anger—what was there to compete over now that Burt admitted he was responsible? If Burt were living opulently then maybe someone could try to insist that Burt sell his personal assets to fund four weeks of severance rather than two, but Burt didn't have any obvious personal wealth, so no one made that request. By making it clear to everyone that he was taking responsibility and had taken a major financial hit in the process of trying to give them better careers, Burt had defused the most emotional competitive shared objectives he had with the people being laid off: who was to blame.

Hiring and firing is how the EL builds his team. Your effectiveness at recruiting people who can help you design and implement successful projects and processes will determine whether your enterprise can survive and prosper. Although not discussed in any detail in this chapter whom you recruit also, as you can well imagine, plays an important role in how culture is formed. You will hire people whose opinion of your leadership will influence how other new hires will perceive your ability and credibility. Early-stage hiring is a series of high-stakes projects. Once an enterprise needs a steady stream of new hires, hiring must become more efficient, and a process must be established with people and resources dedicated to its successful operation. The effectiveness of this process in recruiting people with the right skills and mastery, who fit well into their new peer group, and who feel comfortable in the culture plays a role at least as important as that of the leader in the overall productivity of the enterprise. Because hiring is inherently risky, there will be mistakes. It is critical that the mistakes be resolved quickly and cooperatively so the negative impacts on the enterprise and the employee's career prospects are minimized.

Finally, no matter how excellent and effective the hiring, a new employee can only be as effective as she is enabled to be by the teamwork of her new peers. While effective hiring projects and processes take into account how compatible a new employee is likely to be with his future peers, good teamwork is still essential for employee motivation and productivity. Leading effective teams is the subject of the next chapter.

11

Leading Teams

The part of any enterprise culture that has the greatest impact on employee satisfaction and productivity is the matter of how expectations are set for how people should and should not work in teams. The art and science of knowing when to form teams and how to lead them is poorly understood throughout many enterprises, small and large, which makes leading teams effectively and appropriately an important competitive advantage. Leading teams makes use of all of the core skills of an entrepreneurial leader.

Early in my career, working as an engineer for International Rectifier, I hit upon a potentially valuable insight on how to quickly improve profits.[1] In the early days of the semiconductor industry, yields were a major problem; you often had to produce one hundred devices just to get thirty that worked properly. My insight had nothing to do with yield improvement, although that was my assignment at the time; it had to do with the 70 percent of all devices that didn't work. Each device contained a few cents worth of gold, and I asked the question, "What happens to all the gold in the scrap devices?" It turned out that scrap devices were being thrown away because nobody thought it was cost-effective to reclaim the gold inside them. I did some research on my own time and convinced myself that the reclamation would cost much less than the recovered value of the gold. The company definitely wanted the $500,000 that I estimated was sitting around in rejected devices, so I got the go-ahead to start accumulating all the scrapped devices and setting up a process to reclaim the gold.

I remember calling a meeting to organize my project, with the purpose of introducing myself and explaining my mission. Many people didn't show up to my meeting. Almost everyone who did show up listened politely to my long-winded explanation of the problem and my request for help, then responded with something along the lines of "Good luck with your project, but I have more than a full-time job, and I just can't spare the time to help you with your scrap." The meeting accomplished nothing.

Throughout the rest of that project, I never held another meeting. Instead, I met face-to-face with each person I wanted help from in order to work out some deal (that is, some shared objective) to convince them that helping me could help them. As part of requesting help, I would estimate how much extra profit each manager could expect from reclaiming the gold in their department, and that was enough to get them to agree to help me. We eventually recovered over $500,000 of gold that year, which was almost exactly the total reported profit for the corporation.

I start this chapter with this experience because my first insight on leading teams is that many times you are better off without them. I was much better off working one-on-one on the gold reclamation project. It would have wasted the time of hard-working mid-level managers by asking them to attend meetings and listen to one another describe the details of how they would work directly with me to reclaim gold. Each manager's gold reclamation issues were different, so there was no need to form a team. *You do not need a team unless you need to synchronize information and actions between more than a few people.*

A few years later, when I was promoted to be in charge of a production department, I wanted my small staff to feel like we were a team, so I held a weekly staff meeting. I had no idea what "feeling like a team" actually meant, but I knew enough to know that it wasn't what actually happened in my staff meeting: each staff member just told the group in very general terms what they were working on and then asked for questions, while scowling to make it clear they would consider it inappropriate if any were asked. I did not set objectives in the meeting other than exhorting them, "We have to make our budget!"

I did not give anyone a feeling of special purpose in being on my staff. Everyone wanted to contribute as little as possible to the meeting so as not to get any inputs, or suggestions, or requests of help from any other staff member. Everyone wanted to stay "off the radar." They felt their autonomy was threatened by my staff meeting. The good news was that I was no worse at leading the team than my predecessor, or anyone else in the company for that matter, so nobody really noticed how bad I was at leading.

A LITTLE MOTIVATION DELIVERS A BIG IMPACT

My breakthrough in leading teams came in two steps. The first step came when there was a department that was in trouble and I needed to step in and fix it—fast! Crises like that were not uncommon at IR at that time, because everyone was reticent to bring up problems because it "put them on the radar." The department in question was packaging our newest high-tech device, but we were way behind schedule, and we had only three weeks left before having to announce to our investors that we had failed to keep our promises to our customers that we would ship at least 600,000 of the new devices that quarter. I don't remember exact numbers, but to make our commitment we had to ship something like 350,000 devices in the remaining three weeks—and we had never produced more than 40,000 in *any* week.

My first act as interim leader of that department really upset the top executives: I stopped production and asked to meet in the lunchroom with all members of the department. I told them what we needed to accomplish and why it was important. Everyone in the department knew full well why it was important, but they told me that it couldn't be done: "We have never produced more that 150,000 in a month, and we have less than a month left—no way!"

I went to the whiteboard and mapped out why it was theoretically possible to make the target—we had the capacity and the manpower, we just were not utilizing capacity very effectively. That unleashed a firestorm of reasons why the theoretical capacity could not be met. The department employees shouted out about two dozen meaningful problems preventing the department from producing what was needed. I said, "Let's work as a team, with me being the person who gets your problems solved. I will dedicate myself to eliminating virtually all of the problems you have listed if you promise to help me do whatever it takes to make our numbers."

An hour later, when the team meeting broke up, I was on the phone calling to get the help I would need to solve these two dozen problems. I had no problem getting top priority for the resources I needed, because all the top execs knew what was at stake. The team started working thirteen-hour shifts. My wife, Diana, six months pregnant with our first child, and I worked sixteen-hour shifts. I worked on solving the problems; Diana brought in food for everyone, ran backup machines, and entered information into the computer system. I moved my office to a little table in the corner of the department so everyone could see and hear me working with them. Both of the thirteen-hour shifts met for twenty minutes of overlap at the shift change to brief one another on whatever issues needed extra attention.

Momentum started building quickly as each shift started reporting new record output numbers. To highlight some of the best practices being used, we started various competitions between the shifts for prizes, like having the top execs make them lunch, or leaving two hours early on a Friday (after production had been caught up) to go to the beach for a sunset picnic (there was a beautiful beach just five minutes away from IR). We made our numbers with a day to spare, and we used the extra day to celebrate *and* rest.

I remember sitting down with my wife that weekend and saying to her, "We just accomplished some amazing things; how do we keep that up?" We talked about how there was no "magic bullet" solution and that everyone in the department had a good sense of what was working and what needed fixing. Listening, not second-guessing, and just adding to the collected wisdom had been key success factors. Everyone in the department loved having somebody they felt was dedicated to fixing the things that prevented them from doing a good job. They loved feeling a common purpose. And they all loved "winning" and being acknowledged for it. We had realized the fundamentals of motivating a team: helping the team to feel a purpose, respecting them for being masters at what they do, and making them feel supported in doing their jobs well. Teams feel so let down when they are told to do their jobs well and then not supported with what they feel they need.

DISCOVERING THE VALUE OF DUCKS

Unfortunately, not all my teams after that point were successful. Leading teams was not always as easy as just helping them solve their problems. It took another five years for me to take the second step and figure out why. Before I acquired all the skills required of a successful team leader, I had to understand the role of shared objectives and the importance of duck alignment. This understanding did not come until after I had played a role in the failure of an important team, which forced me to spend the time to think through what I would need to do differently to be a successful team leader.

This fateful failed team worked in our factory in Italy. The production department that was the focus of this improvement project had some important differences from the ones I had worked with before. This department produced a very established product line. It had not changed or improved any of its processes in years. The team was located in Italy where culture and status are more rigid than in the United States. The team reflected this formality. I could not get anyone to stop calling me "*Doctore*," because addressing me without a title made team members feel uncomfortable.

The mission of the team had been to install new software that would directly control critical manufacturing equipment in such a way that it would reduce paperwork for everyone in the department while increasing throughput from 2,000 to 2,400 devices per hour. After two months of work, the team had failed to produce any increase in throughput. The software had worked fine, but nobody in the department felt it helped them with their work, and they wanted to go back to their old methods.

The department manger, Luigi, and I spent several long nights working out the reasons why the very capable people assigned to be on this team could not accomplish what they all had agreed to do. We found five fundamental reasons, which eventually were codified as the comprehension, motivation, skills, resources, and communication "ducks." Our breakthrough in understanding what had gone wrong came when we asked ourselves what our fellow team members really wanted to see happen to them as a result of their being on the team. Thinking about what it would be like in *their* position, not our position, was an epiphany. Around that time I had been reading books and articles about cooperation and competition, so as we discussed what we thought each person wanted from being a member of the team, I tried to figure out how to put what we wanted and what each team member wanted in terms of the shared objectives and desired outcomes that I discussed in Chapter Four. Thinking in terms of shared objectives and figuring out where we cooperated, competed, and retreated proved to be a powerful framework to use to sort out the specific issues we would have to address to make the team successful.

One of the important realizations was that the people assigned to the production throughput team had very different understandings of what the team really needed to accomplish. Getting production throughput up from 2,000 to 2,400 devices per hour sounds like a simple objective to understand. Although the maintenance supervisor on the team certainly wanted production to increase, to him this project was more than just that. This was potentially a very threatening mission, because the project could focus on his group's inability to maintain the software that would be installed. This maintenance supervisor felt the project would be successful if "only a small amount of software was installed." The team included two production workers who were worried that the software threatened their jobs and could make them obsolete. The product engineer on the team was excited because he felt that running the department using advanced software would enable him to design products with tighter tolerances and therefore higher performance. Luigi—the production manager and leader of the team, the person who reported to me—saw this project as a way to demonstrate that he could improve the profitability of his department. Looking back, I "sort of" knew that there was this misalignment in understanding the mission of the team, but I had incorrectly rationalized that the team's objective was so specific that it would solve any misalignment issues. Luigi and I, after thinking about what our team members actually would want from the team, realized that everyone had a very different comprehension of what the team should accomplish. We would later describe this problem as our comprehension duck misalignment.

Luigi and I went on to discuss how we could have aligned each team member's understanding of the project such that they all would have wanted to work toward the same goal. We had previously avoided having any candid discussions about whether the work of the team could have led to any production workers being laid off or to the maintenance department losing responsibility for certain pieces of equipment. Shame on us! Each person on the team wanted to understand how their lives would change by being on the team. Without very frank and candid discussions about the team objective, they would just assume we were holding back on telling them the truth, and they would not trust us. That realization, though it came too late, led Luigi and me to realize that unless we could align each team member's personal motivations with the project's mission it would not make any difference if they understood what we really wanted the team to accomplish. If a team member feared that their actions in support of the team objective could cause them or a friend to lose her job, then that fear (a powerful motivation) would be too strong for them to work diligently toward a solution that would be best for the company. To succeed, we would have to align motivations to be consistent with the team's objectives (duck two).

Not many team leaders make sure everyone has the same clear understanding of the team's mission and that they are personally motivated to achieve it. Without alignment on the details of the mission and also on individual motivations, a team usually is reluctant to agree on anything. When some team members feel that they could be chastised for a lack of agreement, the team will default to just agreeing on noncontroversial actions; in other words, the "least common denominator" solution. This was the case with the team that Luigi and I failed at leading. The team felt they had no choice but to install the software that had been developed, but they used only the software's most basic functionality, so the department derived no measurable benefit. Least common denominator solutions produce mediocrity and, if endemic, result in an enterprise that is uncompetitive and incapable of producing any real value.

Great team leaders are good at aligning their team's understanding of their mission and making sure each team member is motivated to achieve the mission. Many great team leaders impart some vision of what a successful outcome will look and feel like to each member. That vision, if it is detailed and personal enough, will trigger the emotional discussions required to make sure you have alignment, supported by an appropriate motivation—what some call "buy-in." When I had led the new high-tech device production team five years before, I hadn't had to worry about aligning understanding and motivation. Nobody felt threatened by a good outcome, everyone in the department was on the team, nobody felt suspicious of anyone else's motives, and everyone understood that the team would become successful by fixing a list of problems that were preventing us from operating at full capacity. This Italian team was more established and did not have a clear idea of what their future held for them; they were a much greater team leadership challenge. Luigi and I had to create a vision of team success that would be the team's shared objective. Our description of that vision would have to include the benefits for each team member. To achieve a truly great result, we would need to construct a portfolio of cooperative, competitive, and retreating outcomes. This required a great deal of thought and work. A complementary set of shared objectives doesn't just happen when a team leader shows up and asks his team to vote on what to do next.

When we wound up reconstituting a new team after we had caused this one to fail, Luigi and I explicitly decided that we would list a set of the features we wanted the installed software to include, and that we would not let features be vetoed simply because someone felt anxious. We set up a simple process whereby each team member listed the expected benefits of including the feature and also listed the problems the feature could cause. Luigi and I would then judge whether any feature was too problematic to implement. This set up a competitive test for each feature and resulted in everyone's realizing that every feature had been properly considered and debated before it was implemented. We also created a new vision for team success. We realized that, because this was the first production department to implement software control, members of the team, having gained valuable experience, would be in a position to help other departments with their implementations. This was a major status enhancer that we had not even thought about when we set up the original project objectives.

The misalignments of ducks one and two (comprehension and motivation) were not our only leadership failures. We also realized that we had some major skills (duck three) missing from the team. Nobody on the team had known much about training; that meant it was never properly considered in the team's deliberations. Nobody on the team was skilled in software maintenance, something the team also never considered. This team was assembled back in the '80s, when software control was very new and software "administration" was something that made people nervous and few people knew how to deal with. Ultimately, because everyone on the team thought they were masters at their jobs, nobody thought to consider the potential impact of applying different skills to the problem. *Without proper leadership every team thinks they know everything they need to be successful.* A team *needs* outside perspective if they are going to do a good job of knowing what skills they need to call upon. Entrepreneurs can feel a loss of control in seeking outside skills and therefore can selfishly constrain the ability of their teams to perform well.

I committed another major leadership sin when I withdrew some resources that I had promised the team before they were finished with them (I misaligned duck four, resources). I withdrew two different resources. One resource was a part-time project manager who helped the team keep track of their meetings and action items. Without the part-time project manger, due dates slipped and staff became even less accountable for their actions. Luigi tried to fill in this role, but he had his other full-time job to perform, so he struggled to keep up.

The second resource I pulled was a nifty new camera that could read off the temperatures of whatever surface you pointed it at. The team had asked to use this camera to determine how well the software could set furnace temperatures. Today these cameras are inexpensive and common in production environments where you need to make sure temperatures are set properly. But thirty years ago these were expensive devices, and I let another department take the camera for yield enhancement work that I felt was more critical. These two acts of taking back resources I had promised to provide sent a message to the team that I didn't consider their work important. It also caused the team to abandon an entire line of enquiry based on faster and more accurate calibrating of the production furnaces that later proved valuable in increasing throughput. Pulling back resources I had promised to make available also sent a message that I was not trustworthy when it came to promising resources.

A final reason that this team failed was because nobody on the team communicated what they were doing to the people that spent their lives on the production line. We just assumed that everyone would want to help this team be successful. The team did not present their ideas to the production line workers for how the throughput could be improved until it was time to implement the changes. The production line workers gave us a list of reasons why our ideas would not work. Because of my poor leadership and poor coaching of Luigi, the team's actions were just a least common denominator implementation of the new software—features that provided few benefits but still required plenty of training. The production line workers told us they would need significant training, but the training we provided was ineffective. Although we had instructed the production line supervisors to provide individual coaching to each worker, some of the supervisors didn't understand the software themselves. Most of the other reasons we were given that our implementation plan would not work had been thoroughly considered by the team and could have been dealt with easily, but because the production department had felt left out and had not been consulted properly, the tone of the meeting was competitive, not cooperative, or even retreating. We had lost their support before even asking for it—which is a major rationale behind duck five, communications.

LEADERS ADMIT THEIR MISTAKES

After reviewing and analyzing what went wrong, I had to admit that I had really screwed up the assignment. Rather than giving up and moving on, Luigi and I committed ourselves to following our five principles for making sure teams would work and we restarted the project. Luigi and I went back to the entire department, and the engineering and maintenance support personnel, and apologized for our leadership failure. We describe the lessons we had learned. We explained what we wanted to accomplish, and we answered some critical questions before anyone even had to ask.

- No, there will be no layoffs. The increased throughput will reduce unit production costs to the point where we can win more business.
- We realize that we need to provide training to make sure everybody feels they can understand the computer screens.
- We will get together every two weeks; we will tell you about our progress and let you know if anything has changed.
- We will answer your questions whenever you ask, and we will never tell you that we don't have time.

We let everyone understand that by being the first department in our Italian factory to implement the new system, there would be opportunities for team members to help other production departments implement theirs. We asked for volunteers to be on the team; we got plenty, and the team went on to succeed.

THE IMPORTANCE OF STRONG EMOTIONS

Teams of capable people generate emotional debates and strong opinions. Many people fail to be leaders because they are afraid of these strong opinions and emotions. Either they choose complacent and uncommitted people as team members or they distort the team's mission in order to avoid confrontation. Differences of opinion enhance the quality of the output of well-led teams and must be encouraged, not discouraged.

The most extreme form of debate is when one or more parties take an absolutist position such as "I will *never* agree to X!" This happens frequently in poorly led teams because it allows members to manipulate team decisions by de facto vetoing of certain options, irrespective of what is best for the team. Strong differences of opinion happen in well-led teams because team members feel free to express their true emotions. Absolutist positions, and strong feelings in general, do not scare great team leaders or ELs. An emotional confrontation or absolutist position is the result of a previously unrealized comprehension or motivational alignment issue. Dealing with strong disagreements is not about open public debate, where emotions can rage out of control, and it is not about the leader showing the team how good he is at resolving strong disagreements. The leader's challenge is to find the source of the emotion. The source of the emotion will lie in some alternate interpretation of starting assumptions or in some unrealized personal fear (again, a powerful motivation). Asking "Why do you feel that way?" several times over, in order to dig as deep as possible to find the underlying assumption or emotion, is the most time-tested and effective way to proceed. The first couple of answers to your "why" questioning will likely be cursory, like "In my experience that will never work" or "I never agreed to support that." You need to ask follow-on questions: "What specifically is your experience?" or "Why is it disagreeable for you to support that?" Absolutism falls apart quickly under questioning, revealing some underlying motivational misalignment.

Strong disagreements may or may not be resolvable. Strong emotions often involve competitions over status, particularly in judging one rival right and another wrong. A person's feeling about how she may be judged may be more motivating to her than any team mission. In these cases you cannot resolve the issue, and you will need to remove the absolutist from the team. Removing the absolutist only from disagreeable tasks or relevant decision making does not work, because the person could continue to distort information flow or to manipulate others on the team in order to not be proved wrong in the eyes of their rival. Absolutists must be removed from any position where they could covertly impede the success of the team.

In many cases the situation can be resolved once it has been identified, particularly if the team leader has status that he can make part of the team's shared objective. I once led a team chartered to improve the efficiency of IR's military testing department. The department had not changed in many years, and there were many good ideas among the team members about how to make the department work more efficiently. One member, Bill, the head of the department, kept saying "no" to any change. Because he was the head of the department, it was impossible to improve. Even though Bill had agreed to be on the team and had expressed his desire to work with the team, for some reason he did not feel comfortable with any of the proposed improvements.

After a private discussion I learned that he had two fears he had not expressed during the formation of the team. One was that I, as leader of the team, could be construed as the new department head and he might be asked to retire. The second fear was that he didn't trust that changes implemented by the team would conform to military testing regulations. Bill was afraid that the team would take shortcuts in doing the tests to save money and the company would get into trouble (several of our competitors had been caught cheating on their testing, so this was a justified fear). I was able to resolve the problem by volunteering to serve as his direct reporting lieutenant. Thus I was directly responsible to him and he could review any changes before they became final. This made Bill feel secure that productivity improvements would comply with government regulations. He thought my reporting to him was an excellent solution. His status was increased because he had a highly regarded engineer working for him. To make this work, I had to put another project on hold for about six months, and I had to take on additional work. This solution nevertheless enhanced my reputation as an innovative problem solver and team leader. After this agreement was in place the department manager went on to make some excellent suggestions himself, and the team was extremely successful in accomplishing its mission.

In the next sections we will look at two types of teams that are particularly demanding of their team leader but can greatly benefit entrepreneurial leaders: (1) the board of directors and (2) teams of highly talented individuals, like the sales team.

LEADING A BOARD OF DIRECTORS

The board of directors (BOD) is legally responsible for ensuring a company complies with all rules and regulations (also known by other names, such as board of trustees for non-profits, and supervisory board in Europe). The board is a supervisory team whose mission is to make sure the enterprise is under control. If an enterprise has accepted investments or donations from any individual other than the founder, then the board is also responsible for making sure everyone's money is used as intended.

Many boards are made up of just one person: the entrepreneur. Entrepreneurs who started their company in order to not have to work for anyone else resist creating a board of directors, even if it is a team they select themselves and that helps them succeed. A well-led BOD provides broad, experienced, and wise mentorship and extends the influence of the enterprise beyond what any EL could achieve on his own. If the BOD is not properly led, however, it can be a huge distraction and headache.

In the case of an enterprise that has accepted outside money and must have a board with independently chosen members, the effectiveness of the board directly impacts the ability of the enterprise to succeed. When the board consists of a majority of independent directors with potentially misaligned shared objectives, then the founder's job and his control of the company depends on how well he leads this team. A well-led board of directors adds significant value to an enterprise; a poorly led board destroys value.

The entrepreneur wants to be the judge of his own performance and be accountable only to himself; the EL wants to be better than she can be by herself. The EL understands the benefits of using an independent team of people with the experience and motivation to help her reach ambitious objectives.

Leading a board of directors can be more challenging than leading a typical team when the EL cannot choose everyone who is on the board. Independent investors or relatives may insist on choosing some board members. In some countries one or more board members may be dictated by regulation (for example, the head of a union may be a required board member). Boards can therefore include members with shared objectives inconsistent with the EL's. This can make board duck alignment much more difficult.

Many entrepreneurs never make it clear what the board's objectives, responsibilities, and authorities are. You cannot align the comprehension duck of a BOD without defining its purpose and constraints. Government regulations define some BOD responsibilities. You are well advised to have a business lawyer periodically attend your BOD meetings to describe the fiduciary responsibilities of the board. To these fiduciary responsibilities you can add your own expectations for how your board performs its supervisory role. For example, non-profit boards are often expected to help raise or donate money. It is important to set expectations for your board on their responsibilities for helping the enterprise succeed.

Board agendas are set to keep deliberations focused on whatever specific judgments are needed from them. Board agendas also make clear what information the EL will need to provide the board in advance of the meeting to help it be prepared to make the required judgments. Board responsibilities change and expand as enterprises mature, so over time agendas change. A stage one BOD discusses what potential customers have been solicited, what feedback has been received, and how much money remains in the bank account relative to the progress in getting the first revenue-generating customers. They may discuss raising more funds. A stage two BOD needs to understand how quickly new customers are being found and how well the enterprise is retaining existing customers. Stage two boards want to understand how fast improvements—that is, processes—are being implemented. They also want to understand cash flow and make sure it is consistent with funding prospects. In general, board agendas should closely reflect what progress is being made relative to getting to the next stage.

The motivation duck can be particularly hard to align on BODs whose members represent different constituencies and therefore do not have the same shared objectives. VCs sitting on a board do not share all of the founder's desires. To be successful, VCs need to quickly make money for their partnerships even if it means the founder or CEO makes less money than they want. There's a fundamental competition relative to how the wealth created by the enterprise will be divided among the investors, the entrepreneur, and his team. The board and the entrepreneur also compete as to whether the entrepreneur is the best person to create and implement strategy to increase total enterprise valuation. Unless a firm is wildly profitable to the point that both the VC and the founder are sated by their new wealth, there will always be misaligned motivations between the entrepreneur and the investor. Misaligned motivations are competitive shared objectives that require a test to determine a winner and loser. The test is who can get the most board members to support their position for how best to increase the valuation of the enterprise.

Family members also may not share the same motivations for sitting on the board. Family shared objectives can easily conflict with the entrepreneur's objectives for his enterprise. Families always have issues about status, fairness, and emotional well-being, and a family member on the board brings those issues to the enterprise. The entrepreneur may feel obliged for family reasons to invite or allow a family member to become a board member, but that *will* have ramifications.

Entrepreneurial leaders are not naïve about the motivations of the people they ask or approve to be on their board of directors. The best practice for aligning motivation on the BOD is to prescreen potential investors and directors to the point where the EL feels confident he understands their motivations. Very few entrepreneurs do any investigation or reference checking. With a few phone calls, the EL can find out from other people with direct experience with the potential board member how they actually acted in situations where their best interests were not aligned with the best interests of the entrepreneur. I know several ELs who avoided mistakes because they did this investigation. Unfortunately, most entrepreneurs are too excited about the prospect of receiving an investment from a VC to ask any questions that could sour the deal. I can't count the number of entrepreneurs who suffered major setbacks, like being fired or being forced to prematurely sell their enterprise, because board members' motivations did not align with theirs.

That said, ELs may have to adjust their motivation in order to capture a board member or investor that they believe will tangibly increase their chances of success. What ELs are really deciding in such a case is whether to modify the objectives of their enterprise to accommodate the personal objectives of the new board member. Similarly, when dealing with family members on the board, ELs must either accommodate their personal needs or have some explicit agreement about how they will not vote on matters that pose a conflict.

If ELs can remove the board member whose motivations are misaligned, they are advised to do so, but typically they cannot. To prevent board members from acting only in their personal best interest, the United States and some other countries have laws that deal with board conflicts of interest. In the United States, all who serve as a director of a company are legally bound to look after the well-being of the company's investors and stakeholders before their own. Unfortunately, self-interest can be easy to deny as a reason for making any decision, so this law is difficult to apply. ELs have occasionally used the threat of litigation against board members clearly acting in their self-interest to change a crucial vote, particularly when it is a decision related to the future of the company.

The skills and resources available to a board can also be misaligned. Some board members may not have the skills or the time to perform competently. This sorry situation can occur even with board members appointed by professional investors. Again, the EL must investigate potential board members relative to what they know and how much time they agree to invest in board deliberations. No person can do a good job if they are on more than five or six boards. Some overcommitted VCs actually send a delegate to attend board meetings when they don't have time to perform their duties themselves. Inserting a new member into a team always misaligns board ducks! Get your VCs and other board members to promise that they will not send delegates.

Boards of directors are often paranoid about all board communications because lawyers tell them that shareholders can sue them for anything they communicate that later turns out to be untrue or misleading. This is true for both private and public companies. Lawyers counsel boards to say very little to shareholders and to "commit to nothing." Although many entrepreneurs who have raised money from outside investors excuse their poor communications by citing this advice, the EL wants to make sure his ducks are always aligned and will communicate nonetheless. ELs make clear to their company lawyers the critical need to communicate, and they set expectations that their lawyers will help facilitate these needs.

The EL must also take responsibility for all communications to the board. ELs need to organize the information flow to the board and receive feedback from the BOD to ensure they have understood the information. I sent an email every Friday giving my board a snapshot about how the company was doing. I always had a "good news" paragraph and a "bad news" paragraph to accompany the most important performance metrics. If I didn't receive any reply emails from the board on points that I thought they should be happy or concerned about, then I sent them an email asking them what they thought about those points to make sure they read the communication.

In the actual board meeting the EL's responsibility is to make sure the board discusses all relevant issues completely to their satisfaction. The board needs to feel confident that they possess all the information they need and that the information they have received describes all practical options they should consider. In the meeting, the EL must ask any tough questions that should be brought up but that no one else present has raised. *For a board to feel comfortable with the EL and fully support his actions, they need to feel that the EL is at least as demanding of his own performance as they are.* Entrepreneurs who cover up issues or potential options to consider do so at their own peril. It is selfish and counterproductive for the entrepreneur to try and manipulate the board of directors into seeing an issue the same way he does. Boards add value to an enterprise when individual members bring their own complementary experience and expertise to BOD discussions. A BOD that agrees with everything the entrepreneur proposes adds zero value and is a waste of time. The EL who can describe to his team how his board came up with good suggestions and helped to spot potential problems is viewed as wise, in control, and selfless.

LEADING TEAMS OF TALENT

The successful salesperson possesses a skill that is widely coveted, not least by the competition. Leaders of sales teams face challenges associated with aligning the motivations of individually talented individuals who may be more committed to extending the impact of their individual talent than to extending the value of the overall enterprise. Understanding how to lead teams of selfishly motivated people can yield major competitive advantages.

Leaders harness the support of individually talented individuals by committing to help them succeed in the application of their talent. The leader of the sales team, and ultimately the EL, must help all team members

- Objectively measure their sales ability
- Directly benefit from the application of their ability
- Improve their sales skills

Classically, the measurement and the personal benefit of sales ability are tied together through the implementation of a sales commission. If the best salesperson earns commensurately more commission than an average or poor salesperson, then each salesperson will feel properly judged and work passionately to improve the chance for a commission.

Ambitious salespeople want to improve their sales ability, and they want to work for an enterprise that gives them that opportunity. The leader of the sales force must explicitly tell each salesperson how he or she is being given the opportunity to improve. Less experienced salespeople could be offered training or mentorship. More experienced salespeople could be offered new accounts or more sophisticated products or services to sell.

Selfish individuals do not naturally cooperate with one another, and this creates an additional challenge for the EL and his sales force leader. Many sales forces are organized as competitions among salespeople to see who can sell the most. In this type of sales environment, rewards for selling the expected amount of product are substantial, and the constraints placed on the individual salesperson, beyond respecting defined sales territories, are minimized. Some sales leaders foster cooperation by creating sales metrics that result in sales commission being shared among salespeople. This cooperation must be very well defined. For example, every salesperson around the world that sells to the same multinational account may have some or all of their commission on that account paid according to how much is globally sold to that account. This focuses cooperation on maximizing total account sales, but it does not solve the problem of letting all salespeople know how individually talented they are. Creating a "global account" therefore requires that the sales leader give more individual attention and feedback to each salesperson who contributed cooperatively to the global account results. This individual attention can take a great deal of time, so cooperation among salespeople can occur only in very limited areas.

Many entrepreneurs do not understand the needs of their sales force and therefore attract less talented salespeople to work for them. Many an entrepreneur has lost her market opportunity because a competitor with more savvy sales leadership skills had a more motivated sales force. ELs offer to measure, reward, and improve the individual talents of their salespeople or any employee with rare and highly sought-after skills.

Plenty, but not all, work gets done in teams, which means that the ability of an enterprise to produce value and ultimately become self-sustaining is greatly enhanced if the EL can stimulate a culture in which teams routinely meet high expectations and avoid mediocre, least common denominator results. Although not all aspects of a culture are under the EL's control, team expectations are. Armed with an understanding of where to use teams and what teams need to be successful, the EL can coalesce a culture around high team performance expectations by

- Sharing this understanding with everyone asked to lead a team
- Coaching team leaders to be skilled at leading through understanding how to keep ducks aligned
- Rewarding successful teams

ELs create enormous value by ensuring that their enterprise astutely leverages the power of teams.

Leading Through Crises

A *crisis* happens whenever an important underlying assumption about how your enterprise can succeed proves false. All crises have common characteristics: they are threatening to survival, unexpected, and require significant action and resources to contain, mitigate, and resolve. Some crises are preventable, but many are not. Crises strike every enterprise and every entrepreneur. Irrespective of whether the crisis was preventable or not, leaders are expected to lead their teams to success, and no expectations can be set to the contrary.

CRISES ARE INEVITABLE

The survival and success of every enterprise is contingent on many different assumptions, many of which the entrepreneur may not realize. All entrepreneurs start with many assumptions about customers, costs, economic conditions, competitors, and what help they'll be able to find. At the start of an enterprise, every cell in any spreadsheet is an assumption, and many of these are critical assumptions.

Startups go through many crises. It is hard for any entrepreneur to know how potential customers will react to their idea, and many assumptions about customer demand prove false, as do many assumptions about costs, finding people, and whether products can be delivered as planned. The entrepreneur's explicit or implicit assumptions about changes in the economic environment—what society considers important, interesting, and fashionable—must also be tested.

Crises also occur when critical process and project steps are skipped inadvertently. The assumption that all steps will be performed as agreed to is a major underpinning of any new enterprise. Even though crises caused by mistakes are avoidable, they occur often in startups, because very little time and money is available for training or checking work. For example, if money does not get transferred to a critical supplier on time, then the new enterprise could be forced to make additional deposits and may not have the funds to do so, thereby sending the enterprise into crisis. Entrepreneurial leaders lie awake at night worrying about what could go wrong, and although worrying enables ELs to catch some potential crisis-causing mistakes, it cannot ensure that they will catch them all.

Even large, mature enterprises find long-held assumptions suddenly invalid. Andy Grove wrote an excellent book, *Only the Paranoid Survive*, about how Intel's design flaw in its Pentium microprocessors exposed several faulty assumptions about what customers expected and how Intel's culture had to change to satisfy them. Since the late 1980s, crisis leadership has been acknowledged as a field worthy of study, triggered by the misguided handling of the Exxon *Valdez* and the Space Shuttle *Challenger* disasters. Unfortunately, the field of crisis leadership has focused on studying large institutional crises such as these and has ignored the entrepreneur.[1]

THE PHASES OF CRISIS LEADERSHIP

To successfully resolve any crisis, the enterprise must complete five phases:

- *Crisis Identification:* The first step is to understand that there is a crisis. Crises are identified by acknowledging that results differ from what had been assumed.
- *Planning and Deployment:* Projects must be quickly planned and resourced, even before the true source of the problem is completely understood.
- *Crisis Containment and Mitigation:* The problem must be brought under control and the damage mitigated before a permanent

solution can be designed and implemented. This tends to be a project phase.

- *Recovery:* New processes, independent of the original flawed assumption, are designed and implemented.
- *Lessons Learned:* The root cause(s) of the problem are positively identified and long-term permanent changes are implemented so the problem cannot reoccur. The enterprise is stronger as a result.[2]

Many of the entrepreneurial stories we have visited in this book are about crises. Crises are a true test of a leader, and you can tell a great deal about someone's leadership abilities by how they deal with crises—sometimes crises that are not yet realized. Arun, whom we met in Chapter Eight, failed as a leader because, like so many intense entrepreneurs, he failed to acknowledge that 3E was in crisis. Arun astutely anticipated that 3E's new product would likely have design issues that the customer would find once the energy saving equipment was installed; but Arun's "designs-never-work-the-first-time" assumption was not what caused the crisis. 3E's crisis was caused by a failed assumption that the company was properly organized to deal with design problems. Arun led 3E's engineering team to solve the design problems he had anticipated having, but it was his failure to do so effectively that should have actually sounded the alarm.

3E's crisis was preventable, but preventable crises are often the hardest ones to acknowledge. When preventable crises arise, people involved with fighting the symptoms of the problem feel they could be blamed, making them prone to do whatever they can to resolve the issue on their own without asking for help. Hiding the fact that something is not working out as expected makes the problem worse. ELs must look for crises; it is one of their major leadership responsibilities. If Arun could not lead 3E to solve a tricky design problem without the first customer demanding his money back, then Arun's team could not feel confident he would make them successful, despite the enormous potential of the technology. That is why he was replaced.

Max Levchin and Peter Thiel successfully led Confinity and PayPal through at least four crises that they could not have prevented: three different products that not enough people wanted to buy and a fourth crisis when the losses from fraud were causing PayPal to run out of money. If Max and Peter had not acknowledged the fraud problem and not focused on successfully solving it, they would have been replaced as PayPal's leaders, or the company would have failed, as happened to all of their competitors. When Jon in Chapter Six failed in his first attempt to develop leading-edge training courses, EIT was *not* thrown into crisis, because his company could continue its business without that capability. EIT's future may not have been as bright in Jon's eyes, but he remained the leader in the eyes of his team because they felt he'd be able to make them successful without the new capability.

To a certain extent, entrepreneurial leaders *want* crises to occur in stages one and two so that they fix their mistaken assumptions. Max and Peter would have failed if they had not robustly tested their customer demand and money processing assumptions quickly, before they no longer had the funds to respond aggressively. No enterprise can become self-sustaining until all its fundamental underlying assumptions have been tested and proven true. *The more promptly false assumptions are identified and dealt with, the faster the enterprise can mature.*

CRISIS LEADERS ARE SELF-AWARE

Arun didn't want to acknowledge he had a problem. Crisis identification is challenging for everyone, because information is rarely complete or clear about what caused unexpected results. It almost goes without saying that unexpected results are confusing. When a customer rejects a product prototype, it is an obvious problem, but when prototype performance issues haven't been resolved within a week or two, it is not always clear what is making this happen. As in the 3E case, the organizational structure is not what most entrepreneurs would look to as the cause.

For ELs to feel comfortable that they are in position to identify crises as quickly as possible, they need to

- Spend time looking for problems.
- Make it *rewarding* for people throughout the enterprise to point out unexpected results.

- Make sure management and leadership review all unexpected results that prevent the enterprise from progressing to the next stage. In stage one, this review occurs naturally in the huddle. In stage two, unresolved problems would be put on the agenda of the weekly progress meeting. In stage three and beyond, this review would be conducted by the leadership team.
- Require additional review, by people outside the leadership team, for all serious problems that are not resolved as expected.

Once it was clear that 3E's design problems were not getting solved as expected, Arun made the crisis even worse. Many entrepreneurs leading in a crisis insist they know what to do and how to do it. Under stress, most people naturally want to feel like nothing is blocking them from playing to their strengths, because that is what gives them confidence to "win." When the perceived strength is actually a weakness, the leader makes the situation worse. Arun wanted to take control of solving the design problem because he felt he was the smartest and hardest working person at 3E, and because he had the best working relationship with Manuel. Some of 3E's engineers understood that Arun was neither an electrical design person nor a skilled problem solver, but when they offered to help, they were rebuffed. Arun's arrogance made it impossible for anyone to question his misguided decisions.

At 3E the crisis could have been identified as soon as the demonstration equipment began to produce unexpectedly poor or erratic performance and the first and second attempts to solve the problem had failed. Any lingering performance or satisfaction issue with one of the first few customers should be considered a crisis, as it could lead to the loss of the first customer and to a bad reputation that would be hard to overcome.

When a crisis occurs, ELs ask themselves how they need to change to make the situation better, not how to get everyone around them to act more like them. A crisis is not the time for self-doubt. ELs ask not "Am I worthy?" but rather "What can I do differently to make the situation better?" Self-awareness is important in times of crisis, to the extent that it helps entrepreneurs understand that their traits, motivations, and skills make them vulnerable to repeatedly making certain types of mistakes. Without this level of self-awareness they are unprepared to change and do not recognize when they make crises worse.

BABY STEPPING THROUGH A CRISIS

After the EL has identified a crisis, a plan must quickly be formulated to contain the problem and prevent it from potentially spreading and getting worse. Nobody yet understands the extent of the problem, let alone its cause, and there is no time to wait until definitive answers are found. How do you line up your ducks for the project when you do not know what steps, skills, resources, and communications may be needed? The effective strategy in a crisis is to break the huge problem of crisis resolution into a series of very small subprojects—what some people refer to as "baby steps." Each subproject is chosen so as to reduce the risk and scope associated with subsequent projects, thereby making best use of limited resources. Some of the initial subprojects will be trial-and-error experiments, or investigations. Some of these subprojects may focus on the acquisition of missing information, skills, or resources. The completion of each subproject fills in a missing piece of the crisis cause and resolution puzzle. Each successful subproject is viewed as a sign of progress, and failed subprojects are not viewed as major setbacks.

As soon as unexplained problems (or opportunities!) arise that could impact the enterprise's performance and well-being, the EL must quickly form a crisis team. Crisis teams are formed differently from the project and process teams the EL would normally commission to build the enterprise. Crisis teams immediately become the highest priority activity in the enterprise, with time being a critical factor. The EL must be prepared to put on hold any, perhaps even all, discretionary activities pending the resolution of the crisis. The crisis team should be selected with duck alignment in mind. Because a crisis team is often formed before the actual problem has been identified, ducks are aligned using a different strategy than in the case of premeditated change. Although many people may be drafted into helping the crisis team, the team itself is limited in size by the leader's ability to align the shared objectives of the team members while satisfying their own personal motivations. A team with six people is much easier to align than a ten-person team. The EL wants to pick a team size he feels comfortable leading, with a balance of these elements:

- *Team members who are available full time, relieved of conflicting priorities for the duration of the crisis.*
- *People with skills clearly pertinent to finding and solving the problem.* What's most important for the team are best-in-class levels of any specialized skills required to assess the available information. The team must have the expertise to understand what the data are telling them. Although problem solving is a very well-defined skill in itself (in industry there are certified problem solvers, and you can take problem-solving classes) and is very useful to have available to the team, it doesn't necessarily have to be on the team.
- *People who will provide the resources needed by the team.* Although the EL has authority for demanding any resource within the enterprise, he is well advised to team up with the people who will provide these resources, to give them as much visibility as possible. The visibility given to resource providers averts follow-on crises brought on by the diversion of critical resources to the crisis team. If significant amounts of money may be required, a financial person should be on the team.
- *Someone who is good at communicating and can take responsibility for aligning the communication duck.*

Arun never formed a crisis team, so he was doomed to fail as a crisis leader. The best possible outcome, given Arun's teamwork fears, would have been to consider Arun and Manuel as a two-man problem-solving team—as one of the subprojects I alluded to earlier. Arun would have had to make it clear to Manuel that he was responsible for identifying the root cause of the problem and Arun was on the team to provide whatever help and resources Manuel needed. I would have also hired a best-in-class problem-solving consultant whom Manuel respected to facilitate these subproject meetings and advise on best problem-solving practices. Arun then could have formed the formal high-level crisis team with 3E employees who could best deal with the customer and provide the resources to quickly make required modifications to the demonstration equipment.

As a first action with the crisis team, the EL must decide on the *ultimate minimum objective* (UMO) to achieve. Choosing the UMO is equivalent to deciding which of the core business assumptions must be maintained for the enterprise to continue to preserve as much of its value as possible. Examples of typical UMOs are for the enterprise "to find and fix poor-quality products to preserve as many of the existing orders as possible" or for the enterprise "to find a work-around for the delivery bottleneck in order to preserve the relationship with critical partner X." The UMO is equivalent to the mission of the crisis team. The UMO is important because it sets a general direction and level of expectation for all other decisions. In a crisis it is very important that the EL set the UMO. The future of the enterprise is at stake, and everyone wants to feel assured that the EL knows that and supports the plan to resolve the crisis. In the case of Arun, his UMO could have been simply stated as, "Identify and resolve the failure of the installed demonstration equipment to meet minimum specifications in order to preserve our first customer." This UMO has nothing to do with evaluating the organizational structure of 3E, because Arun is not yet aware that this is a problem. Most UMOs are originally focused on solving a symptom, not on the root cause of the problem—the team will focus on the root cause later, when they have better information and visibility.

With the UMO in place, the crisis team must quickly decide on its next few steps. There is no time to plan out a complete solution to the crisis, because crisis situations are volatile and the available information is incomplete and suspect. Furthermore, widespread uncontrolled emotions can impair the enterprise's ability to respond and can damage its reputation, so it is imperative that the EL appears in charge as soon as possible after the crisis has been acknowledged. Taking successful and rational initial steps restores some of the eroded stakeholder confidence.

Aligning the comprehension duck requires that everyone on the team have an identical understanding of the project objectives. In a crisis there is little time to debate and modify the UMO or subproject objectives. The EL must choose and subsequently modify the crisis team's composition such that he feels the team is completely aligned with the chosen UMO. ELs must remove from the team anyone who objects to the UMO. Because crises threaten the well-being of all stakeholders, the entrepreneurial leader can act selfishly at this point to remove UMO dissenters from the crisis team to ensure alignment, although in practice UMOs tend not to be very controversial.

In a crisis situation the EL also does not have time to align the motivations of each team member (duck two). Fortunately, most members of the enterprise want to see the enterprise survive, and they naturally share this motivation. The EL should keep in mind that individuals or groups that feel they could be blamed for the crisis may have a strong motivation to prove there is no crisis or that the crisis could be solved in ways that mitigate their responsibility. This is the common source of motivational misalignment in a crisis. The team does not have time or the resources to be distracted by any team members who are less than highly motivated. Anyone who is not motivated to see the enterprise achieve the UMO should be removed from the team, quickly.

I made my previous recommendation that Manuel not be on the crisis team but instead be used exclusively to find the cause of the problem, bearing in mind the motivational duck alignment challenge. Manuel was motivated to see the equipment he invented work properly, and he wanted to understand the sources of the problems, but he was not motivated to see others get status and recognition for being able to fix problems for which he may have been responsible.

The skills duck—making sure the project team has, or has control of, the needed skills—is a relatively tricky duck to align in a crisis. Crises are often caused because of a mistaken assumption that a certain skill was not required by the enterprise or that a needed skill was present when in fact it was not. A classic example occurs when the EL feels that the enterprise does not yet need to spend money on a financially skilled person, and the company unexpectedly runs out of cash due to poor cash management. Another classic example of a missing skill–induced crisis arises when a critical process is outsourced to another group that did not itself have the skills to deliver on their responsibilities. A third classic missing skills–induced crisis happens when an enterprise finds that it is unintentionally producing inferior product because it did not have appropriate product testing skills.

Breaking the crisis response into small manageable subprojects is an excellent strategy for mitigating missing skills. Finding a person who can quickly and temporarily test a product for a specific type of defect is much more straightforward and amenable to duck alignment than acquiring or accessing the skills required to create an experienced product testing group. I think Arun needed a skilled problem solver to work with his problem identification subteam—namely himself and Manuel. The fact that the design problem was difficult to identify indicates that Arun needed to find some expertise in heavy electrical equipment design. Manuel, being an academic, likely did not understand many of the subtleties that go into designing big pieces of electrical equipment that are connected to the power grid.

Many crises spin out of control because the enterprise did not allocate the appropriate resources (duck four) to its containment. Crises by their very nature are hard to control, and the EL must quickly make a list of all the resources that *could* be required. In a crisis ELs cannot flinch from taking resources from anywhere within their enterprise or anywhere else they may be available. Crises are very dangerous and not a time for formal requisitioning or a debate on relative priorities. As already mentioned, breaking the crisis into subprojects is a good strategy for not wasting considerable resources yet still deploying all the resources necessary for crisis containment and solution. In the case of 3E, Arun did call upon all his engineering resources when he needed them. Arun was not shy in this respect.

Duck five, communications, aligns by making sure everyone impacted by the project understands its importance. It is the single toughest challenge in a crisis. Emotions run high. People feel insecure and anxious. A lack of relevant information feeds insecurity and anxiety. Communication shapes the perception of how a crisis is being led and whether people inside and outside the firm feel satisfied with the ultimate solution and crisis cleanup. It can misalign for two reasons:

- The crisis team leaves a critical constituency out of its communication plans (for example, it may not have the resources to communicate with everyone).
- The crisis team did not trust a critical constituency with all the information it needed. Unilateral filtering of potentially useful information creates a needless competition at an already emotional time. Each constituency wants to feel they have all the information they need to develop their view of the importance of the enterprise's crisis response. Do not expect to "fool" any constituency into supporting your efforts, particularly when your own actions cause distrust.

Leaders tend to lose their jobs because they didn't pay enough attention to duck five. Immature leaders often leave out the board of directors and investors as distinct constituencies requiring their own communications. Erstwhile ELs are often afraid or too distracted to compose board-specific communications. Arun didn't communicate with the board because he feared they would judge him to be at fault for the problem. Similarly, an enterprise's reputation is invariably hurt when customers do not receive direct crisis communications. If the press is involved, then they require their own communications to help them independently assess the importance of the crisis. Considerable resources must be spent communicating to constituencies in a crisis; being stingy with communication resources causes more problems at a time when you can least effectively deal with them.

Arun did not do a good job of leading communications with the employees of 3E, his board of directors, or the customer. He used the exact wrong communications strategy: "tell people only what they need to know." Need-to-know communication strategies may be appropriate for spying, but they are not good for aligning action among people whose help you need. Everyone knows there is a problem when unexpected things start happening and expected things don't happen. Need-to-know strategies make everyone feel they are not trusted. Need-to-know is a great way to destroy trust with your board of directors, particularly when the board is legally responsible for looking after the interests of outside investors. Arun could not have had the time to do all the communicating he needed to do. As I mentioned previously, I would have composed the 3E team to include a person who would manage all the communications, with Arun personally briefing the board on his evolving plans and 3E's progress at least weekly.

LEARNING YOUR LESSONS

Duck alignment skills are critical to enabling a leader to identify, contain, solve, and clean up the inevitable crises that any enterprise faces. Unfortunately, leaders often forget the essential last step, lessons learned: What did we learn and what do we need to change in order to not suffer similar crises in the future?

Any crisis that reoccurs will result in the leader losing his job. ELs do not let their enterprise relax until the root causes of the crisis are completely understood and mitigated. Solving the crisis and cleaning up the mess as quickly as possible doesn't mean that you have fixed the root cause(s) that could cause a related crisis to occur. Root causes are often hard to identify and hard to fix. In the case of 3E, the problem wasn't just that Manuel made a mistake in his ground fault circuit design because he wasn't as skilled in electric equipment design as everyone had thought. Innovative enterprises always have the problem that they don't know all the skills they need to implement their innovations. Well-led innovative enterprises are on the lookout for missing skills, and innovative enterprises are organized so as not to overload the leader and innovators with noncritical tasks. There were three root causes of the problems at 3E. First, 3E lacked a culture that could question whether the enterprise, and Arun and Manuel specifically, lacked essential skills. Innovative companies have cultures that are always on the lookout for missing skills (in Chapter Five we described how Dean Kamen gave top priority to acquiring missing skills). Second, 3E was designed in such a way that it was virtually impossible to respond to crises. Third, Arun didn't respond to the crisis as a leader should; he never formed a crisis team, and his ducks were never aligned.

Finding the root causes and thus the lessons that need learning is best done by a small team working independently of the original crisis team. The crisis project team will be exhausted by the time the cleanup is finished. Team members are also emotional about how their lives have been dramatically and unexpectedly impacted by the crisis. Though the crisis team has plenty of opinions about what happened and what to do about it, these opinions have a high emotional content. A smaller independent "lessons learned" team will identify more accurate root causes and will come up with more economical mitigations. It is good to put the enterprise's most objective and outspoken problem finders on the team (there are people who have a natural ability to find problems, and they love to be acknowledged for this ability). Of course, the "lessons learned" team must work with members of the original crisis team to access to their accumulated experience in dealing with the crisis. They will need to work very closely with the EL on implementing the changes they recommend.

The too often forgotten final critical step of all "lessons learned" teams is to thank each individual involved with successfully overcoming the threat to the well-being of the enterprise. Any founder or CEO that forgets to say thank you will be considered a selfish entrepreneur and not a selfless leader.

THE CRITICAL IMPORTANCE OF SLACK TIME

Successfully solving a major crisis always requires the EL's full attention. The EL will be called upon to deal with crises continually in stage one, and sporadically in subsequent stages. Because ELs cannot take a chance on failing to lead their enterprise successfully through the crises they should naturally expect, they keep slack time in their schedules to be used when, inevitably, they must deal with crises big and small. Most entrepreneurs allocate all their time to doing the tasks they like best or the tasks required of them to keep the enterprise going. Entrepreneurs typically do not create the slack time necessary to understand where problems are occurring that could turn into crises. When critical processes or projects in the enterprise rely on tasks performed by the entrepreneur, then he cannot pay enough attention to either his appointed tasks or the tasks required to line up the ducks when a crisis hits. Without leadership slack time the enterprise will automatically have to endure two crises instead of one!

Because the EL must be able to assume responsibility for leading a crisis team at any time, the EL must not be essential to any make-or-break projects or any critical processes during noncrisis times. This doesn't mean that ELs sit on a sideline waiting for a crisis to occur; rather, they need to construct the teams and activities in which they participate so that these can be performed without them. ELs can participate fully in activities when there is no crisis, but they cannot play an essential role. Too often the requirement for leaders to have slack time is realized as a lesson learned, but then it is too late to save the job of the leader.

Leading an enterprise successfully through a crisis builds trust in the leadership credentials of the EL with everyone that was impacted. Any other outcome can quickly lead to the EL's downfall.

13

The Selfish Rewards of Selfless Entrepreneurial Acts

Most of the protagonists in this book eventually succeeded as entrepreneurial leaders, but in almost every case it required one or more major traumatic experiences to realize they needed to make changes. A few of our protagonists refused to change or did not change fast enough, in spite of their traumatic experiences, and they ultimately failed, despite their intelligence, talent, education, and experience. Everyone who wants to succeed in taking an idea and turning it into a value-producing, self-sustaining enterprise will have to change—and this is inevitably a more or less painful experience: more if the change is unwelcome and the entrepreneur resists it; less if she accepts the necessity and embraces the change. I hope this book will help some people avoid the more traumatic experiences of change.

As we have seen, change requires a strong motivation to drive it, whether you are the leader of the change or a participant. This chapter is about how to find your entrepreneurial motivations. These motivations will help you whether you are thinking about starting your own enterprise (which half the working population will ultimately attempt), helping someone start theirs, or deciding whether to propose starting a new department or product line at the place where you now work.

Adam, our first entrepreneurial protagonist from Chapter One, did not launch his second venture for money, but it took him a while to figure out what made him do it. Adam had left Gale Solutions shortly after Gerry, the VC, hired a new CEO. Adam did not feel comfortable working for a person who did not seem to care about his opinions. He felt like a failure, like someone who had let down people who had sacrificed their careers to help him. He started to see a therapist. Adam became almost obsessive about figuring out how he could have done a better job as Gale's leader. He asked his wife, his therapist, his best friends, and former Gale Solutions colleagues for their opinions. He read blogs and books. He made notes that almost filled a notebook. It seemed to Adam that there were so many reasons for his failure that he could never learn how to overcome them all.

Fifteen months after leaving Gale Solutions, Adam received a call from Gerry letting him know that the company was about to be sold to a much larger software company for the substantial sum of $65 million, making Adam wealthy enough (through his founder's stock and stock options) that he no longer needed to work. The news of the sale shook Adam out of his perpetually gloomy mood. His mood shifted not because of the money he would receive, but because the sale made him realize that he had not been a complete failure as an entrepreneur. If the company could be sold for a significant amount of money so soon after he left, he must have done a pretty good job of putting the company on a decent foundation. His wife, friends, and former colleagues had been telling him he had done a great job starting Gale Solutions, but he had not believed them before he heard this news. Adam then realized that he would have been much better off if he had listened to the suggestions and inputs of his wife and friends all along. He had been closed minded in thinking that no one else could really understand *his* situation.

Serial entrepreneurs start new ventures when they feel motivationally unfulfilled by their earlier attempts. Adam felt unfulfilled in his identity as a successful entrepreneur, despite the fact that Gale Solutions had been sold for enough money that he no longer needed to work. Adam felt capable but not fulfilled in his new frame of mind; he was energized to start working on a new software solution he had been thinking about that could download and analyze large amounts of information from public websites. Adam felt particularly excited that he could develop software that could do a better job searching government websites for jobs and contract opportunities that were hard to search using Google or other tools. This information could also enable anyone to quickly summarize all the money spent by every government agency anywhere in the country or the world—so it would also be a powerful tool for collecting market research. The day after hearing about the sale of Gale Solutions, Adam sat down and jotted notes about what he wanted his new company to do and how he thought he could describe its value to potential clients. He already understood the economics of software companies well enough that he didn't feel the need to write down any of the other critical aspects of the business model outlined in Chapter Eight.

Indeed, that day Adam spent much more time summarizing the inputs he had received over the previous year about how he could have succeeded as the leader of Gale Solutions. Adam spent hours on the floor of his living room organizing small file cards, each with a different piece of advice taken from his notes. He organized similar ideas into piles, and then summarized the insight from one or two piles into "overarching" pieces of advice. By dinnertime Adam had written down three short statements on a piece of paper—his equivalent of a personal leadership strategy—which he decided to keep in a frame on his desk:

Lessons Learned

Adam wanted to make sure he always was actively learning from the results of his actions. To that end, Adam started a new notebook in which he wrote down each lesson learned.

Debates, Not Disputes

Adam knew that his demise at Gale Solutions had been partly caused by his aversion to conflict. Working with his therapist, he had already created a simple checklist that reminded him to focus on outlining what he perceived as dispute issues—shared objectives, in the parlance of this book—and each person's position in the dispute; that is, their desired outcomes. Adam had come to realize how debates added value, whereas competitive disputes only sap energy and dissipate value.

Ask, Don't Guess

Adam felt he had caused his own downfall because he had thought he could figure out the solution to any problem on his own. He had been arrogant. He resolved to always seek the advice of others who were more experienced.

The next day Adam started making phone calls, tracking down people who might be excited to help him fulfill his vision and his destiny. Adam used his own money to hire two of the most dynamic and capable people he knew in the field of market research, both of whom he had met as clients. He also hired two star software people from Gale Solutions (Adam's agreement to not hire anyone from Gale for a period of one year had expired) and another software person who worked for a competitor whom he respected and whom he had met a couple of times at conferences. He felt good about how he had found and hired people at Gale Solutions, and this gave him confidence to move quickly hiring good people for his next venture.

As soon as G2 Solutions was incorporated, in spite of the fact that he had not taken any money from outside investors, Adam formed a board of directors of people whom he wanted as advisors. There were three people other than Adam on the board. One was a CEO of a very profitable medium-sized market research firm that had been a client of Gale Solutions; Adam felt he was a great business person and understood how information could be structured to create value. He also invited onto the board another software entrepreneur whom he had met several years before and with whom he had stayed in touch. The final person on the board was a friend from college who had just been appointed an assistant professor of marketing at a well-regarded business school. Feeling he had direct access to excellent business experience and advice, and wanting to focus his attention entirely on making G2 a major success, Adam stopped seeing his therapist. Adam felt his board would give him good advice and make it easy for him to "ask, not guess."

Adam was not the only entrepreneur who saw the potential for capturing information from public websites, and the domain already had several competitors. Adam was soon compelled, based on the inputs from potential customers, to pivot from his original idea to a more immediately useful business model focused on the data-scrubbing aspects of his software. Within eight months his experienced and highly motivated small team developed software that proved particularly good at improving the quality and consistency of information downloaded from public websites. The value of this software was quickly appreciated by any firm experienced in collecting information from many different sources of inconsistent quality.

The firm grew quickly. Adam funded the venture himself for eighteen months before he decided to accept money from a VC in order to grow G2 fast enough to satisfy his growing list of clients. Adam's situation in raising money was now very different from when he had accepted money from Gerry. Several VCs had been soliciting Adam to let them invest in his enterprise, so Adam could decide on the terms of the investment he was willing to accept. Adam remained firmly in control, as he sold only 25 percent of his company for $3.5 million. Because G2 turned cash flow positive in its third year, Adam never had to raise any more money from investors.

Today Adam remains CEO of a highly profitable firm in a field we now call "big data." G2 Solutions has grown to over two hundred people and moved beyond its original software products. Adam has led G2 to successfully develop a set of services they offer to companies needing to create their own "big data" capabilities. Within five years of its founding, G2 had matured through all four stages. Many larger software companies have expressed interest in buying G2 for considerable sums of money, but for now Adam is not interested in selling. He feels fulfilled.

ELs SELFISHLY HELP OTHERS

Turning ideas into value-producing, self-sustaining enterprises is a broad and powerful capability. The concepts discussed in this book can be applied to more than starting and growing a company. Teachers are potential ELs. Athletes are potential ELs. Shop owners and other business owners are potential ELs. ELs can help their colleagues at large companies create new capabilities and processes. Anyone who interacts with other people with a purpose to create new value can be an EL. Your vision of how you are going to deliver new value to your students, your teammates, your employees, and existing customers *is* your idea. It is your gift, not someone else's. It is the source of your selfishness.

The value you envision creating will be delivered through projects and processes that will depend on others. You will have to make sure everyone who helps you create value will be successful. Your success will come from the success of your students, your teammates, your employees, and your customers. You will be responsible for making sure the projects and processes used to deliver the value you envision are designed well and implemented efficiently. Everyone will watch you. Everyone will adjust their actions accordingly, thereby creating a culture based on what they see creates the greatest reward for them.

Adam failed at leading Gale Solutions because he didn't understand what his enterprise needed from him and what he needed to do to align his team to work together. He had not been self-aware or skilled enough in relationship building or in motivating others to ask anyone to change what they were doing, even when advised that setting such expectations was what was needed. Adam understood he could be happy only if he could fulfill his ambition to become a successful entrepreneur in total control of a very profitable enterprise. It was not until Gale Solutions had been successfully sold by his nemesis, Gerry, that Adam felt capable enough to seriously change and acquire the skills of an entrepreneurial leader.

Each profiled entrepreneur with the strong enough motivation to want to see his or her vision become a reality ultimately reached the same conclusion as Adam: change or fail. Success for ELs is determined not so much by intelligence, education, or experience as it is by whether they decide to focus their actions on selflessly giving their enterprise and the people they hire what they need to be successful. Each of our protagonists was ultimately a very strong person; indeed, Adam had to become a stronger person in order to finally succeed. Entrepreneurs find their real opportunities *after* they decide to change.

THE ATTRACTION OF SINCERE SELFISHNESS

Besides a burning ambition to be a successful entrepreneur (whatever the strong underlying motivation is), the only other prerequisite for success is an idea, or vision, of how to create value in the world. The major challenge then becomes balancing the powerful selfishness that comes with a vision and a strong motivation to succeed, with the selflessness required to get others passionately dedicated to help you, ultimately making the personal changes that allow the enterprise to flourish. *Selfishness is a requirement.* Without selfishness, the entrepreneurial vision is not strong enough to be successful.

A strong vision also is required to motivate followers: nobody wants to dedicate their working life to help another person fulfill an entrepreneurial vision to which they are not dedicated. *ELs must be selfish about their vision, but their vision must be a selfless one.* Your selfish side wants to control your vision and the emotional and economic power that it creates. But the EL must be willing to share the vision to the point that other people feel emotionally and economically attached to it. Indeed, ELs will create and structure their enterprise in order to sincerely attract others to help them. ELs will then do whatever they need to do to make those they have attracted feel fulfilled in the work they do.

This sincere attracting, this doing whatever is needed—these have been the focus of this book. This willingness and ability to channel selfish vision for selfless ends is the catalyst for turning an entrepreneur into an entrepreneurial leader—someone capable of navigating an enterprise through the four stages of development from inception to self-sustaining value.

Acting as an entrepreneurial leader requires five straightforward skills, none of them inborn:

- *Self-awareness:* You must understand your motivations well enough that you understand what drives you to act. You must understand your traits and skills so that you can realistically understand your strengths and weaknesses and what you can realistically contribute to your enterprise. You must understand what skills you need to acquire—either on your own or by working with others.

- *Enterprise basics:* You must understand the basics of how enterprises operate—through projects, processes, and culture—and how enterprises mature—through four stages from inception to sustained value—in order to understand what your enterprise and all its stakeholders expect from you.

- *Relationship building:* You must understand what constitutes relationships—a web of shared objectives experienced through competition, cooperation, or retreat—and how to create, structure, and manage relationships to support your vision. Relationship building makes you a better communicator; this is essential, because communicating is the most basic of all relationships and is integral to all enterprise activities.

- *Motivating others:* You must understand how to make the people who help you to fulfill your vision feel autonomous, masterful, and purposeful. Motivations vary among people, and some motivating forces are stronger than others at various stages of an enterprise's development.

- *Leading change:* You must understand how to put in place and keep in place those five prerequisites for change, the five ducks: comprehension, motivation, skills, resources, and communication.

A major vision-threatening shock—often an enterprise failure or the entrepreneur's ouster as leader—is usually required to get the typical entrepreneur to realize she needs to acquire one or more of these basic skills. My hope is that by reading this book you can alleviate the need for such a shock. Specifically, the creation of a personal leadership strategy, as described in Chapter Seven, can prepare you to lead crises and grow your vision into a self-sustaining, value-creating enterprise. The PLS is an outline of the changes you determine you must make; its function is to help you hold yourself accountable to those changes. *Without personal accountability to your PLS, you will require a vision-threatening shock to make these changes.* Use a PLS. It's much less traumatic.

Armed with a vision, a powerful personal motivation, and a mastery of these five skills, the EL can avoid the common causes for startup failures: poor hiring and firing, unproductive teams, misguided strategies, unleadable organizational structures, and unresolved crises. It is clearly worth it for the EL to learn the five basic skills of self-awareness, enterprise basics, relationship building, motivating others, and leading change to avoid the need for vision-threatening shocks.

VALUABLE IDEAS ARE EVERYWHERE

In this book we have dealt with protagonists who already knew how they wanted to create value. To answer the question "Is it worth it?" for anyone who is still seeking that exciting idea, I will briefly outline a simple thought process associated with finding or validating the value potential of an idea. Although it is outside the scope of this book to describe completely how to find ideas that create value, both practicing and potential entrepreneurs need to have a realistic estimate of the potential reward they could receive from their idea. This is as true for somebody starting her fifth company as it is for the entrepreneur who has already started her enterprise and must decide how to lead the firm all the way through stage four. It is also true for entrepreneurially minded leaders within bigger institutions. The value potential of an idea hinges on two things: is this something you *really* can figure out how to do, and does it *really* excite enough people to motivate you?

Not all ideas can work, and not all ideas can produce value, *but there are always an infinite number of ideas that can produce value.*[1] People everywhere in the world are looking to embrace new products and services that will help them improve their lives or just be happier. It really is that simple: *value is produced by improving people's lives or by making them happier, either in their personal life or at work.* It can get complicated when you want to improve the professional life of someone in a sophisticated profession, and it can get complicated when you want to use leading-edge technology to deliver your product or service, but the fundamental value you deliver always comes back to making somebody's life better.

Making people feel better, saving people time, saving people money, and making people feel more secure are the prime examples of how you deliver value. Virtually everyone already provides value to friends, family, or colleagues at work. You can probably think of more ways you could deliver value, particularly if you augment your skills. Augmenting skills requires an investment of time and possibly some money, so this limits what it is practical to achieve. You may be able to find a mentor who will help you develop the skills you want to improve, and there are many classes and programs that teach skills. Unfortunately, skills learned in classes can get you only so far without real-world practice, but a well-placed job can allow you to practice a skill while observing first-hand how people with best-in-class skills get things done. Most entrepreneurs learn the skills they use to start their enterprise on the job. This applies to entrepreneurial leaders as well.

Finding an idea that adds value to the world is not a daunting challenge; it is fairly straightforward. The real challenge is deciding whether or not you are deeply motivated to selfishly capture for yourself any of the value you know how to create for others. How you change your idea to fit the needs of others is the focus of stage one. Without completing stage one, your idea can become, at best, only a hobby.

Beyond stage one, you need to figure out how to deliver your idea and how to find others who need and want your idea. You have a great deal at risk in this stage two discovery. The investment in projects accelerates, finally resulting in some basic processes; yet, as Max Levchin and Peter Thiel discovered four times with PayPal, customer demand may not be what you expected. The point is, worthwhile ideas for new enterprises abound, and entrepreneurs are finding them all the time. Entrepreneurs transform potentially valuable ideas into something that real people actually find useful and valuable; entrepreneurial leaders also do this, but they are motivated enough to be willing and able to selflessly lead through each of the stages we have reviewed, to the point where the world can rely on the EL's enterprise to keep on delivering products and services that make our lives better.

Most entrepreneurs take their enterprises no further than just putting into place the most basic processes that enable them to survive. If your primary motivation is to be your own boss, be in total control of all decisions, and not care about making more money than to satisfy some basic needs, then most will argue that there is no reason to go any further. There is a critical flaw in this thinking, and that is that no market and no customer base is static. Any enterprise that cannot complete stage three will start to atrophy and decay; it is just a matter of time. This atrophy and decay makes entrepreneurship an ongoing emotional and financial struggle for most. No tangible asset value has been created until an enterprise consistently creates value under stressful competitive and economic conditions. As I mentioned before, over half of the enterprises that reach stage three do not complete the stage and either shrink in size or must be rescued by selling the company for a low price or finding a more capable leader to take over.

I would argue that being an entrepreneur is likely not worth it, emotionally or financially, unless you are willing and able to take your enterprise all the way to the end of stage three. But the value of an enterprise remains highly discounted at this point, because atrophy and decay are still underlying assumptions in any professional valuation. That is why most stage three enterprises are valued at a very low multiples of their annual cash flow. Without the stage four rejuvenation processes in place, long-term value creation cannot be demonstrated. It is at this point that the entrepreneurial leader receives his financial reward and his fulfillment. Even if the firm is sold sometime after completing stage four, legacies remain.

You likely have more at stake now than when you started reading this book. You probably now have more possibilities to consider, and those possibilities are more real and less dreamy. This alone reduces the risk and increases the potential value of your ideas. Do you want to move forward, transforming one of your ideas into a tangible reality, or do you want to maintain status quo? You understand enterprises. Enterprises transform ideas into tangible realities. *Your ideas can become tangible realities.*

Now you must decide. Making no decision means you do not want change. Going forward with your idea means embracing and navigating profound changes in your approach to entrepreneurship—with greatly improved chances of building and leading an enterprise that is both personally satisfying and a source of value to you, your stakeholders, and the world.

APPENDIX A

Motivations, Traits, and Skills

Motivations, traits, and skills define you; they are distinct but interrelated.

Motivations drive your actions. They are your basic desires and fears. Your strongest motivations arise from the things that are the source of your happiness or that protect you from your primal fears.

Traits are the physiological and psychological characteristics that you are born with or that develop early in life. Traits are virtually impossible to change. Each trait has characteristics that make it harder or easier to master the skills of an EL. These traits affect your ability to perform the essential skills of an entrepreneurial leader:

- Traits determined by the Myers-Briggs Personality Type Indicator (MBTI)
- Learning preferences
- Intelligence
- Ability to detect and understand other people's emotions
- Physical stamina
- Mental focus
- Neuroticism (emotional intensity created in reaction to stress and unknowns)

Skills are abilities to perform prescribed tasks. You learn skills, and your ability to perform them is affected by your traits and your motivations. Your proficiency in a skill can be measured as

- *Basic:* Can perform the task under nonstressful conditions

- *Competent:* Can perform the task under varying conditions with acceptable outcomes
- *Master:* Can consistently perform the task under very stressful conditions
- *Best-in-Class:* Can consistently perform the task under the most extreme possible conditions

Your skills proficiency can improve with practice and with experienced coaching, but the level of mastery you can achieve also depends on your motivations and traits.

APPENDIX B

The Five Essential Entrepreneurial Leadership Skills

Self-awareness: You must understand your motivations well enough that you understand what drives you to act. You must understand your traits and skills so that you can realistically understand your strengths and weaknesses and what you can realistically contribute to your enterprise. You must understand what skills you need to acquire—either on your own or by working with others.

Enterprise basics: You must understand the basics of how enterprises operate—through projects, processes, and culture—and how enterprises mature—through four stages from inception to sustained value—in order to understand what your enterprise and all its stakeholders expect from you.

Relationship building: You must understand what constitutes relationships—a web of shared objectives experienced through competition, cooperation, or retreat—and how to create, structure, and manage relationships to support your vision. Relationship building will make you a better communicator; this is essential, because communicating is the most basic of all relationships and is integral to all enterprise endeavors of every size and type.

Motivating others: You must understand how to make the people who help you to fulfill your vision feel autonomous, masterful, and purposeful. Motivations vary among people, and some motivating forces are stronger than others at various stages of an enterprise's development.

Leading change: You must understand how to put in place and keep in place those five prerequisites for change, the five ducks: comprehension, motivation, skills, resources, and communication.

APPENDIX C

Characteristics of Projects, Processes, and Culture

A *project* is a set of tasks performed by a team of people to create something new or to make something better.

A *process* is a set of tasks that people repetitively perform to transform materials and information into something more valuable.

A *culture* is a shared set of understanding held by an enterprise's stakeholders about how contributions are valued and rewards are given.

Projects	Processes
Have never done this before.	Do the same thing repetitively.
Goals are about creating something new or about implementing a change.	Goal is to create value by repetitively performing a task.
Much less efficient than processes for transforming some inputs into an output (think of building a custom house versus houses built in a housing tract).	Processes are created by projects and therefore have an up-front cost of creation. This up-front cost is partially recovered each time the process is performed, as processes are much more efficient than projects.

Projects	Processes
Project status is monitored through achievement of milestones and the time and resources expended. The quality of project output is variable.	Process status is monitored through in-process measurements, often using statistical tools. The output quality of a process is typically greater and more uniform than the output quality of a project.
Projects are achieved by assembling people *temporarily* into a team with the skills and motivations required to achieve the project objective.	Processes are performed by people assigned *permanently* and who are trained in the required skills.
Project objectives and plans can be changed by whoever gives the project team its mandate and resources, provided the team also agrees.	Processes can be successfully changed only with significant planning and investment (a project is required to change a process).
Significant leadership is required to plan and execute a successful project.	Processes are managed, not led, unless they are to be changed.
Projects carry a greater risk of not achieving a successful outcome, relative to processes, because they do something new.	Process risks are well defined by statistics.
Projects create change.	Processes resist change.

APPENDIX D

Characteristics of Enterprises and Their Leaders in Stages One Through Four

STAGE ONE: CUSTOMER VALIDATION

Stage one starts when someone commits to forming an enterprise around an idea and ends when a customer commits to using the product or service.

The activities in this stage are organized as a major project, perhaps with some subprojects.

A nascent culture forms, based on how the team perceives the founder makes decisions and rewards independent actions.

This stage is most effectively led through a series of ad hoc huddles, called whenever there is new information to discuss and whenever the project plan needs to be adjusted.

The planning horizon for the leader extends only as far as necessary to fulfill what has been promised to potential customers.

The enterprise is controlled simply with a checkbook.

A key goal of stage one is naturally motivating to people who find it stimulating to work on projects, particularly trying to do things that have not been done before.

In stage one the strategic imperative—the focus of all actions—is to find, as quickly as possible, potential customers who align with what you think you know how to deliver. Strategic thinking in stage one focuses on answering these higher-level versions of the ten strategic questions:

- *How can I best (fastest, with least effort) find real customers?* This will ultimately lead to understanding who will be your customers.

- *How can I make a very basic product (also known as the minimum viable product or MVP) attractive enough so some customer will actually agree to try it?* This will ultimately require you to understand your value proposition.
- *How can I deliver the MVP when I find a customer willing to try it?* This will lead to understanding the initial projects and processes required to make and deliver your product.

STAGE TWO: OPERATIONAL VALIDATION

Stage two starts with a customer committing to use the product or service.

This stage ends when basic processes are used to deliver the product, ensure that customers are satisfied, capture new customers, and simply administrate the enterprise (that is, pay employees, pay bills, inventory and purchase supplies, keep basic accounting records). Existing customers must be satisfied with their product to confirm the potential of the enterprise to create substantial value.

The activities of this stage are organized as at least three projects with a mission to establish processes for them: (1) delivery of the product, (2) finding and satisfying customers, (3) administrating the enterprise. Other projects may be necessary to raise money or deal with special regulatory requirements. Before the entrepreneur knows exactly how to implement these three capabilities, she must have answered all ten strategic questions. The strategic imperative of stage two is to implement these core capabilities as simply and reliably as possible.

The activities of this stage are most effectively led by regular meetings of the EL with her project leaders, where progress against project milestones is reviewed along with customer feedback.

During stage two the planning horizon reviewed in the regular meeting should extend only as far as the time required to capture new customers or to manage the supply chain for the delivery of products promised to customers, whichever is longer.

Culture continues to solidify, based on how new processes are conceived and managed and how much autonomy is given to new and veteran employees.

The enterprise is controlled based on cash flow projections.

Stage two enterprises are naturally motivating to people who like to figure out how to make things work better. The EL should want his stage two hires to feel they can be masters at making things work better. He must recognize and reward them for this mastery.

The EL makes people and teams feel autonomous in stage two by setting clear expectations about what improvements he wants in place and what he uses as criteria to judge improvement.

Employees working in a stage two enterprise feel purpose because they can see their improvements become embedded into the fabric of how the enterprise operates. They also feel purpose in being associated with the mission of the enterprise.

Employees feel highly motivated and proud when the EL tells them he can recognize their specific contribution in the design of how the enterprise operates.

The mantra of the EL in stage two is "How can we make it simpler?"

STAGE THREE: FINANCIAL VALIDATION

Stage three starts when the value proposition has been confirmed and basic processes are reliably in place to deliver the product, capture and satisfy customers, and administrate the enterprise.

This stage ends when the company is able to produce consistent value under stressful competitive and economic conditions by operating with scalable processes that manage all aspects of the enterprise, with no process relying on any particular individuals.

The enterprise is led based on continual review of operational, customer, and financial metrics and a forecast of operational, customer, and financial performance.

The planning horizon is one year.

The culture solidifies around how processes are managed and how rewards are distributed throughout the enterprise.

The enterprise is controlled based on a forecast of profits or fiscal surpluses.

Stage three is when the EL hires people for specific expertise of which they are very proud. The feeling of autonomy in stage three comes from pride in perfecting skills and from working on teams that work autonomously.

Employees newly hired in stage three should be chosen because they are proud of their ability to perform tasks at a high level of mastery, and they derive purpose from helping others improve.

In stage three it is important for the EL to create opportunities and support for career advancement.

The strategic imperative of stage three is to create a sustainable balance in the enterprise processes between effectively generating significant value and being flexible enough to meet the expectations of existing and potential customers. Finding the proper balance requires making forecasts on how revenues and costs can change with time, economic conditions, added investment, and competitive pressure and under any number of other conditions that may be specific to the market place or regulatory environment.

In stage three all processes must operate without the direct involvement of the entrepreneur or any other individual person or supplier.

STAGE FOUR: SELF-SUSTAINABILITY

Stage four starts when the leader initiates a project to create an innovative new product or service that captures new customers. Stage four does *not* start automatically when stage three ends, for many enterprises it starts years after stage three has ended, or never starts at all.

Stage four ends when the new product or service produces consistent value for the enterprise and a process has been established to produce more innovative products.

The planning horizon expands out to however many years are required to see new innovation projects create positive value.

Once an enterprise has completed stage four, it is a fully mature enterprise.

The EL's biggest motivational challenge in stage four is to ensure that the enterprise's culture is equally supportive of innovators and those who want to improve efficiency.

In stage four, career tracks must be modified to provide equally motivating autonomy and mastery opportunities for those innovative people who want to change everything and those enormously productive people who want to improve what they already do.

The strategic imperative of stage four is for the enterprise to implement a process that enables itself to be renewed. This renewal can come in the form of introducing significant new types of products, making major leaps in existing capabilities that set new product or service benchmarks, creating new business models, or opening up entirely new markets. Innovation can also come through acquiring innovative enterprises and preserving their innovative culture.

APPENDIX E

Relationship Building and the Benefits and Costs of Cooperation, Competition, and Retreat

All relationships are formed when two people have at least one shared objective. A *shared objective* is any change that two people care about, but they do not have to agree how the change should be accomplished.

There are three types of relationships:

- *Cooperative:* When both parties agree how they will share the costs and benefits of achieving the shared objective
- *Competitive:* When either or both parties do not agree how they will share the costs and benefits of achieving the shared objective
- *Retreating:* When either or both parties do not care how the costs or benefits of achieving the shared objective will be shared

Each category of relationship has its benefits and costs.

Benefits	Costs
Cooperation	
Is the most efficient method to create new value or capability Is the lowest-risk path to desired outcome	Requires largest investment in time and resources Requires continuous investment of time and resources to ensure desired outcomes continue to meet expectations

Benefits	Costs
	Has inconsistent quality when practiced by unskilled relationship builders (for example, they are prone to "least common denominator" solutions)
Competition	
Is the most efficient and effective way to test a solution Is more suited to those people who perform skills better when competing	Destroys value and assets to perform the test Is the highest-risk path to achieving a desired outcome Often creates feelings of anxiety
Retreat	
Enables independence, which refreshes energy and resources Often enables creativity and innovative thinking Is the equivalent of buying an option on achieving future desired outcomes	Requires forgoing desired outcomes Can generate feelings of isolation

Competition supersedes both cooperation and retreat. Retreat supersedes cooperation.

Relationship building is the exercise of the ability to improve the expected desired outcomes of shared objectives, thereby making relationships stronger, more productive, and more satisfying. The fundamental strategy of relationship building is to

- Ensure that all competitive shared objectives create valid performance tests. Each competition should yield a valuable new insight into how to improve the performance of the enterprise.

- Shift other competitions into retreat or cooperation by offering to modify the shared objectives.
- Shift some acts of retreat, when the potential benefits are high enough, to cooperation by offering to modify the shared objectives.

APPENDIX F

The Five Prerequisites of Change
(The Five Ducks)

*D*uck One, *Comprehension:* All members of the team responsible for designing and implementing the change must all share the same understanding of the change objectives.

Duck Two, *Motivation:* All members of the team implementing the change must be motivated to see that the change is successfully accomplished.

Duck Three, *Skills:* The project team must possess or have under their control the skills necessary to design and implement the change.

Duck Four, *Resources:* All the resources required to perform the project must be made available to the team as they are requested.

Duck Five, *Communication:* Everyone impacted by the change must understand its importance.

APPENDIX G

Ten Basic Strategic Questions

Who will want to buy your product?

You need to be able to describe the customers who will want to buy your product or service. The more you understand your customers—who they are, what they think, how they spend their time, and so on—the more comfortable you can make them feel with being your customer.

Why will they want to buy your product?

The EL must eventually understand what benefits the customer will get from buying her product. Benefits are those aspects of the product that make the customer feel better. This is called the "value proposition."

How can they know they want to buy your product?

You need to understand how you will find potential customers to tell them or show them what you have to offer. Will you be going to trade shows, or advertising, going door-to-door, or (using our example) giving out free samples at the Firemen's Fair?

Where will they want to buy your product?

Will customers buy your product on the Internet, in a store, directly from a salesperson who visits their office, or some other way?

How much will they be willing to pay?

Until you know how much customers are willing to pay, you cannot be sure your idea can ever produce value. Unless a similar product or service already exists, this is a hard question to answer definitively until real customers have had the opportunity to actually buy the product.

What process will you use to make and deliver the product?

You must understand how you can create your product. It is a waste of time to test a product idea that is impractical to produce and deliver.

Are any special skills required for the enterprise to succeed?

Most types of enterprises require some special skills to start and to lead. Many types of enterprises require licensing (such as real estate brokers) or certification of skill levels (such as CPAs). Starting certain tech companies can require a very specialized set of skills.

Are there any critical enablers to making and delivering the product?

ELs take the time to discover who could prevent them from making their product (for example, someone owns a patent to make the product, or a regulatory agency has to certify that the product as safe), and also who could be willing to help them as a partner.

How much will it cost to make and deliver the product?

The cost to make the product has three components: (1) the cost of the input materials or services, (2) the cost to operate the processes to make, test, and deliver the product, and (3) the overall costs associated with any waste or losses associated with the process.

How much money will it take to set up your rudimentary (stage two) processes for delivering the product, finding and satisfying customers, and administrating the enterprise?

You need to estimate how much investment you will need to set up your enterprise and its rudimentary processes in order to know how much money you will need to have on hand or be prepared to raise.

APPENDIX H

Five Phases of Crisis Resolution

To successfully resolve any crisis, the enterprise must complete five phases:[1]

- *Crisis Identification:* The first step is to understand that there is a crisis. Crises are identified by acknowledging that results differ from what had been assumed.
- *Planning and Deployment:* Projects must be quickly planned and resourced, even before the true source of the problem is completely understood.
- *Crisis Containment and Mitigation:* The problem must be brought under control and the damage mitigated before a permanent solution can be designed and implemented. This tends to be a project phase.
- *Recovery:* New processes, independent of the original flawed assumption, are designed and implemented.
- *Lessons Learned:* The root cause(s) of the problem are positively identified and long-term permanent changes are implemented so the problem cannot reoccur. The enterprise is stronger as a result.

NOTES

Preface

1. The specific information on the contribution of new firms to jobs growth came from a recent Kauffman Foundation research report, "The Importance of Startups in Job Creation and Job Destruction," The Kauffman Foundation Research Series: Firm Foundation and Economic Growth, July 2010.

2. For an understanding of the facts of entrepreneurship and how it drives growth, the best single overview is Shane, *The Illusions of Entrepreneurship* (New Haven, CT: Yale Press, 2008). Pages 106 to 108 are particularly relevant to my discussion in the introduction. Another important reference is Reynolds, *Entrepreneurship in the United States: The Future Is Now* (New York: Springer, 2007). On page 13 you will find the surprising extrapolation that almost half of the working population in the United States will have attempted to be an entrepreneur at some point in their career.

3. The fact that most firms decay after they have started to create value, sometimes significant value, is best illustrated in some studies on *Inc.* magazine's annual "*Inc.* 500 list of fastest growing companies in the US." See Buchanan, "Life After the *Inc.* 500: Fortune, Flameout, and Self-Discovery," *Inc.*, Aug. 21, 2012, http://www.inc.com/magazine/201209/leigh -buchanan/life-after-the-inc-500-fortune-flameout-self-discovery.html. Virtually all *Inc.* 500 companies have reached Stage 3, or else they could not have grown so quickly. Only about 32 percent of the *Inc.* 500 companies between 2000 and 2006 had grown larger or had gone public by 2010. Another 32 percent were sold, but 57 percent of these sales (around 18 percent of all companies) resulted in the founder's continuing in a regular job at the acquirer—not the ideal entrepreneurial exit. So well over half of all *Inc.* 500 companies were not able to become self-sustaining and create consistent positive value.

4. My estimate that fewer than one in fifty entrepreneurs lead their enterprises to the point where they are value producing and self-sustaining is an extrapolation of the fact cited by Shane (page 155) that only one startup in forty-three has any employees ten years after starting.

Chapter One

1. Adam is a composite character. Many real-world entrepreneurial trajectories parallel the elements of his story.

2. Relevant to the character of Adam or any entrepreneur who takes money from professional investors is the major irony that in the real world the more successful the startup, the more likely the CEO will be fired and replaced by a professional manager. This startling fact can be found in a well-regarded research paper by Noam Wasserman, "Founder-CEO Succession and the Paradox of Entrepreneurial Success," *Organization Science*, 14 (2003): 149–172. The more valuable a company becomes, the more its investors want to ensure that the enterprise is led by someone who will maximize its value. The analogous reasoning: if after years of intense searching you finally discover buried treasure, who would you want to guard the treasure on the way to the bank: the person that designed the super special metal detector that found the treasure, or a retired Navy SEAL?

3. Throughout this book I use the classic definition of *entrepreneur*: "Someone who works to start a business as well as someone who leads a business they have started." Nonetheless, entrepreneur is also commonly associated with many other definitions, so be sure you understand exactly which definition any writer or speaker is using—if they even know. The spectrum of usage ranges from "the rare hero who founds a company that grows quickly and creates hundreds of jobs" to "the characteristic that is within virtually everyone to take risks in order to maximize personal economic well-being." In the case of the hero definition, "entrepreneur" would apply to only a few dozen people a year in the United States. My definition applies to approximately six million working Americans, according to the Reynolds book cited previously (see Preface, n. 2).

4. The facts on how many entrepreneurs actually get a first customer, or survive for five years, are based on the summary of entrepreneurial research described by Shane.

Chapter Two

1. Brian O'Kelley is a real person. Most of the facts I have used in the chapter, particularly those pertaining to Brian's motivations, come from direct interviews with Brian as well as some employees who work directly for Brian or for AppNexus. A very interesting recording of Brian talking about his entrepreneurial failures can be found in "Brian O'Kelley: Three Failures and a (Big) Success: The Evolution of a Startup CEO," http://www.youtube.com/watch?v=pGVSsg_5zkk.

2. The research on the motivations of entrepreneurs in starting their enterprises is problematic, because motivations have been self-reported, therefore being subject to many individual and interpretive biases. I am not aware of any studies in which trained and objective motivational experts determined motivations. The entrepreneurial research community is aware of this issue; see Shane et al., "Entrepreneurial Motivation," *Human Resources Management Review*, 13 (2003): 257–279; Xu and Ruef, "The Myth of the Risk-Tolerant Entrepreneur," *Strategic Organization*, 2 (4) (2004): 331–355. An interesting valuable summary of self-reported motivations can be found in Wasserman, *Founder's Dilemmas* (Princeton, NJ: Princeton University Press, 2012), chapters 2 and 11.

3. The most famous exposition of the motivation by an entrepreneur, using the "if I were to die today reasoning," was made by Steve Jobs in his 2005 Commencement Speech at Stanford University. See http://www.youtube.com/watch?v=UF8uR6Z6KLc. There are many other lists of questions for finding your true motivation; for example, http://www.oprah.com/spirit/How-to-Get-Motivated-to-Change-Your-Lifestyle -LLuminari-Guide; http://www.ineedmotivation.com/blog/2008/04/7-questions-to-finding

-your-true-passion/; http://voices.yahoo.com/questions-determine-personal-motivation
-6119820.html; http://www.billgeorge.org/files/media/true-north1/epilogue-exercises.pdf.

4. A well-regarded book on finding your own sources of motivation is Martha Beck, *Finding Your Own North Star* (New York: Three Rivers Press, 2001).

5. Some free online personality tests can be found at http://www.personalitytest.net/ipip /ipipneo1.htm, and http://pstypes.blogspot.com/2009/03/free-jungian-type-tests.html. Free IQ testing can be found at http://www.free-iqtest.net/. Free EQ testing can be found at http://www.ihhp.com/?page=freeEQquiz. You can find out your learning style at http://sunburst.usd.edu/~bwjames/tut/learning-style/.

6. The two most common models of personality traits supported by academic research are The Five Factor Model and Myers-Briggs. Each of these trait models is supported with a strong base of empirical research demonstrating their ability to describe most personalities across culturally diverse populations. The best starting references for these two models are Costa and McCrae, "Four Ways Five-Factors Are Basic," *Personality and Individual Differences*, 13 (1992): 653–665; Myers, *Gifts Differing* (Mountain View, CA: CPP, 1980). The Five Factor Model and Myers-Briggs are highly correlated to one another; see McCrae & Costa, "Reinterpreting the Myers-Briggs Type Indicator from the Perspective of the Five Factor Model of Personality," *Journal of Personality*, 57 (1) (1989): 17–40.

7. Note that your ability to control your emotions is equivalent to the Neuroticism measure used in the Five Factor Model of personalities.

8. You can find many thousands of profiles of entrepreneurs online or in books; see, for example, http://entrepreneurs.about.com/od/famousentrepreneurs/Famous_Entrepreneurs .htm. Two of my favorites are Koehn, *Brand New: How Entrepreneurs Earned Consumers' Trust from Wedgwood to Dell* (Boston: Harvard Business School Press, 2001); Evans, *They Made America* (New York: Little Brown, 2004).

Chapter Three

1. Wendy Kopp is a real person and has been widely interviewed. Her book *One Day, All Children* is a very poignant story about how Teach For America was launched and Wendy's personal journey to become an entrepreneurial leader (although she never refers to herself as such). I have interviewed Wendy Kopp to capture additional color for this chapter.

2. My information on TFA's latest financial numbers came from http://www.teachforamerica .org/sites/default/files/FY2011AuditedFinancialStatements.pdf.

3. Today, "processes" are sometimes referred to as "workflows," with the differentiation that process references action sequences in factories, whereas workflow applies to all sequences of actions, even those performed by computers. Some consultants use the word "system" as an overarching term describing interrelated processes that are often facilitated by specific hardware and software. I use "processes" as the all-inclusive term.

4. Much has been written about the stages or transitions organizations go through in their life cycle, even in the startup phase. Unfortunately, most definitions of stages that startups go through have been written by academics and have not focused on the causes of stress on the leadership of rapidly growing organizations. The four stages I define are similar to those described as the first four stages in the academic treatise *Growing Pains* (4th ed.) by Eric Framholtz and Yvonne Randle (San Francisco: Jossey-Bass, 2008). They are also similar to the three stages described in the popular practitioner's treatise *The Four Steps to the Epiphany* by Steve Blank (self-published, 2007), except that I split the "Process-Managed Execution and Growth" phase into two distinct parts. Relative to both books, my focus is specifically about what is expected of the entrepreneurial leader in each stage.

5. Wendy Kopp, "An Argument and Plan for the Creation of the Teachers Corporation," Princeton University senior thesis (1989).

6. The value created by an enterprise can be measured using different metrics, but the most common are profit, EBITDA (earnings before interest, taxes, depreciation, and amortization), and cash flow. In the case of Teach For America, it would be measured in terms of fiscal surplus.

7. See Preface, n. 3.

8. Clayton M. Christensen, *The Innovator's Dilemma* (Boston: Harvard Business Press, 1997).

Chapter Four

1. Michael, Laura, and Larry are composite characters.

2. The original insight that relationships among people fall into the categories of competitive, cooperative, or individualistic came from a seminal analysis of primitive cultures by Margaret Mead. She found she could not describe all cultures using only competitive and cooperative models. Margaret Mead, *Cooperation and Competition Among Primitive People* (New York: McGraw-Hill, 1937). The section titled "Interpretive Statement" is the first outline of this framework for analyzing relationships that I am aware of. In the study of interpersonal communication as well as the study of negotiations, analogous terms and concepts are used. Many interpersonal communications experts classify communications as aggressive, assertive, or passive; see, for example, Robert Bolton, *People Skills* (Simon & Schuster, New York, 1979). Some negotiation experts analyze negotiating positions as competitor, accommodator, avoider; see, for example, Robert Mnookin, *Beyond Winning* (Cambridge, MA: Harvard University Press, 2000).

3. A good question is whether we can form relationships with entities and other living beings as well as with people. Pet owners know that they have relationships with their pets and other animals; at a basic level you share space and food (we often *retreat* from having shared objectives with many of the insects around us, although we have limits as to how much we are willing to share space with cockroaches, which compels us to *compete* with them). The tougher question is whether your relationship is with an organization or with the specific individuals within the organization, such as the customer service person on the phone helping you solve some problem. In my view, anyone can create a relationship with anything that they believe shares an objective. If somebody believes the organization has the power to decide how to share the benefits of a shared objective, then a real *cooperative* relationship can occur. Ultimately, within an organization, some person or group of people controls the actual decision making associated with sharing any of the organization's outcome, but because the decision making is now often carried out with software that renders scripts for customer service employees to read, this can become an essentially irrelevant distinction.

4. Most academic study has focused on the cooperation-versus-competition dynamic as modeled by the prisoner's dilemma; very few have studied the resulting game theory as a three-way dynamic, with the inclusion of *retreat*. Morton Deutsch, in his classic study *The Resolution of Conflict* (New Haven, CT: Yale University Press, 1973), explicitly maps out the retreat case of "non-interdependence of goals" on p. 21, later referencing a book by R. K. Merton, *Social Theory and Social Structure* (Glencoe, IL: Free Press, 1957), for an analysis of "individual" states within society (see pp. 139–157). More recently, the concept of retreat as voluntary participation has been analyzed by Hauert et al., "Volunteering as Red Queen Mechanism for Cooperation in Public Goods Games," *Science*, 296 (5570) (May 10, 2002): 1129–1132.

5. For an alternative discussion on how to communicate more effectively, see Bolton, *People Skills: How to Assert Yourself, Listen to Others, and Resolve Conflicts* (New York: Touchstone, 1979).

Chapter Five

1. For more details on the sources of motivation, see Ryan and Deci, "Self-Determination Theory and the Facilitation of Intrinsic Motivation, Social Development, and Well-Being," *American Psychologist* (January 2000): 68–78. Alternatively, you can read Daniel Pink's book *Drive*.

2. It is impractical to build relationships with more than a handful of people at any given time. The number of potential primary shared objectives grows exponentially in relation to the number of people in a group, so other alignment techniques are required.

3. Dean Kamen is a real person. He has been widely interviewed. Much of the material used in this chapter can be found in Kemper, *Reinventing the Wheel* (New York: Harper Business, 2003).

4. The concept of *intrinsically motivating* is fully developed in the previously cited work by Ryan and Deci and described in very accessible terms in the book *Drive*.

5. The concept of self-actualization was introduced in 1939 by Kurt Goldstein and further developed by Maslow as the ultimate feeling of personal well-being. A good introduction to Maslow and self-actualization can be found at http://www.simplypsychology.org/maslow.html

Chapter Six

1. Jon is a composite character.

2. This chapter makes use of my article "Duck Alignment Theory: Going Beyond Classic Project Management to Maximize Project Success," *Project Management Journal* (December 1999). Another practical recipe for leading change that touches on the same points but is written for the leader of fully matured enterprises is Kotter, *Leading Change* (Boston: Harvard Business School Press, 1996).

Chapter Seven

1. Keri is a composite character.

2. You can find other outlines for personal leadership plans on the Internet. One of the most highly respected, used at Harvard Business School, is available at http://www.billgeorge.org/files/media/true-north1/epilogue-exercises.pdf. This version and all other leadership plans are designed for building a general leadership vision and plan—they are not, however, specific to entrepreneurial leadership.

Chapter Eight

1. Max Levchin and Peter Thiel are all real people who have been interviewed widely. A good reference for the material on Max Levchin and Peter Thiel is Jessica Livingston, *Founders at Work* (New York: Apress, 2008), pp. 1–17.

2. The effectual strategic process is described in Read et al., *Effectual Entrepreneurship* (London: Routledge, 2011).

Chapter Nine

1. Arun is a composite character.

2. The Army has cared about which organizations work best under stressful situations for a long time. A good recent study of the problem that Arun suffered can be found in Galbraith, "Organizational Design: An Information Processing View," *Army Organizational Effectiveness Journal*, 1 (1984): 21–26. A more general source of organizational design insights

can be found in Huber and McDaniel, "The Decision-Making Paradigm of Organizational Design," *Management Science*, 32 (5) (May 1986): 572–589.

Chapter Ten

1. Nate, Jennifer, Burt, and all the protagonists in this chapter are composite characters.

Chapter Eleven

1. I worked at International Rectifier (IR) from 1976 to 1999. The company was founded by my father and grandfather in 1947 and went public in 1956. At the time of the stories in this chapter, my father was still CEO of the company.

Chapter Twelve

1. Most programs and books on crisis leadership target government officials and executives of large corporations. Two very accessible references are Pearson and Mitroff, "From Crisis Prone to Crisis Prepared: A Framework for Crisis Management," *Academy of Management Executive*, 7 (1993): 48–59; Augustine, "Managing the Crisis You Tried to Prevent," *Harvard Business Review*, 73.6 (1995): 147–158.

2. These five phases are not universally adopted in the field of crisis leadership. Norm Augustine's article cites six stages; Pearson and Mitroff describe five. I use a combination of both to put it into a context most useful for the leader of a fragile enterprise.

Chapter Thirteen

1. You can find very compelling demonstrations of the point that good business ideas are everywhere throughout Tina Seelig's wonderful book, *What I Wish I Knew When I Was 20* (San Francisco: HarperOne, 2009), as well as the book *Why Not?* by Nalebuff and Ayres (Boston: Harvard Business Review Press, 2006).

Appendix H

1. See Chapter Twelve notes.

ACKNOWLEDGMENTS

The contents and themes of *Startup Leadership* were inspired and encouraged over the past forty years by legions of passionate and brilliant entrepreneurs, business people, academics, venture capitalists, students, and personal friends. This book has been possible only because hundreds of people have been willing to share their candid thoughts, experiences, and ideas with me.

The team I worked with at iSuppli, led by Lloyd Kaplan, Greg Sheppard, and Joe Armstrong and coached by brilliant and successful business strategists like Bruce Hack, Gene Richter, Rich Levin, Darren Cohen, and Peary Spaeght, played pivotal roles in the development of my leadership abilities and insights. We ultimately always figured out how to meet the high expectations we set for our team and ourselves.

I similarly want to acknowledge the many people at Princeton University who enticed me to create and teach a class on entrepreneurial leadership. Vince Poor, the dean of the School of Engineering and Applied Science, took a big gamble inviting me to teach based on an inspired suggestion from his colleague Jane Maggard. My success as a professor is directly related to the support and coaching I received from the fantastic team at Princeton's Keller Center for Innovation in Engineering Education. Sharid Malik, then director; Sanj Kulkarni, now director; along with Cornelia Huellstrunk, Victoria Dorman, Stephanie Landers, and Beth Jarvie have done everything in their power to help me develop new and innovative classes, while developing the material, research, and insights contained in *Startup Leadership*. I also received essential help from Steve Kauffman, Noam Wasserman, and Mike Roberts at Harvard Business School; Steve Blank and Irv Grousbeck at Stanford; and Martin Lautman at Wharton, not to mention Ed Zschau, John Danner, and Martin Reuf here at Princeton.

I am very grateful to Ricardo Levy and Jeremey Donovan for essential advice and wisdom they shared as the book was being written. Steven Haines also provided great inputs into the process.

I want to particularly thank Brian O'Kelley for being so open about his entrepreneurial experiences, good and bad. I feel very lucky that Brian was so generous with his time and with sharing his feelings about his journey in becoming an entrepreneurial leader. I also want to thank Wendy Kopp for generously sharing her time in giving me extra color on her entrepreneurial leadership journey. I am thankful to all the entrepreneurs who have shared their stories and journeys with me.

I know the book has benefited greatly from the scores of students at Princeton who have challenged me to explain my concepts in the clearest possible terms. The book has also directly benefited from the close reading of the manuscript by Leah Cohen-Shohet, Danielle Cohen-Shohet, Lang Wang, Jeffrey Westheimer, Natasha Gajewski, Arel Lidow, and Teel Lidow.

I also owe a great deal to several key people who also believed in this book project. My agent, Jeffrey Krames, has taught me more than I ever dreamed I would need to know about the publishing world. Genoveva Llosa took on the project at Jossey-Bass. Clancy Drake always challenged me, with good reason, to improve the manuscript; she really helped me find my voice. John Maas has been a wonderful publishing partner. Mary Garrett has been a wonderful production editor.

Finally, my wife, Diana, has been my loving partner and supporter through the entire project: reading and editing countless drafts and providing great suggestions, an essential alternate point of view, and constant encouragement and love over the seemingly endless months.

I am a truly lucky person.

ABOUT THE AUTHOR

Derek Lidow teaches entrepreneurship at Princeton University, where he created and teaches two very popular classes: Entrepreneurial Leadership and Creativity, Innovation, and Design. When not teaching and helping Princeton students start enterprises of all sorts, Derek lectures widely on the subject of startup leadership, coaches startups and entrepreneurial leaders, and sits on a few boards of directors.

Before joining Princeton's faculty, Derek was founder, president, and CEO of iSuppli Corporation, which was acquired in 2010 by IHS. Derek founded iSuppli to serve the critical need for data and analysis that can improve the performance of the global electronics industry value chain. iSuppli accomplishes this by gathering and disseminating unique value-chain data and by collaborating with its clients to use this information to make smarter business decisions. Derek is also acknowledged as one of the world's experts on the global electronics industry. His analysis of the electronics value chain is used by top executives and key government officials around the globe, influencing decisions at corporations such as Sony, Samsung, Dell, Philips, Goldman Sachs, and IBM, and his comments on the electronics industry have received extensive global media coverage in such outlets as the *Economist*, *New York Times*, *Wall Street Journal*, *BusinessWeek*, *Forbes*, *Bloomberg*, *Nikkei*, *Reuters*, and *Taipei Times*, as well as the tech blogosphere.

Prior to founding iSuppli, Derek was CEO of International Rectifier (IR), a leading power semiconductor company. Derek earned a bachelor of science degree summa cum laude in electrical engineering from Princeton University and a PhD in applied physics from Stanford University as a Hertz Foundation Fellow.

For more information, please visit dereklidow.com.

INDEX

FREE RESOURCES
FOR ENTREPRENEURS

VISIT **DEREKLIDOW.COM** FOR THESE RESOURCES

CREATE YOUR OWN
PERSONAL LEADERSHIP STRATEGY

Create a compelling personal leadership strategy using the very same questions and evaluations Derek Lidow uses when working with entrepreneurs.

Each strategy is unique to the individual entrepreneur. This assessment will help you explore your own motivations and traits so you can leverage your strengths and mitigate your weaknesses. This is also a great way to develop a stronger bond with your mentors and others you want to help you.

STARTUP LEADERSHIP MAP

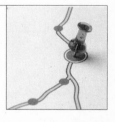

Successful entrepreneurs must be leaders. How do you beat the long odds of becoming an entrepreneurial leader and creating a successful enterprise?

This diagram turns into a great poster and highlights how the concepts in *Startup Leadership* help entrepreneurs and teams overcome the many challenges they face as their enterprise matures through four stages.